2⊬ 10

FRENCH LITERATURE
AND ITS BACKGROUND

3

The Eighteenth Century

FRENCH
LITERATURE
AND ITS
BACKGROUND

EDITED BY

JOHN CRUICKSHANK

3

The Eighteenth Century

OXFORD UNIVERSITY PRESS

LONDON   OXFORD   NEW YORK
1968

Oxford University Press

LONDON OXFORD NEW YORK
GLASGOW TORONTO MELBOURNE WELLINGTON
CAPE TOWN SALISBURY IBADAN NAIROBI LUSAKA ADDIS ABABA
BOMBAY CALCUTTA MADRAS KARACHI LAHORE DACCA
KUALA LUMPUR HONG KONG TOKYO

© OXFORD UNIVERSITY PRESS, 1968

FIRST PUBLISHED BY
OXFORD UNIVERSITY PRESS, LONDON, 1968

PRINTED IN GREAT BRITAIN

Contents

Introduction

THIS is the third of six volumes under the collective title: *French Literature and its Background*. It deals with various aspects—literary, intellectual, political, social—of eighteenth-century France. There is no attempt to give the type of exhaustive coverage normally associated with more traditionally conceived histories of literature. On the contrary, each of these volumes is the outcome of many meetings among a group of scholars who agreed, after lengthy discussion, on a dozen or so fundamental topics which they wished to examine in relation to a given century. In this eighteenth-century volume, for example, the *Mémoires* of Saint-Simon were eventually omitted as were other important figures (but not, in our view, figures of the first importance) such as Restif de la Bretonne, Buffon, Bernardin de Saint-Pierre, Fontenelle, Marmontel, etc. We limited ourselves to four indisputably major figures—Voltaire, Montesquieu, Diderot, and Rousseau—while also giving a good deal of attention to both Marivaux and Beaumarchais. Some writers such as Chénier, active towards the end of the century, are examined in the next volume because of their significance for early-nineteenth-century studies.

Although exhaustive coverage has not been our aim, the scheme outlined above has made it possible for us to pay some attention, in a thematic way, to important aspects of intellectual and social history. Chapters of the first kind are devoted to 'The Heritage of Newton and Locke' and to 'The Problem of Evil'. A sociologist's analysis of the meaning and function of the intellectuals' role in eighteenth-century France is contained in 'The New Intelligentsia'. In addition, the widespread eighteenth-century view of literature (novels and plays as well as discursive writings) as a means to polemical or propagandist ends is studied in 'The Literature of

Persuasion'. Chapters of this kind, apart from their intrinsic interest, also allow one to see the historical significance, within a given context, of writers who are otherwise not of major literary importance. It is in such chapters that reference is made to Condillac, Helvétius, d'Alembert, d'Holbach, Condorcet, etc.

The general arrangement of each of these volumes inevitably means that a major writer is not necessarily treated fully in any one chapter. For example, there are important comments on Voltaire and Diderot, viewed from a series of different angles, in at least half a dozen chapters, and much the same is true of Rousseau. More precisely, Marivaux is discussed as a novelist in one chapter and as a dramatist in another. This means that the Index to the volume should be frequently consulted.

Finally, we have included a 'Chronology' which is designed to serve various purposes. It enables one to relate eighteenth-century French literature to historical events (mainly French), to the literature of England and Germany, to the main European painters and composers of the period, and to major works of ideas, from Newton's *Principia* to Paley's *Evidences*, which influenced European intellectual life in the eighteenth century.

JOHN CRUICKSHANK

University of Sussex
March 1967

1. Voltaire

No individual can ever be said to be fully representative of his age,
but Voltaire probably comes nearer to achieving this distinction
than any other man of modern times. When he was born, in 1694,
Racine and La Fontaine were publishing their last works; Louis XIV
reigned in autocratic splendour and the Church spoke with an
authority few dared to question on practically every subject of
human inquiry. When he died, on the other hand, in 1778, Napoleon,
Hegel, Wordsworth, and Coleridge were already of school age, the
American Revolution was in progress, the nineteenth century was
at hand. In the intervening years the intellectual edifice of the
modern world was being constructed and if others contributed more
durable pieces of masonry to it, none was more ubiquitously and
ceaselessly active than Voltaire. From 1718, when he first gained
fame with his tragedy *Œdipe*, until his death, his reputation never
ceased to grow. The esteem in which he came to be held can be
judged from the fact that his last home at Ferney, on the outskirts of
Geneva, became a place of pilgrimage which no European traveller
with pretensions to enlightenment could omit from his itinerary.
When he returned to Paris at the end of his life he was the object
of an outburst of popular enthusiasm such as no earlier writer had
ever known. In 1791, his mortal remains were transferred to the
Pantheon with all the pomp and circumstance which the young
Revolution could bestow on such an occasion. The inscription on his
sarcophagus reads: 'Il vengea Calas, La Barre, Sirven, et Mont-
bailly. Poëte, philosophe, historien, il a fait prendre un grand essor
à l'esprit humain, et nous a préparés à devenir libres.'

The epitaph showed admirable judgement. The achievement to
which it gave pride of place, the vindication of the memory of victims
of religious intolerance and barbarous legislation, might perhaps

seem an evanescent one, for most of these cases are now forgotten. Yet the passion for justice which prompted Voltaire to spend many years in lengthy legal battles was an outstanding trait of his personality and one of the main reasons for his popularity and influence. The other aspect of his activity which the Revolutionaries chose to stress was more obvious—by freeing the human spirit from the shackles of dogma, by his constant championing of political liberty within the law, he had indeed prepared the way for all that was most liberal in the work of the Revolution itself.

However, the epitaph is relatively brief on what to us seems perhaps the most outstanding characteristic of Voltaire—the encyclopedic breadth of his interests. 'Poëte, philosophe, historien' hardly does him justice and the Revolutionaries could easily have gone further. Had they so wished, they could have spoken of him as a brilliant popularizer of new ideas in science and political thought; they could have described the new universality and new social awareness visible in his historical writings; they could have catalogued the pious frauds destroyed by his mocking satire; they might even (though the solemnity of the occasion would scarcely have allowed this) have mentioned that he was the author of some of the wittiest short stories ever written.

No doubt they thought that such additional praise was superfluous, believing that Voltaire was assured of the gratitude of posterity. They could not foresee that immediate posterity, in the shape of the Bourbon Restoration, was to remove his remains from the resting-place in which they had so proudly placed them. Nor could they foretell a later posterity's judgement on his work. Had they been able to do so, their reactions might well have been a mixture of self-congratulation and bewildered incomprehension. How right they had been to stress the passionate love of freedom and justice in one whose pleas for tolerance and humanity were to re-echo down the corridors of the nineteenth century and beyond. Yet how puzzling that one of the images of their hero which was to take shape during the same period was that of a shallow, mocking, self-satisfied nihilist. How right had been their emphasis on the range of Voltaire's literary output, yet how disconcerting to find that a little over a century later the greater part of it (with the outstanding exception of the *contes* they failed to mention) would remain more or less permanently on the library shelves.

They might, it is true, have received early warning of posterity's judgement from Diderot's cryptic phrase: 'Cet homme n'est que le second dans tous les genres.' The generalization is unfair, but it contains enough truth to serve to highlight the paradox of Voltaire: the literary work by which he and his contemporaries set the greatest store has failed to stand the test of time; for the most part it is the writings which he regarded as transient which have proved lasting.

Tastes may change, but there seems little likelihood that Voltaire's epic and dramatic poetry will ever again command the respect which even a Romantic like Byron could feel for it. If, nevertheless, it deserves pride of place in any account of Voltaire, this is primarily for historical reasons. To his contemporaries he was first and foremost a poet—the great poet of the century—and even his numerous enemies usually coupled their denunciations of his religious and political ideas with eulogies, however grudging, of his poetic genius. Nor, given the taste of the age, was this an altogether unreasonable view, for he epitomized the neo-classical spirit better than any other Frenchman. Even today his work is not without some appeal: there is wit and grace in many of his slighter poems; there is a ring of sincerity in some of his more serious philosophical ones (such as the *Ode sur le désastre de Lisbonne*) which makes them more than rhetorical commonplaces; there are descriptive passages (in *La Henriade*, for example) which reveal something of the vivacity and the eye for significant detail more normally characteristic of his prose style. His plays, too, though in later years they tend to relapse into pathos and propaganda, are not without their merits. *Œdipe* may be something of a rehash of Sophocles and Corneille (with Racine thrown in for good measure), yet something of the intensity of Voltaire's own feelings comes through in the note of revolt which characterizes its tragic ending. *Zaïre* may be a French *Othello* (though Voltaire's debt to Shakespeare has often been exaggerated), but it has its moments of poetic inspiration, a classical clarity of exposition and a tragic dignity which is never allowed to lapse into sentimentality.

Yet all this, if it adds up to a certain distinction, does not constitute greatness. Voltaire himself was perspicacious enough to put his finger on one of the reasons for this when he remarked that after a period of great artistic achievement such as the French Classical age, 'on est réduit ou à imiter ou à s'égarer'. If to innovate was to go astray, then imitation was the safest path, especially if imitation meant following the classical rules which to him, as to the majority of his contemporaries, were 'discovered not devised'. So imitate he did. In *La Henriade*, the epic poem in praise of Henri IV, he produced a work which was hailed by contemporaries as the long-awaited French epic, but to us appears as a rather uninspired pastiche of Virgil. In his many tragedies he followed all (or nearly all) the classical rules and adopted the *style noble* of Corneille and Racine.

Such a policy need not necessarily be condemned; had not Virgil and Racine themselves imitated the forms of others? But they had infused them with a poetic magic of their own, and this Voltaire (who lacked both poetical inspiration and psychological insight) was in no position to do. Nor did he really try to do so. Racine had spent a year over most of his plays and longer over his last masterpieces. Voltaire, for the most part, wrote his plays in haste; the theatre was his favourite art; nevertheless, he had other fish to fry.

Moreover, despite his admiration for the classical rules, despite his fear that to innovate was to go astray, he nevertheless wanted to innovate; rightly so, for his own genius was cast in a different mould. Indeed, he did innovate, especially in his plays. His theatre may be 'French Classical', but it introduces a greater degree of action and spectacle to the stage, chooses its subjects from French history or from more exotic lands (*Alzire*, *L'Orphelin de la Chine*), and even departs from classical norms of reason to the extent of introducing 'Shakespearian' ghosts (*Éryphile*, *Sémiramis*). Above all it is propagandist. In the earliest plays the propaganda—anti-Christian and anti-monarchical—is visible only in occasional lines, but later it becomes central to the plot and is often made even more explicit in the printed version by lengthy prefaces which foreshadow those of Dumas *fils* or Bernard Shaw. Indeed, if he was far from being a revolutionary in matters theatrical (despite a mild flirtation with the new *drame bourgeois*), he contributed not a little to the evolution which was to prepare the way for the Romantic upheaval, though no doubt he would have rejected Romanticism as a return to the barbarism of Shakespeare whose genius he admired, but whose influence he deplored.

Yet if his innovations are historically significant, they are aesthetically unconvincing; the new spirit of 'philosophical' propaganda could not be adequately conveyed by an artificial language fixed almost a century earlier or by an artistic form designed to reveal the underlying motives of human behaviour. Voltaire never recognized this consciously; it would, indeed, have been difficult for him to do so when contemporaries were unanimous in their praise of his poetic genius. Subconsciously, however, he may have sensed the truth, for though he never abandoned poetry and drama, he also sought other forms of expression better adapted both to his literary gifts and to the message he wished to convey.

For if Voltaire the poet belongs primarily to the realms of literary history, Voltaire the *philosophe* (and nearly all his prose writing and a good deal of his verse too may be described as 'philosophic') belongs to posterity. Not only was he the tireless exponent of ideas which, novel in their day, have since become part of the fabric of our civilization, but he brought to the task of expressing them superlative literary qualities. The vividness, clarity, and wit which he possessed in abundance rarely penetrated the constricting form of classical verse, but in his prose writing, above all perhaps in his masterpieces, the philosophical *contes*, they found their fullest expression.

In the eighteenth century, of course, the word *philosophe* meant something very different from what it does today. In one sense its meaning was wider, for a *philosophe* could be anyone who approached the problems of philosophy, religion, science, or politics, or simply the problem of living, in a spirit of free inquiry untrammelled by dogmatic preconceptions. In another sense, however, it was narrower, for, particularly in the second half of the century, the term was appropriated by a group of writers who could perhaps most simply be described as liberal propagandists. Deists, atheists, and, more rarely, Catholics in religion, they were united in their advocacy of toleration. Royalists or democrats in politics, they were at one in affirming the need for reform of the French State. Aristocratic or bourgeois in origin, they nearly all sought the abolition of feudal privilege, greater social equality, and more political liberty. Most of the great writers of the century belonged in some way to this 'philosophic' movement even if, like Rousseau, they ended by breaking away from it. Voltaire, its most prolific and its greatest writer, was extolled by the others (though some, like Diderot, had their reservations) as the *philosophe par excellence.*

To be a great *philosophe* in this sense it was not essential to be a great philosopher in the modern meaning of the term, and certainly the reader who looks to Voltaire in the hope of finding philosophical profundity or rigorous logical argument is likely to be disappointed. He once described himself as being like one of those little brooks which are very clear because they are not very deep, and it would not be unfair to add that there are times when the currents seem to be running in opposite directions. On the whole, he was a typical eighteenth-century empiricist, cautious, factual, mistrustful of system-building, an avowed disciple of Locke, proud to proclaim himself, as he does in the title of one of his works, *le philosophe ignorant.* Yet when he was defending his belief in 'un dieu créateur, rémunérateur et vengeur' he could throw caution to the winds. For this sceptic who spent a large part of his life ridiculing revealed religion in general and orthodox Catholicism in particular, nevertheless believed in a God whose existence he 'proved' by *a priori* arguments and to whom, particularly in his later years, he attributed many of the qualities of the Christian divinity. So intense, indeed, were the religious feelings he expressed that some critics have even spoken of 'Voltaire the mystic'. The conflict between these different approaches ran through many aspects of his thought, but it crystallized particularly around the problem of evil. 'Reason' affirmed the existence of a just and omnipotent God; experience showed that mankind was a prey to moral and physical evil. In vain Voltaire sought, as in his poem on the Lisbon earthquake of 1755, to reconcile these conflicting views and if for a moment—the moment of his masterpiece, *Candide*—he was to urge men to stop trying to solve the problem, he was, in the long run, quite incapable of heeding his own advice.[1]

[1] See Chapter 12 for a general account of the various eighteenth-century discussions of the problem of evil.

Nor is he very satisfying as a political philosopher. He is consistent in his advocacy of certain general principles: liberty, toleration, humanitarianism, the rule of law. But if we ask him what form of society and government is needed to achieve these ends, we find that the consistency has disappeared. On the one hand there is a 'republican' Voltaire who defends the right of peoples to govern themselves and who is one of the great creators of the *mystique* of democracy. Yet he is no doctrinaire democrat, and the admired *peuple* can suddenly become the despised *populace*, the debates of virtuous republicans can be transformed into the factional bickerings of self-seeking pressure-groups, and Voltaire (though he never uses the term) can insist on the eminent desirability of enlightened despotism and can fall at the feet of a Frederick or a Catherine the Great. If we look in his work for a consistent political philosophy, we can only agree that he has created what Émile Faguet called 'un chaos d'idées claires'.

His philosophy of history, again, influential though it is, can hardly be said to rank with those of a Vico, a Montesquieu, or a Herder. On the one hand, he is fascinated by the achievement of outstanding individuals—Louis XIV or Peter the Great—and often exaggerates their historical role. At the other extreme, he delights in demonstrating the complete unpredictability of history—the most trivial causes can have the most momentous consequences. He has a belief in progress and is capable, at times, of producing masterly analyses of how various social and economic factors have brought it about, but he also has a very narrow concept of the consistency of human nature which makes him judge the ancient Babylonians as if they were contemporary Parisians and often vitiates his appreciation of distant historical epochs. If he coins the phrase 'philosophy of history', he is not one of the outstanding creators of the reality behind it.

However, if we turn from Voltaire the philosopher to Voltaire the *philosophe*, a very different picture emerges and we begin to see how the greatness of the man transcends his limitations as a systematic thinker. 'Jean-Jacques n'écrit que pour écrire,' he once wrote, 'moi j'écris pour agir', and if the statement is unfair to Rousseau it reveals the essence of Voltaire. His immense energy was primarily directed not towards a theoretical understanding of man and the universe, but towards the practical amelioration of the human condition; contemplation was all very well, but what really mattered was action:

Looked at in this light, the contradictions of his philosophy do not disappear, but they take on a new significance. Epistemology, metaphysics, the philosophies of history and politics all matter to Voltaire, but, consciously or unconsciously, they are all subordinated to an overriding concern for the moral improvement of mankind. His consistent opposition to Christianity, for example, epitomized in the slogan 'écrasez l'infâme' and expounded in countless anti-biblical works of the sixties and seventies, was not based primarily on a dispassionate investigation of the New Testament (though this played its part) but on a profound revulsion against the barbarities of the Old, on the horror he felt at events like the massacre of St. Bartholomew's Day and, more recently, the executions of a Calas or a La Barre, above all on the fact that the Church continued to justify such atrocities. It was based perhaps too (though here we are in the realms of conjecture) on early personal experiences which caused him to hate the image of a gloomy vengeful divinity. The task, if humanity were to prosper, was to destroy this doctrine of sin, atonement, and damnation and replace it with something both truer (so that it would be widely accepted) and more positive (since it would be more useful to the progress of humanity). A thoroughgoing materialism might have fulfilled the first prerequisite, but could it have fulfilled the second? The problem confronted many eighteenth-century thinkers, among them the clear-sighted Diderot, who expressed his rage at his inability to solve it. Voltaire, however, never posed it, at any rate not openly. He felt the need for a divine authority to sanction his universal moral standards and this feeling was converted into certainty by the 'Newtonian' proofs of God's existence. The result may not have been entirely satisfactory from the point of view of logical consistency, but as a weapon against 'l'infâme' it was far more effective than dogmatic atheism which unnecessarily antagonized both the authorities and the public (had not the publication of Helvétius's *De l'esprit* nearly killed the *Encyclopédie*?) and could lead to a total breakdown of moral standards. If Voltaire wished to 'act' on men's minds he had chosen the ideal combination of ideas.

If his political philosophy is considered in a similar light, then once again the 'chaos d'idées claires' resolves itself not into consistency but into a meaningful pattern. Once again his basic purpose was the moral improvement of human society. This could be furthered by the achievement of specific aims: the rule of law, respect for the liberty of the individual and his property, freedom from arbitrary arrest and from the barbarities of judicial torture and inhuman punishments. It could be achieved by more equitable taxation, by a reduction of the barriers between classes, by greater concern for the welfare of the labouring poor. Voltaire's great strategic aim was to bring about these reforms. Just how they were to be achieved and by whom were questions which he regarded as relatively minor tactical matters. If it looked as though an enlightened despot would succeed, one should support the despot; if a limited monarchy seemed capable of producing the desired result, it should be encouraged; if a popular assembly of the majority of the citizens had the power and the will, it too should be supported. All these situations Voltaire saw as existing in the Europe of his own day. In France he supported the reforming ministries of Louis XV and Louis XVI rather than the venal, intolerant, and aristocratic Parlements; in England he extolled the virtues of the mixed monarchy resulting from the Revolution settlement of 1688; in Geneva, on the other hand, he supported first the bourgeois and then the relatively plebeian *natifs* in their struggle against the patrician *conseil*, for they seemed to him to be an enlightened, educated majority capable of ruling and reforming their city state.

Voltaire's philosophy of history, for all its theoretical weakness, was no less geared to action. In the first place, the action of actually writing history. Montesquieu's preoccupation with the analysis of different forces leading to historical change led to a major sociological study, but one devoid of historical continuity. Voltaire, on the other hand (and if the sheer volume of his work is anything to judge by, this is one of his major achievements), rewrote, in narrative form, practically the whole history of the human race from the Creation to the middle of the eighteenth century. Yet he had a second and perhaps more important practical aim—that of providing modern, enlightened man with the title-deeds to his inheritance. He

consciously rewrote history as 'l'histoire de l'esprit humain'—not as
a chronicle of kings and their wars but as the story of the gradual
development of human society, its arts, its sciences, its industry, its
social institutions. If the kings and battles were there too, they were
there to serve as reminders of a barbarism which had been overcome
and which must never be allowed to return. Moreover, not only did
he give history a new meaning, he also struck at the roots of an old
one—that of the Church. It was absurd to try to compress the early
history of mankind into the four thousand years which, according to
biblical chronology, had elapsed between the Creation and the
coming of Christ; it was absurd to believe in the repopulation of the
earth by the grandsons of Noah after the Flood. It was ridiculous to
write, as Bossuet had done, as if nothing significant had happened
outside the confines of the Middle East and Europe, and still more
so to descry the finger of God constantly controlling the events of
universal history to reward or punish the Jews or the Christian
Church. If Voltaire liked to dwell on the insignificant causes of great
events it was partly in order to show the absurdity of this naïve view
of the providential control of human history, just as his emphasis
on the achievements of great men was linked with his belief in
human freedom and his exhortations to his own contemporaries to
carry progress yet further.

Voltaire the *philosophe* was, then, essentially a man of action. Yet,
while his actions would in themselves have ensured him a place in
history, they would not have placed him among the great figures of
the history of literature. His position there is maintained by the
qualities which characterize his writing: a remarkable power of
organization and presentation of his material; a lucid and engaging
style; above all, an unsurpassed wit.

He was, in the best sense of the term, a superb journalist. From
the vast amount of material at his disposal (he read voraciously and
his memory was prodigious) he chose with a sure instinct the facts
which best fitted his case (for he usually had a case to make) and
which were most likely to arouse the immediate interest of his
readers. He then presented them in their most telling form, using
aphorism, dramatization, irony, wit. The process is seen again
and again in his works, but nowhere more clearly than in his first

masterpiece in which description and propaganda are combined: the *Lettres philosophiques* of 1734, which both described all that was most significant in the life of the England from which he had just returned and constituted, in Lanson's phrase, 'la première bombe lancée contre l'ancien régime'. Just how effectively Voltaire seizes on the essentials of the English scene can be judged from any comparison of his work with earlier travellers' accounts. These are more concerned with geographical description and colourful anecdote. Voltaire ignores geography, keeps anecdote firmly in its place, and describes instead religion, government, science, philosophy, literature. But he does so in such a way that nearly everything he says in praise of English institutions leads up to, or at least implies, criticism of the corresponding institutions in the France which had exiled him, and at the same time puts forward a general argument for liberal reform. The Letter 'Sur le commerce', for example, after speaking approvingly of the social status enjoyed by the English merchant class and of the freedom of the nobility to indulge in commerce, concludes:

En France est marquis qui veut; et quiconque arrive à Paris du fond d'une province avec de l'argent à dépenser et un nom en *ac* ou en *ille*, peut dire: 'Un homme comme moi, un homme de ma qualité', et mépriser souverainement un négociant... Je ne sais pourtant lequel est le plus utile à un État, ou un seigneur bien poudré qui sait précisément à quelle heure le roi se lève, à quelle heure il se couche, et qui se donne des airs de grandeur en jouant le rôle d'esclave dans l'antichambre d'un ministre, ou un négociant qui enrichit son pays, donne de son cabinet des ordres à Surate et au Caire, et contribue au bonheur du monde.

The whole letter leads up to the demand for greater social equality and social utility implicit in the withering irony of this paragraph.

Of course, Voltaire has his models. The lively dramatic form which he uses in the letters on the Quakers echoes that of Pascal's *Lettres provinciales*. There is a greater debt to Montesquieu, whose *Lettres persanes* constituted the first great satire on eighteenth-century France. However, the differences between the two works are significant. Montesquieu can be more profound in his discussions and more subtle in his portraiture, but his work is more diffuse and he can become engrossed in the picturesque detail or the romantic complications of his plot. Voltaire, on the other hand, hardly ever loses sight of his aim—the promotion of tolerance, freedom of thought, and political liberty.

The clarity and force of his style are clearly visible in the *Lettres*, as in the passage quoted above or in aphoristic phrases such as 'La Chambre des Pairs et celle des Communes sont les arbitres de la nation, le roi est le sur-arbitre', or 'S'il n'y avait en Angleterre qu'une religion, le despotisme serait à craindre, s'il y en avait deux, elles se couperaient la gorge; mais il y en a trente, et elles vivent en paix heureuses', or again, in a different key, 'le mérite de cet auteur [Shakespeare] a perdu le théâtre anglais'. And his ability to enliven more erudite subjects can be seen from the opening phrases of his discussion of the Newtonian revolution:

Un Français qui arrive à Londres trouve les choses bien changées, en philosophie comme dans tout le reste. Il a laissé le monde plein; il le trouve vide. A Paris on voit l'univers composé de tourbillons de matière subtile; à Londres on ne voit rien de cela. Chez nous, c'est la pression de la lune qui cause le flux de la mer; chez les Anglais, c'est la mer qui gravite vers la lune.

The slightly colloquial letter form, allowing as it does a telling directness of approach, was well suited to Voltaire. But the same sinewy vigour is to be found in other and more formal works—in his histories, for example, and above all in the first and most 'literary' of these, the *Histoire de Charles XII* of 1731. The account of Charles's defeat at Poltava and his subsequent flight to Turkey is an admirably vivid piece of narrative writing. The parallel of the two opposing monarchs, Charles and Peter the Great, though using a traditional rhetorical form, is a model of its kind:

Charles XII illustre par neuf années de victoires; Pierre Alexiowitz par neuf années de peines, prises pour former des troupes égales aux troupes suédoises; l'un glorieux d'avoir donné des États, l'autre d'avoir civilisé les siens; Charles aimant les dangers et ne combattant que pour la gloire; Alexiowitz ne fuyant point le péril, et ne faisant la guerre que pour ses intérêts; le monarque suédois libéral par grandeur d'âme, le moscovite ne donnant jamais que par quelque vue...

There were times, moreover, when Voltaire succeeded in coupling this vigour with an expression of the emotional intensity which characterized him as a man and in achieving something of the grandeur of the Bossuet whose prose he so much admired. The *Traité sur la tolérance*, for example, the most important single work in his long stuggle to vindicate the memory of Calas, ends with a moving prayer. Yet such moments were rare, for this was not really Voltaire's way. His essential appeal was to the intellect and his sharpest weapons not eloquence, but irony and wit.

His wit has an exuberance which one would be tempted to describe as youthful were it not for the fact that it increased as he got older. It is visible in dozens of books and pamphlets ridiculing the Church and its doctrines, mocking pretentious pedants in the spheres of science and history, poking fun at a whole host of *idées reçues*. It permeates the *Dictionnaire philosophique*—the one-man encyclopedia which he began in the fifties and kept on expanding. However, it really comes into its own in the philosophical *conte*—the genre which Voltaire largely created for himself and which was most perfectly adapted to his gifts.

For the *conte* gave scope to all his qualities. As it was philosophical —that is to say argumentative or propagandist—it allowed him to express his message, religious, political, or social. As it was in origin a tale of adventure, swift-moving, packed with incident, a sort of compressed picaresque novel, it gave full range to his narrative skill without demanding of him qualities of psychological insight which he did not possess. As it sprang from both the black humour of Swift and the more delicate irony of Boccaccio, it gave free rein to all the shades of his own wit and humour.

Voltaire only discovered the genre late in life and the first of his *contes* were not published until he was over fifty. They are not all masterpieces. Sometimes, as in the earliest of them, the tolerant, easy-going message is lacking in bite. Sometimes, as in *L'Homme aux quarante écus*, Voltaire tries to hit too many targets with one shot. Sometimes, as in the *Histoire de Jenni*, the story gets forgotten and the work becomes a philosophical dialogue. Yet in the best of them—for example in *Micromégas*, *L'Ingénu*, or *La Princesse de Babylone*—Voltaire achieves a real fusion of subject-matter and style. Above all, this is the case with *Candide*. Here the central theme—the ridiculing of the absurdity of philosophical optimism epitomized in Pangloss's 'tout est bien'—dominates the tale from beginning to end and the message is conveyed by the story itself rather than by the comments of the author or the characters. The characters themselves, however, by their puppet-like simplicity and by their habit of reappearing in different parts of the world after they have been assumed to be dead, contribute to the general picture Voltaire is trying to create of a universe without plan or purpose. So too does the style with its sudden descents from apparent high seriousness into bathos or even bawdry, with its magic-lantern-like succession of shots of different places and people. The way in which its sudden changes of perspective can drive home the argument is nowhere better illustrated than in this description of a battle in which what at first sight appears to be a glorification of war is suddenly transformed into an account of its horrors:

Rien n'était si beau, si leste, si brillant, si bien ordonné que les deux armées. Les trompettes, les fifres, les hautbois, les tambours, les canons, formaient une harmonie telle qu'il n'y en eut jamais en enfer. Les canons renversèrent d'abord à peu près six mille hommes de chaque côté; ensuite la mousqueterie ôta du meilleur des mondes environ neuf à dix mille coquins qui en infectaient la surface. La baïonnette fut aussi la raison suffisante de la mort de quelques milliers d'hommes.

Candide epitomizes Voltaire because it compresses into a small space two basic aspects of his personality—his 'realistic' philosophical pessimism and his fundamental personal optimism. Human life has no 'meaning'; the cosmos cannot be explained. Yet even whilst explaining that it cannot be explained, Voltaire is in some sense imposing a pattern on it just as he believes that man can impose a significant pattern on his own life by 'cultivating his garden'.

The miracle of *Candide* remains unique, but all its qualities are to be found, if in a more diffuse form, in his other writings. Perhaps, indeed, too much has been made of this one masterpiece. The reader who turns from it to the rest of Voltaire will find much to recompense him.

NOTE

FRANÇOIS-MARIE AROUET DE VOLTAIRE, 1694-1778, son of a Parisian notary, soon gained fame as poet and dramatist and notoriety as deist and satirist. Two years' exile in England (1726-8) left a deep impression. Return to France was followed by further literary success (e.g. *Histoire de Charles XII*, *Zaïre*) and further scandal (e.g. the pro-English *Lettres philosophiques* of 1734). A spell of favour at Court proved brief, as did his 'honeymoon' with Frederick the Great (1750-3). Later he settled at Geneva (1755) and Ferney (1760) whence he dominated the 'philosophic' movement, pouring forth liberal and deistic propaganda and intervening in favour of victims of injustice. He died shortly after a triumphant return to Paris.

Editions. See G. Bengesco, *Voltaire: bibliographie de ses œuvres* (1882-90). There are three major complete editions: (*a*) by Beaumarchais and others (1784-9); (*b*) by Beuchot (1828-40); (*c*) by Moland (1877-85). For the *Correspondance*, these are superseded by Besterman's edition (1953-64). Among other modern editions, the following are noteworthy: *La Henriade* (ed. Taylor, 1965); *Œuvres historiques* (ed. Pomeau, 1957); *Lettres philosophiques* (ed. Lanson, revised Rousseau, 1964); *Traité de métaphysique* (ed. Patterson, 1937); *Micromégas* (ed. Wade, 1950); *Essai sur les mœurs* (ed. Pomeau, 1963); *Candide* (ed. Morize, 1913, and Pomeau, 1959); *Dictionnaire philosophique* (ed. Benda and Naves, 1935-6); *La Philosophie de l'histoire* (ed. Brumfitt, 1963); *Le Philosophe ignorant* (ed. Carr, 1965); *L'Ingénu* (ed. Jones, 1936).

Criticism. G. Desnoiresterres's biography, *Voltaire et la société au XVIIIᵉ siècle* (1869-76: 8 vols.), though outdated, remains basic. Excellent general studies include G. Lanson (revised edn., 1965), H. N. Brailsford (1935), R. Naves (1942), and N. Torrey (*The Spirit of Voltaire*, 1938). On specific topics, see G. Pellissier, *Voltaire philosophe* (1908); R. Pomeau, *La Religion de Voltaire* (1956); P. Gay, *Voltaire's Politics* (1959); J. H. Brumfitt, *Voltaire, Historian* (1958); R. Naves, *Le Goût de Voltaire* (1938); R. S. Ridgeway, *La Propagande philosophique dans les tragédies de Voltaire* (1961); W. H. Barber, *Voltaire's 'Candide'* (1960); I. O. Wade, *Voltaire and 'Candide'* (1959). Many recent studies are to be found in the Institut Voltaire's *Studies on Voltaire and the Eighteenth Century* (1955-).

2. The Heritage of Newton and Locke

THOUGH Voltaire is the most universal figure of the French Enlightenment, he perhaps fails to reveal both its inner core of enthusiasm and what is most original in its doctrine. He is too all-embracing and too superficial to be a first-rate systematic thinker and something of the depth and rigour of the philosophy of the Enlightenment escapes him. Moreover, he is too much the incarnation of sceptical common sense to share the more optimistic visions of some of his contemporaries. The Enlightenment strove to create a new Utopia; to construct what Carl Becker called 'The Heavenly City of the Eighteenth-Century Philosophers'. Voltaire never believed that man would get much further than a tolerably habitable garden suburb.

If Voltaire does not adequately reflect the Enlightenment vision, the same can also be said of other outstanding individuals of the century. Montesquieu, for all the novelty of his method, is far too much a cautious traditionalist in his view of man and society. Rousseau is often in conscious revolt against the spirit of his age. Diderot comes much nearer to being the characteristic man of the Enlightenment, but in many ways he transcends its limitations and he too can revolt against it when he finds that it is in danger of becoming an intellectual strait-jacket. To appreciate its full savour one has to turn from the men of genius to others who, though distinguished, are of lesser stature: to Condillac and d'Alembert, to La Mettrie and Helvétius, to d'Holbach and Condorcet. It is they who are the principal architects of the 'heavenly city'.

Yet if they are men of second rank, they are nevertheless disciples and interpreters of two men of genius, for the basic intellectual inspiration of the Enlightenment stems from two great Englishmen of the late seventeenth century—Newton and Locke. It was they who provided the essential ideas which were to be combined and developed (and at times distorted) into a new and fruitful synthesis.

To understand why the seeds of Locke's and Newton's thought developed as they did, one must first examine the ground on which they fell. Survivors of the revolutionary upheaval at the end of the century could look back on the Old Regime as an age of 'la douceur de vivre'. It had never been that for more than a privileged minority, but it had been a period of social stability and material progress without parallel in previous history. The great scourges of the human race, war, pestilence, and famine, had none of them been abolished, but they had all, in Western Europe at least, been confined within acceptable limits. Man's inhumanity to man appeared to have lessened: the horrors of the previous century such as the devastations of the Thirty Years War or the laying-waste of the Palatinate seemed to be things of the past, and if wars continued to be fought, they had become relatively gentlemanly encounters between small professional armies ('Messieurs les Anglais, tirez les premiers', as a French commander at Fontenoy is reputed to have said). With the vast expansion of European trade and with the beginnings of what were later to be known as the Industrial and Agricultural Revolutions, economic prosperity, education, all the attributes of civilized life became available to new strata of society. All social classes (except perhaps the peasantry) sensed the reality of this progress and all desired its continuation; but it was primarily the bourgeoisie which gave concrete form to such aspirations. They had contributed most and had gained most and were perhaps therefore the most optimistic. However, as they grew in wealth, they became increasingly aware of their unsatisfactory position in a society which was still nominally, and in many ways practically, dominated by a feudal nobility and clergy. As a result the philosophy of the Enlightenment was to be something more than a mere affirmation that progress had taken place and a desire to see a theory of progress established on a rational scientific basis; it was to contain in addition a demand for the radical intensification of that progress particularly in the direction of social equality.

At first sight the mathematical and cosmological theories of Newton and the epistemological investigations of Locke seem remote from such preoccupations. Nor was their initial acceptance based on any clear awareness of their potentially revolutionary implications. Yet they did, in fact, provide the spark which was to set the Enlightenment ablaze.

The philosophy of Descartes, when it first appeared in the early seventeenth century, had aroused the suspicions of the orthodox. Yet by the early eighteenth century it had itself acquired the status of orthodoxy. In doing so, however, it had become transformed. Descartes had preached, if he had not always practised, the virtues of observation and experiment, and he had insisted almost as strongly as did the men of the Enlightenment that 'philosophy' must contribute to the material well-being of humanity. However, this 'revolutionary' Descartes was fast becoming forgotten. Instead there emerged the image—a true if incomplete one—of the creator of a great deductive system which started from a very few self-evident truths but arrived at conclusions which were very far from being self-evident, such as the explanation of the universe based on the theory of vortices or whirlpools of 'subtle matter' which accounted for the movement of heavenly bodies, the assertion that animals, having no souls, were purely mechanical beings, and the affirmation that many of man's fundamental ideas were born with him.

Descartes himself strove to reconcile his views with Christian orthodoxy and the greatest of his disciples, Malebranche, was to continue this process, though in so doing he was to depart even further from the 'common sense' his master had preached. This very fact may partly account for the Enlightenment's reaction against his philosophy. Not only had it become less 'reasonable', but it had become associated with a Church which they rejected not only because they could not believe its doctrines, but also because they saw in it one of the main pillars of a social organization they wished to alter. Some of them, it is true, recognized the greatness of Descartes, but others, Voltaire among them, adopted a predominantly hostile attitude. This was somewhat unjust, for the Enlightenment as a whole, though it started off by being intensely suspicious of Descartes's system-building, was itself to erect a system which was often at variance with the facts of human nature, and in this it was to be more 'Cartesian' than it was willing to admit.

However, if the ideas of Newton and Locke were to triumph over those of Descartes, this was not primarily the result of some shrewd calculation of possible political utility, but rather the growing conviction that the theories of Newton and Locke fitted the facts, whereas those of Descartes did not. This conviction, however, especially in the case of Newton, was slow to develop.

Newton's fame spread to France in the early eighteenth century, but this was not because of his *Principia mathematica* of 1687 in which he propounded the theory of gravity with which his name was to become indissolubly linked. Rather was it the result of a celebrated controversy between his disciples and those of Leibniz as to who had first invented the infinitesimal calculus, and of his *Optics* of 1704 which soon won a large measure of approval. The *Principia* was at first ignored, but this neglect was replaced, in the second decade of the century, by an attitude of open hostility.

The reasons for this attitude are instructive. On the whole, the Newtonian law of gravity seemed to fit the known facts well whereas the Cartesian principle of vortices of subtle matter appeared less satisfactory because the planets did not behave quite as they might have been expected to do if carried round in a whirlpool; they appeared, for example, to speed up at times when they ought to have slowed down. However, there were important, and what at the time seemed more powerful, arguments on the other side. The Cartesian explanation of the universe was based on a hypothesis of the sort that Newton was refusing to make when he made his famous statement, '*hypotheses non fingo*', for the vortices of subtle matter which accounted for the motion of the heavenly bodies could not be perceived and hence their existence (though assumed to be a physical fact) could not be verified. Yet at least they were based on a clear and distinct idea and on a principle of propulsion which was comprehensible to common sense and corresponded to the observable realities of the physical world. This could not be said of the Newtonian view. The idea of attraction at a distance across 'empty' space could not be comprehended in terms of human experience and seemed contrary to common sense. Was Newton asserting that this power of attraction was a quality inherent in matter, and if so was he not reviving one of the 'occult qualities' of medieval scholastics and leading physics back from intelligibility to obscurity? In fact Newton took great care to insist that he was making no such claim and that he was merely using the term 'attraction' to describe an existential mathematical relationship between bodies, the fundamental cause and nature of which he did not pretend to be able to explain. This caution was not, however, shared by all his disciples, and many of them, following the lead of Cotes in his preface to the second edition of the *Principia* (1713), made attraction a primary quality of matter.

Hence the opposition to Newtonianism in France, which is expressed by reputable scientists such as Jacques Cassini, Dortus de Mairan, and Jean Bernoulli, as well as by the outstanding popularizer of scientific thought and Perpetual Secretary of the Academy, Fontenelle. All reject Newton's views and seek to defend the Cartesian theory. Yet their attempts never quite succeed in making the theory fit the facts and gradually certain features of Newtonianism become accepted. How far this was the case can be seen from Fontenelle's *Éloge de Newton* which he gave to the Academy of Sciences after the English scientist's death in 1727 and which contained a parallel of Descartes and Newton in which the balance was tipped only very slightly in favour of the Frenchman. The diffusion of Newtonianism was furthered by a number of works, among them Coste's translation of the *Optics* in 1720, and two books by disciples: Keill's *Introductio ad veram astronomiam* of 1718 and Pemberton's *A View of Sir Isaac Newton's Philosophy* of 1728. Equally important, as far as France was concerned, was the acceptance of Newtonianism in Holland, particularly by the leading Dutch physicist's Gravesande, whose *Physices Elementa* appeared in 1720–1.

Yet the breakthrough did not occur until the late thirties and it was brought about largely by two men who had come into contact with Newtonianism in England. The first of these was Voltaire, who had been in England at the time of Newton's state funeral in Westminster Abbey and who could hardly have avoided learning about him from Samuel Clarke, the Latin translator of the *Optics*, who was one of Voltaire's principal mentors in matters of English philosophy and theology. Voltaire's initial conversion, however, was largely an act of faith, for he had little knowledge of Newton and little scientific training. It was not until he was back in France that he really began to study Newtonianism with the help of scientists such as Clairault and Maupertuis, and his correspondence with the latter shows that his remaining ignorance was still extensive. It had only partly diminished when he published the *Lettres philosophiques*; his information came mainly from the works of Maupertuis and Pemberton, and very possibly he had not read Newton himself. The chapters on Newton in the *Lettres philosophiques* aroused relatively little interest compared with the more provocative ones on English philosophy and religion. Nevertheless, the great success of the work meant that a favourable account of Newton's theories reached a far wider French public than ever before.

Between Voltaire's visit to England and the publication of his *Lettres philosophiques* there occurred another, and from the scientific point of view more reputable, conversion to Newtonianism—that of Maupertuis, who spent six months in England in 1728, was in close touch with Pemberton and Keill, and was elected to the Royal Society. In 1732 he published his *Discours sur les différentes figures des astres* which expounded Newtonian theories. Reactions were still hostile, but the opposition was weakening. In 1736, Deslandes, a disciple of the Dutch physicist Musschenbroek, published his *Recueil de différents traités de physique* in which, following his master, he propounded the Newtonian viewpoint. Meanwhile, Voltaire, partly under the influence of Mme du Châtelet and partly under the tutelage of 's Gravesande (whom he visited in Leyden), had deepened his knowledge and in 1738 produced his *Éléments de la philosophie de Newton*. Mme du Châtelet, for her part, was busy translating the *Principia* and writing a celebrated commentary on it.

By the middle of the century, when d'Alembert was writing his *Discours préliminaire* for the *Encyclopédie*, the triumph of Newton seemed assured. In a wider historical perspective, the word 'triumph' is perhaps inappropriate, for Newton can be seen not as a complete innovator, but rather as the culminating figure of a seventeenth-century scientific revolution of which Descartes was one of the founders. Yet to many contemporaries Newton's achievement seemed far more revolutionary than this.

> Nature and Nature's laws were hid in night,
> God said: 'Let Newton be', and all was light.

These famous lines of Pope's were echoed, if less poetically, by d'Alembert, who, after praising Newton for giving science 'une forme qu'elle semble devoir conserver', concluded:

> Ce que nous pourrions ajouter à l'éloge de ce grand philosophe, serait fort au-dessous du témoignage universel qu'on rend aujourd'hui à ses découvertes presque innombrables, et à son génie tout à la fois étendu, juste et profond.

By this time, however, Newtonianism was beginning to change its nature. Its original triumph was due to the fact that its mathematics fitted observable phenomena better than did those of Descartes. Yet once it was accepted, Newtonianism, like Cartesianism, began to grow into a system. Newton began to be looked on not just as a great mathematician and scientist who, by a combination of analytical method and creative hypothesis, had placed many phenomena of nature in a new perspective, but as a supreme visionary who had discovered the ultimate law of things. Newton had not attempted to explain how the system of the universe came into being, but he was convinced, as the eighteenth-century deists were to be, that the architecture of the cosmos necessarily implied the existence of an architect. Moreover, the Newtonian explanation captured and stimulated the imagination by its very simplicity. The phenomena of the universe, from the fall of an apple to the movement of the planets, could all be explained by one simple formula. At last man seemed to hold the key to the cosmos.

However, the poet who had praised Newton for illuminating nature's laws had also observed that the proper study of mankind was man. Nature having been reduced to simplicity, it is hardly surprising that men began to ask whether human nature too did not have its simple laws. If so, could they be discovered? and further (and here a more dazzling prospect began to unfold itself) could they be controlled and utilized by man for his own ends? It is at this point that Newton is joined by Locke.

Locke himself, of course, had no such revolutionary ideas. It is true that he had been something of a revolutionary in the political sense and that the *Treatise on Civil Government* was a justification of the Revolution of 1688. But it was not till the later eighteenth century, especially through its impact on Rousseau, that Locke's political thought became influential in France, and we shall not consider it here. His major philosophical work, the *Essay concerning Human Understanding* of 1690, appeared much less provocative. It was mainly concerned with an analytical investigation of how man's ideas were formed and developed, and its method was closely linked with that of the seventeenth-century scientific revolution. Locke began, in his First Book, by refuting the view that certain ideas were innate in man. In the Second Book he proceeded to assert that the mind was like a sheet of blank paper on which experience inscribed its messages, and to show how ideas arose from sense-impressions and from man's reflections on them, how they were combined, how abstract ideas arose, etc. The Third Book dealt with the relationship between ideas and language, and the Fourth attempted to distinguish the fields in which man could acquire certain knowledge from those in which he had to be content with probability.

If Locke's work aroused a measure of hostility both in England and in France, this was very largely due to one brief passage in the Fourth Book where, discussing the limitations of human knowledge, he had suggested that it was impossible for man to know whether or not it was within God's power to give thought to matter. Locke's critics suggested that if He could, then matter was capable of thought, and accused Locke of opening the door to atheistic materialism. However, Locke's main arguments, despite the fact that his attack on innate ideas was a refutation of the Cartesian position, did not provoke hostile French criticism as those of Newton had done. Some criticism there certainly was from the disciples of Descartes and Malebranche, but on the whole the diffusion of Locke's ideas was rapid. Indeed, through a summary of the *Essay* published in 1688 in Jean Leclerc's *Bibliothèque universelle*, they were known in France before they were known in England. In 1700 there appeared the authoritative French translation by Coste, who had worked under Locke's direction, and in 1720 a translation of Wynne's *Abridgement of Mr Locke's Essay*. A new edition of the Coste translation appeared in 1729 and included details of the debate between Locke and Bishop Stillingfleet over the question of thinking matter. These works, together with many favourable reviews in journals, helped to spread Locke's influence. The Jesuit *Journal de Trévoux* was particularly friendly (perhaps because the Jansenists were hostile) and it was a Jesuit philosopher, Buffier, who, in his *Traité des premières vérités* of 1724, was the first Frenchman to produce a major philosophical work influenced by Locke's thought. Others of less orthodox views were also influenced. In 1702 Pierre Bayle, author of the celebrated *Dictionnaire historique et critique*, declared his agreement with the Lockean position on innate ideas. The *Réflexions critiques* of Du Bos, an important work on aesthetic theory, also owed much to Locke's ideas, and other precursors of the *philosophes*, such as Boulainvilliers, lent their support.

However, in becoming accepted, Locke's thought was also to some extent transformed. Emphasis came to be laid on the first two books, with their insistence on the primacy of experience and on the brief passage which deals with the possibility of thinking matter. This last point was taken up by the atheist *curé* Jean Meslier as well as by Voltaire, who stressed it in his *Lettres philosophiques*. It was later to be developed further by the materialist La Mettrie in his *Histoire naturelle de l'âme* of 1745.

Voltaire's *Lettres philosophiques*, by their success and by the scandal they aroused, did much to popularize Locke (though not so much as Voltaire himself later claimed). Not that Voltaire's knowledge was profound; he, like others, stressed, apart from the question of *matière pensante*, the general principles of the first two books and had very little to say about the rest of Lockean epistemology. However, by mid-century Locke had won his battle against Descartes not only among the *philosophes* but among many of the orthodox too, as was to be shown by the Lockean theses of de Prades and de Brienne which the Sorbonne at first accepted before the rising tide of avowed sensationalist materialism forced it to reconsider its position. The esteem in which the *philosophes* held Locke is once again best illustrated by d'Alembert's *Discours préliminaire*: 'Ce que Newton n'avait osé, ou n'aurait peut-être pas pu faire, Locke l'entreprit et l'exécuta avec succès. On peut dire qu'il créa la métaphysique à peu près comme Newton avait créé la physique.'

Locke's thought, however, was soon to become the starting-point for a new and more comprehensive theory of human psychology.

This development was the work of Condillac, probably the greatest *philosopher* among the *philosophes*. Condillac himself was an admirer of Newton and in his *Traité des systèmes* his praise of the Newtonian system formed a unique exception to his general condemnation of philosophical system-building. Even more, he was an admirer of Locke, but he found the Lockean system incomplete and, in his *Traité des sensations* of 1754, set about the task of completing it by a more rigorous use of analytical method.

Locke had traced the origin of all our ideas back to experience, but he had not attempted to reduce the whole of human thought to such an origin. As well as ideas resulting from sensation, man also had faculties of reflection—will, judgement, imagination, and memory. These Locke took for granted without attempting to investigate their source. To Condillac, this was to leave the problem only half solved, and the *Traité des sensations* was an attempt to show that these reflective faculties also owed their origin to sensation. Condillac's method of illustrating his contention was to take an imaginary statue and endow it, one by one, with the various human senses, starting with what seemed the simplest—the sense of smell. Even reduced to one sense alone, he argued, it would be possible for the statue, confronted by a variety of smells which in turn aroused pleasure or distaste (why they should do either, he does not tell us), to develop the faculties of memory and judgement. As further senses were added, the psychology of the statue became more complex until, once they were all there, it approximated to that of a human being. By this type of analysis Condillac thought he had arrived at a simple and basic law of human nature just as Newtonian analysis had discovered the simple basic law of the material universe.

Condillac's ideas won general acceptance in the later eighteenth century and indeed in much of the early nineteenth too. However, Condillac himself remained an academic philosopher, and it was left to others to draw out the implications of his psychology and to transform his descriptive analysis into a new faith. In this transformation the most important role was to be played by Helvétius— a former financier, a friend of the *philosophes* and an enthusiast for progress. Helvétius's *De l'esprit* of 1758 and to a lesser extent his posthumous *De l'homme* (published in 1772) were among the most influential works of the later eighteenth century and their influence extends well into the nineteenth—to Stendhal, for example, or to the English utilitarians. If modern critics such as Cassirer find his work both derivative and unconvincing, it nevertheless drew together the main doctrines of the age and attempted to present them in a new perspective which offered not merely a consistent explanation of human nature, but a theory of how man, master at last of his own destiny, could develop and control human nature for his own purposes. A convinced Newtonian, Helvétius saw, in the combination of Condillac's extreme form of sensationalism with the Lockean suggestion that matter might have sensitivity, the basis on which a scientific theory of man could be constructed. Man, as he explained particularly in *De l'homme*, was motivated solely by the basic instincts of self-preservation and pleasure-seeking. Otherwise his ideas— even his judgements—were purely the result of his sensations; that is to say of his environment. Human psychology, then, could be reduced to Newtonian simplicity. Helvétius's proof of this contained some crude oversimplifications, and his reduction of man to a pleasure-seeking animal (and particularly a sexually pleasure-seeking animal) led Diderot in his *Réfutation* to protest that Helvétius had ignored both the complexity and the dignity of human nature. Yet Helvétius's purpose was far from being that of extolling self-centred pleasure-seeking; on the contrary it was profoundly moral. Once the basic equality and basic structure of human nature had been understood, then it would be possible to create a society which both took account of and gave direction to man's basic impulses and which, founded on a new scientific utilitarianism, could lead him towards a new Utopia. How far Helvétius was from being a mere hedonist is illustrated by the fact that he risked and even to some extent suffered persecution by publishing his work. For the religious authorities which had accepted Condillac reacted sharply against *De l'esprit*, and other works too, the *Encyclopédie* in particular, were to suffer as a result.

Yet rash though he was, Helvétius had taken some precautions and his work did not openly attack established religious and social principles. It was left to d'Holbach and the group of *philosophes* who collaborated with him to present the new thesis not as an abstract study, but as a concrete programme of reform, for they, publishing for the most part anonymously, had no need for reticence. In the work of d'Holbach—in his *Système de la nature* of 1770 and his *Politique naturelle* and *Système social* of 1773—the synthesis of Newton, Condillac, and Helvétius was presented in combination with a radical attack on all forms of social privilege and all varieties of religious belief. D'Holbach aimed both to sweep away the past and to construct the new, scientific, Utopian future. Nor was he alone in this venture. Morelly, the advocate of communistic egalitarianism, held similar views and was to set the fashion, which lasted into the nineteenth century, of applying Newtonian phraseology to human beings and speaking of men as being activated by laws of attraction and repulsion.

After Helvétius and d'Holbach, however, one further major step remained to be taken: that of synthesizing past, present, and future. It was indeed a most important step, for the most serious criticism that can be levelled against the Newtonian view of the universe is that it is a static one. Newton made no attempt to explain how the solar system had come into being and presumably thought that it had been created in its present form by divine power. The Newtonian, mathematical approach, applied as it was to the biological and then to the nascent social sciences, contained no place for evolution and transformation. Dazzled as they were by the splendour of Newton's achievement, the *philosophes* were often unaware of its limitations and only the more acute minds, such as Maupertuis or Diderot, saw that Newtonian method was not universally applicable. On the purely human level, the philosophy of Condillac reintroduced ideas of change and progress into the philosophical scene, but these ideas, as expressed by Helvétius and d'Holbach, referred essentially to the future. Earlier Enlightenment historical writing, as reflected above all in the work of its greatest exponent, Voltaire, had indeed been aware of the reality of historical progress and had also sought the continuation of this progress. But Voltaire was too much a Newtonian, too much a believer in the constancy of human nature (and perhaps too good a historian) to believe in the inevitability of progress. In his *Discours en Sorbonne* in 1750, the young Turgot had described history as a continuous upward movement of the human spirit, but he did not claim that this progress was the inevitable result of human nature. Such an optimistic proclamation was reserved for Condorcet, one of the last of the eighteenth-century *philosophes* and an outstanding intellectual leader of the Revolution. It was made, however, at an inauspicious moment, for in 1794, when he was writing, the Revolutionary Terror was at its height and Condorcet himself, an advocate of more moderate policies, was soon to be arrested and to die, probably by his own hand. Yet his *Esquisse d'un tableau historique des progrès de l'esprit humain* is the last great testament of Enlightenment thought—the culminating manifesto of the Lockean-Newtonian synthesis. In his preface he demonstrated on sensationalist principles that human progress, once begun, must be continuous and unlimited, for as man is the product of his experience his nature will improve as his environment improves, his improved nature will result in a better environment, and so on *ad infinitum*. In the body of the *Esquisse* he sought to show that the history of mankind was in fact a history of this sort of progress, and in his final chapter he suggested, with all the enthusiasm of one who believed that mankind was now on the threshold of Utopia, some of the ways in which this progress could be continued and directed.

It is easy to seize on the tragic irony of the situation in which this work was written and to see in it a symbolic condemnation of Enlightenment philosophy at the bar of history. Nor is it altogether unreasonable to do so, for there was much that was unduly naïve in the optimism of the age. After the Revolution, men were sadder and perhaps wiser. Yet the heritage of the Enlightenment, if it was to be transformed, was not to be destroyed. Bentham was to make the utilitarianism of Helvétius his point of departure; Saint-Simon was to entitle his supreme legislative body 'le conseil de Newton'; Fourier was to make the principle of attraction the motive force of his socialistic Utopia; Comte was to see in Condorcet the precursor of positive science. Nineteenth-century social reform, and more remotely that of our own day, owe no small debt to the zeal which inspired the disciples of Newton and Locke.

NOTE

ÉTIENNE BONNOT DE CONDILLAC, 1715–80, was for many years tutor to the Prince of Parma. Often known as 'le philosophe des *philosophes*', he was more of an academic philosopher than a social reformer. His main works are *Essai sur l'origine des connaissances humaines* (1746), *Traité des systèmes* (1749), and *Traité des sensations* (1754).

CLAUDE-ADRIEN HELVÉTIUS, 1715–71, after a Jesuit education, became a *fermier-général* at the age of twenty-three, but later devoted much of his time to the 'philosophic' cause. His main works are *De l'esprit* (1758), which was officially condemned, and the posthumous *De l'homme* (1772).

PAUL-HENRI THIRY, BARON D'HOLBACH, 1723–89, was born in the Palatinate, but lived most of his life in Paris where his *salon* became a principal meeting-place of the *philosophes*. He translated scientific works and wrote many 'philosophical' and anti-religious books of which the best known is the *Système de la nature* (1770).

JEAN-ANTOINE-NICOLAS DE CARITAT, MARQUIS DE CONDORCET, 1743–94, was a distinguished mathematician and, from 1785, *secrétaire perpétuel* of the Académie des Sciences. Elected to the Assemblée Législative and later to the Convention, he played an important role in revolutionary politics. His best-known work is his posthumous *Esquisse d'un tableau historique des progrès de l'esprit humain* (1794).

Modern editions. The following are noteworthy: Voltaire, *Lettres philosophiques* (ed. Lanson, revised Rousseau, 1964); Condillac, *Traité des sensations* (ed. Picavet, 1885); d'Alembert, *Discours préliminaire de l'Encyclopédie* (ed. Picavet, 1912); d'Holbach, *Système de la nature* (ed. Belaval, 1966); Condorcet, *Esquisse...* (ed. Prior, 1936).

Criticism. General works: E. Cassirer, *The Philosophy of the Enlightenment* (1951); L. G. Crocker, *An Age of Crisis* (1959); K. Martin, *French Liberal Thought in the Eighteenth Century* (1929); E. Halévy, *The Growth of Philosophic Radicalism* (1934). Detailed studies: G. Bonno, *La Culture et la civilisation britanniques devant l'opinion française de la Paix d'Utrecht aux Lettres philoso- phiques* (1948); P. Brunet, *L'Introduction des théories de Newton en France au XVIIIᵉ siècle* (1931); G. Buchdahl, *The Image of Newton and Locke in the Age of Reason* (1961); R. Grimsley, *Jean d'Alembert* (1963); A. Koyré, *Newtonian Studies* (1965); D. W. Smith, *Helvétius* (1965); P. Naville, *Paul Thiry d'Holbach* (1943).

3. Montesquieu

THE spirit of free rational inquiry which characterizes the French Enlightenment is to be found nowhere more clearly than in the writings of Montesquieu. Cosmopolitan in outlook, and fascinated by the diversity of human societies, he believed that behind this diversity there lay intelligible principles discoverable by reason. His interest in the motley spectacle of man's social life is the main inspiration of his writings, and his search for underlying principles goes back, according to his own account, to the days when he began the study of law: 'au sortir du collège, on me mit dans les mains des livres de droit; j'en cherchai l'esprit.' Something of this inquiring attitude appears in his early scientific and philosophical essays and, more obviously, in his first published work, the *Lettres persanes* (1721). Henceforth his studies and travels were to be directed to this end, as can be seen from his *Pensées, Voyages,* and *Spicilège,* notebooks in which he accumulates facts and ideas on almost every aspect of human activity. His career thus has a definite direction and, after the publication of the *Considérations* (1734), in which he shows how an intelligible pattern can be discerned behind the facts of history, culminates in the *Esprit des lois* (1748), where he seeks to lay bare the principles underlying the bewildering complexity of laws and political institutions.

Human diversity is the theme of the *Lettres persanes,* the correspondence of two Persians, Usbek and Rica, who leave their country in search of wisdom and spend some ten years in Europe, mainly in Paris. The letters written by the two travellers are a lively satirical picture of western society, while those they receive from Persia are a vivid portrayal of certain aspects of life in the East. In fact the work is basically a contrast of eastern and western values, and in using the

Persian literary device to make this contrast possible, Montesquieu was following a well-established tradition. Since the previous century the French had enjoyed reading travellers' accounts (truthful or fictitious) of exotic foreign lands, and alongside such writings there had grown up a genre in which foreign travellers gave amusing or satirical descriptions of Europe. Montesquieu was influenced by a number of such satires, particularly by *L'Espion dans les cours* (1684), a translation of a popular Italian work by Marana, in which a Turkish spy describes the France of Louis XIV. He may also have known the Persian letters published by J. F. Bernard in his *Réflexions morales, comiques et satiriques* (1715). Montesquieu was thus by no means the first writer to describe France as seen through the eyes of oriental travellers: he takes up this familiar genre and exploits to the full its possibilities—humorous, satirical, and philosophical.

In some of the letters Montesquieu simply extracts the maximum comic effect of the contrast between the eastern and western ways of life. In letter 24 Rica, bewildered at the strangeness of his new surroundings, gives an amusing account of the streets of Paris and expresses his amazement at the height of French houses, 'si hautes qu'on jugerait qu'elles ne sont habitées que par des astrologues', while in letter 26 Usbek describes how he is shocked to discover that European women do not wear veils and are not attended by eunuchs. In such letters the Persian way of looking at things never fails to amuse by making the familiar seem new and unusual. But the Persians' detachment from western values is also a powerful weapon of irony and satire. Rica, unfamiliar with the traditions of the French monarchy, thinks that Louis XIV is 'un grand magicien' whose power includes that of changing at will the value of currency; having no knowledge of Christian dogma, he sees in the Pope another 'grand magicien' who can make people believe that one is three and three are one (letter 24). Men of common sense and reason, the Persians have a sharp eye for inconsistency and hypocrisy. Their searching examination of the behaviour of women, clerics, magistrates, journalists, and others is a bitter comment on human vice and folly. In a series of character-sketches not unworthy of La Bruyère, they portray with biting irony such social types as the tax-farmer and the 'directeur de conscience' (letter 48). Keeping

abreast of the political events of the period, they satirize unmerci-
fully the corruption of the closing years of the reign of Louis XIV
and the financial muddles of the Regency.

The two Persians, and particularly Usbek, are, like their creator,
not satisfied with a description of the mere surface of things. They
seek to penetrate to the principles governing human conduct, and
many of the letters are reflections on religion, morals, and politics.
Usbek is struck by the variety of religious creeds, but convinced that
dogma, the source of intolerance, is based on credulity or superstition, he rejects the prevailing religions of both East and West. His
faith is a simple deistic one in the existence of God, the creator of an
intelligible universe and the source of natural justice (letter 83). In
politics Usbek is hostile to despotism, oriental and western, considers monarchy unstable (letter 102) and, while admiring the liberty
of the ancient republics, believes that the kind of government 'le plus
conforme à la raison' is simply 'celui qui va à son but à moins de
frais' (letter 80). With regard to morals, he believes that there is an
immutable principle of eternal justice (letter 83), and in the story of
the Troglodytes (letters 11–14) he shows that a society based on the
unbridled selfishness of individuals will necessarily perish, that
moral virtue and self-restraint are essential if the State is to
survive.

The interest of the two Persians in diversity does not make them
relativists in any true sense of the term. They believe that there are
certain moral principles discoverable by reason, and departure of
individuals or governments from these principles they see as a
legitimate target of satire. They see the universe as having a rational
structure, and underlying even the most seemingly inexplicable
phenomena there is an intelligible order. This is so not only of the
physical universe (letter 97), but also of man's life in society, and in a
remarkable series of letters on the problem of depopulation (113–22)
Usbek shows how the number of the earth's inhabitants is related
to certain 'causes physiques' and 'causes morales' such as climate,
geography, religion, customs, and political policy. In this we see
Montesquieu seeking principles behind diversity in a way which
anticipates his later works.

Although they are vehicles of the author's ideas, Usbek and Rica are not disembodied voices of reason, but as Persian as Montesquieu can make them. He borrows local colour from contemporary travel literature, and supplies Usbek (though not the younger Rica) with what he no doubt considered an essential appurtenance of every self-respecting Persian, a harem. The letters Usbek receives from his wives and eunuchs not only describe the East but, taken together, form a story of infidelity and violence, culminating in revolt. This story has often been considered a mere framework, something of an hors-d'œuvre in which Montesquieu panders to his eighteenth-century readers' love of the exotic and near-pornographic. However, the harem story is an essential part of the *Lettres persanes*, for there is in the work as a whole, if not a plot, at least a general direction, which is reflected simultaneously in the two sides of the correspondence: the growing disorder in the harem is parallel to the increasing confusion of the Regency, and the rejection of Usbek's despotic rule by his wives is similar to his own refusal, in the name of reason, nature, and justice, of the values of the East. That the women have been acting instinctively on what are in fact the implications of Usbek's own principles becomes clear when Roxane, his favourite wife and leader of the revolt, writes to him in the last letter: 'J'ai ré-formé tes lois sur celles de la Nature.' In the last resort the revolt is a triumph of nature and justice over despotism, and an unexpected depth of irony is added to the work when Usbek, the brilliant satirist, becomes himself the victim of satire.

The *Lettres persanes* is a work of astonishing variety. Its mixture of styles—the elaborate and the sober, the mocking and the deadly serious, the playful and the bitterly ironic—and the number of subjects discussed reflect Montesquieu's wide interests, his Gascon wit and humour, and his serious intellectual pursuits. A great work in its own right, it anticipates many of the ideas of the *Considérations* and the *Esprit des lois*.

The *Considérations sur les causes de la grandeur des Romains et de leur décadence* is not a history of Rome, but an essay in historical method. Previous writers had, on the whole, tended to ascribe historical events to the workings of Divine Providence, or simply to see in them the operation of blind chance. Montesquieu, rejecting both of these ways of writing history, believes that historical events can be explained rationally:

Comme les hommes ont eu dans tous les temps les mêmes passions, les occasions qui produisent les grands changements sont différentes, mais les causes sont toujours les mêmes. (Chapter 1)

Ce n'est pas la fortune qui domine le monde... Il y a des causes générales, soit morales, soit physiques, qui agissent dans chaque monarchie, l'élèvent, la maintiennent, ou la précipitent; tous les accidents sont soumis à ces causes; et, si le hasard d'une bataille, c'est-à-dire une cause particulière, a ruiné un état, il y avait une cause générale qui faisait que cet état devait périr par une seule bataille... (Chapter 18)

In these important methodological pronouncements we have the essentials of Montesquieu's historical method: his distinction between occasion and cause, his conviction that historical experience is continuous and that historical events are related to the various physical and moral factors that influence man's social life.

The work is an application of this method, and in a style remarkable for its polished restraint and dignity, Montesquieu shows how Rome's greatness depended mainly on its laws, its military organization, and its policy of assimilating conquered peoples. This led to growth, and this growth, causing a loss of control from the centre and a decline in the spirit of citizenship, brought about an inevitable degeneration. In the course of his analysis he shows how such factors as climate, religion, and customs played an important part in shaping life in Roman society, thereby influencing its history. Although the *Considérations* is not without serious shortcomings, particularly in its uncritical handling of source-material, it is a landmark in the history of historiography, an attempt to show that history is neither a branch of theology nor a mere jumble of facts, but a serious intellectual discipline in its own right.

The *Esprit des lois* is the culmination of Montesquieu's genius. Here he offers a more profound reflection on many of the problems discussed in the *Lettres persanes*, and applies, with greater subtlety and to a much wider subject, the ideas on history developed in the

Considérations. More than twenty years in the making, it draws on the accumulated wisdom of the *Pensées*, *Voyages*, and *Spicilège*, and can truly be said to be his life's work.

In the preface to the *Esprit des lois* Montesquieu reaffirms his conviction that behind the diversity of man's social life there are discoverable principles: 'J'ai d'abord examiné les hommes, et j'ai cru que, dans cette infinie diversité de lois et de mœurs, ils n'étaient pas uniquement conduits par leurs fantaisies.' He relates how, in his attempt to understand this diversity, he was often submerged by factual details which at first resisted all attempt at rational explanation; but in the end he discovered principles, in the light of which the material began to fall into an intelligible pattern: 'J'ai posé les principes, et j'ai vu les cas particuliers s'y plier comme d'eux-mêmes; les histoires de toutes les nations n'en être que les suites; et chaque loi particulière liée avec une autre loi, ou dépendre d'une autre plus générale.'

Montesquieu's critics have never been in agreement as to whether the principles to which he refers in the preface are, like those of Descartes, *a priori*, discoverable by reason alone, or whether they are inductive principles, begun as hypotheses which, if they stand the test of the facts, have the status of scientific laws. There is no doubt that Montesquieu is most un-Cartesian in the attention he pays to historical and social facts, and in much of his inquiry he seems to be working from facts to principles rather than the contrary. At the same time, however, in the preface, he insists that his principles are drawn from 'la nature des choses', and 'la nature des choses' is a metaphysical term which refers not to empirical data, but to essence. Montesquieu—like Descartes in this respect—believes that the universe has an inherent rational order, and although he believes that empirical inquiry will reveal much of this order, particularly in the realm of the physical universe, he is convinced that we also have insight into it by reason alone. The principles which he draws from 'la nature des choses' must be the rational principles which he defines in Book I.

Montesquieu begins the work with his definition of laws as 'les rapports nécessaires qui dérivent de la nature des choses', and it becomes clear, from the examples he gives, that this general definition refers both to scientific and to moral laws. Referring to the material universe, he says: 'il faut que ses mouvements aient des lois invariables', and gives a number of examples from mechanics. Speaking of the non-material universe, he produces a mathematical image to prove that there is an immutable moral law—the Natural Law—anterior to all man-made or positive laws: 'Dire qu'il n'y a rien de juste ni d'injuste que ce qu'ordonnent ou défendent les lois positives, c'est dire qu'avant qu'on eût tracé de cercle, tous les rayons n'étaient pas égaux.' If Montesquieu can speak of the laws of motion and the laws of morals in the same breath, it is because both seem to him to be inherent in the rational structure of the universe. If his general definition of laws as relationships seems more appropriate to the descriptive laws of science than to the normative laws of morals, it is a reflection of the prestige of science in his day, and of the tendency of thinkers at the time to assimilate morals to science or, in the words of Locke, to 'place morality amongst the sciences capable of demonstration'. Montesquieu is writing in the tradition of seventeenth-century jurists like Grotius who see the moral law not simply as the command of a superior, but as a 'rapport de convenance', a rule of reason inherent in the very nature of things, and binding even on God.

Having demonstrated the rational order of the material and the non-material universe, Montesquieu proceeds to examine the place of man in the general scheme of things. As a physical being man is subject to the laws of the material world: 'L'homme, comme être physique, est, ainsi que les autres corps, gouverné par des lois invariables.' As a rational being he is governed by the Natural Law, but in fact he commonly violates this law of his nature: 'Comme être intelligent, il viole sans cesse les lois que Dieu a établies, et change celles qu'il établit lui-même.' There are reasons for this: 'les êtres particuliers intelligents sont bornés par leur nature, et par conséquent sujets à l'erreur; et, d'un autre côté, il est de leur nature qu'ils agissent par eux-mêmes', and besides, man 'comme créature sensible, ... devient sujet à mille passions'. The idea of man as a rational creature, endowed with free will, but weak and liable to be misled by his passions, was a commonplace of moral thought. For Montesquieu it is an important truth about human nature, an important principle which he will make use of in his examination of laws, and particularly in his account of bad laws and corrupt forms of government.

In Book I, Chapter 2, Montesquieu considers man in the state of nature, before the formation of civil societies. Here his thought is original and, anticipating Jean-Jacques Rousseau's second *Discours*, he portrays natural man as a timid animal-like creature who has not yet acquired the faculty of reason. As natural man is pre-rational so is he pre-moral, and the 'lois de la nature' at this stage of his development are purely physical ones: desire to live in peace, feeding oneself, the sexual instinct, and a desire to live in the society of other men. To these four laws Montesquieu adds a fifth: religion, which he says is the first in order of importance, though he makes it clear that chronologically it is later than the other four, depending on the development of man's reason.

In Chapter 3 Montesquieu turns to positive laws. The development of the social instinct, by bringing men together, led to a state of chaos, the 'state of war' which Hobbes had attributed to the state of nature. Montesquieu, having rejected the idea that a state of war is natural to pre-social man, also rejects the idea that it is natural to man in society, for man, at this stage, is in possession of his reason, and having become a moral as well as a physical being, provides himself with positive laws which produce order. It is important to quote Montesquieu's definition of these laws: 'La loi, en général, est la raison humaine, en tant qu'elle gouverne tous les peuples de la terre; et les lois politiques et civiles de chaque nation ne doivent être que les cas particuliers où s'applique cette raison humaine.' Produced by 'la raison humaine', and a source of order in man's social life, these laws will be a reflection of the 'raison primitive' inherent in the created universe. However, man must come to terms with his environment and his needs, and as positive laws are not Primitive Reason in its purity, but simply 'cas particuliers' of the application of human reason, they will vary from one nation to another: 'Elles doivent être tellement propres au peuple pour lequel elles sont faites, que c'est un très grand hasard si celles d'une nation peuvent convenir à une autre.' They will vary, first of all, according to the kind of government in force or to be established; and secondly, depending

on the influence of a number of factors which Montesquieu enu-
merates:

> Elles doivent être relatives au *physique* du pays; au climat glacé, brûlant
> ou tempéré; à la qualité du terrain, à sa situation, à sa grandeur; au genre
> de vie des peuples, laboureurs, chasseurs ou pasteurs; elles doivent se
> rapporter au degré de liberté que la constitution peut souffrir; à la
> religion des habitants, à leurs inclinations, à leurs richesses, à leur nombre,
> à leur commerce, à leurs mœurs, à leurs manières. Enfin elles ont des
> rapports entre elles; elles en ont avec leur origine, avec l'objet du légis-
> lateur, avec l'ordre des choses sur lesquelles elles sont établies.

Thus Montesquieu, having begun with definitions of Natural
Law, concludes Book I by outlining what is usually taken to be a
programme of empirical and historical research into positive laws.
It has been maintained by many of his critics that at this point he
simply turns his back on abstract ideas, on Natural Law, and carries
out a sociological inquiry in which he is concerned not with what
laws ought to be, but with what they are. This is, however, an over-
simplification. It is not to be denied that he establishes inductively
the effect of climate and other factors on man's social life, but at the
same time even a casual reading of the *Esprit des lois* will reveal that
he is also concerned with morals. Indeed, his aim is partly to combine
the task of the lawyer and historian with that of the philosopher and
moralist, to relate positive laws to Natural Law. This was not possible
so long as the traditional views expressed by Grotius, Pufendorf,
and others were accepted, that whereas Natural Law was a law of
reason, positive laws were in fact merely the arbitrary commands of
legislators. Montesquieu bridges the gap between the two kinds of
law with his definition of positive laws as 'la raison humaine', a solution to the problem which he probably owed to his study of Plato:
'C'est une pensée admirable de Platon que les lois sont faites pour
annoncer les ordres de la Raison à ceux qui ne peuvent les recevoir
immédiatement d'elle' (*Pensées*, 208). He is sufficiently optimistic
about human nature to believe that men are not 'uniquement conduits par leurs fantaisies', and positive laws he sees as embodying to
a greater or lesser degree, depending on how enlightened people and
legislators are, something of natural reason and justice. Indeed, it is
one of the most striking things about the *Esprit des lois* that even

in apparently absurd laws Montesquieu frequently discerns traces
of reason. While not underestimating the influence of climate,
religion, and other factors on man's life in society, he sees legislation
as a creative moral activity carried out in the light of principles which
are not empirically based. Or at least this is so when man is truly
human and in possession of his reason, for, as he frequently demonstrates, when men are dominated by passion and refuse to act in
conformity with their rational and moral nature, then laws are
more likely to be determined by non-moral factors, such as physical
environment.

The diversity of positive laws he relates in the first place to the
kind of government in force (Books II–VIII). He distinguishes three
types of government: republic (democracy and aristocracy), monarchy, and despotism, and he defines each according to its 'nature' and
'principe', terms which he defines thus: 'sa nature est ce qui le fait
être tel, et son principe ce qui le fait agir. L'une est sa structure particulière, et l'autre les passions humaines qui le font mouvoir.' Speaking
of the 'nature' of each of the three forms, he says that in republics
power is in the hands of a large or small number of citizens. The distinction between democracy and aristocracy he does not think
sufficiently important to make a separate classification and, indeed,
he has no clear notion of what today we think of as democracy, his
models being mainly those of classical antiquity in which, he notes
with approval, legislators divided citizens into distinct classes. His
definition of monarchy was more up to date, being based on the
French monarchy—not as it actually was, but as he thought it
should be. In monarchy power is exercised by one man, but according to fixed laws, and his power is restrained by 'pouvoirs inter-
médiaires' (the nobility and the clergy) and by a 'dépôt des lois' (the
parlements). In despotism power is likewise in the hands of one, but
the despot rules according to his own unbridled will and knows of no
legal restraint.

The 'principe' of each of the three forms of government Montesquieu sees as more fundamental and, if it is not kept intact, there
will follow an inevitable degeneration. In republics the 'principe' is
virtue: respect for the laws, self-restraint—in short, good citizenship.
Montesquieu's idea is that when power is shared among a number of

people, and when there is no external restraint on them, restraint must come from within the individuals themselves. In monarchy the 'principe' is honour, which is not a form of moral virtue, but self-interest, each citizen seeking his own advancement within his rank. In despotism there is no need for either virtue or honour: all that is needed is blind obedience to the ruler, and the 'principe' is fear.

Montesquieu's analysis of the different forms of government—and of the various intermediate degenerate or degenerating forms—draws on his historical researches and travels; but the actual classification is based on his ideas on human nature as described in Book I. If man is faithful to his true rational and moral nature, it will be possible for him to be a virtuous citizen, and the corresponding form of government is republic. On the other hand, if he is entirely corrupt and dominated by his passions, he will be fit only for despotism, in which the ruler is idle and voluptuous, and the subjects barely human. However, man, while being neither totally corrupt, nor yet attaining a high standard of virtue, may be sufficiently rational to channel his self-interest in such a way that it adds to the general welfare, and this, as Montesquieu understands it, is the 'principe' of honour in monarchy. It is monarchy that he most admires, for, while not demanding an almost inhuman standard of virtue, it can achieve political and civil liberty.

The way in which political liberty can be achieved in monarchy he describes in Book XI, Chapter 6, his famous analysis of the British constitution. Political liberty he sees in practice as a question of distributing power so that it will not be abused: 'Pour qu'on ne puisse abuser du pouvoir, il faut que, par la disposition des choses, le pouvoir arrête le pouvoir', and this, he believes, has been carried out in England, where the legislative, executive, and judicial powers are distributed in such a way that no one person or body of men has complete control of more than one of the three powers. The legislative power is vested in the Lords and Commons, and—a point Montesquieu insists on twice in this chapter—the King has a share in the legislative power by his right of veto. The executive power is in the hands of the King, and the judicial power is vested in juries— Montesquieu rather curiously making no clear reference in this context to the power of judges. In this ingenious system the King,

the Lords, and the representatives of the people have a share in
legislation, and though the King is supreme in the executive sphere,
his ministers, if they disobey the laws, can be punished by the Lords
and Commons sitting as a judicial body (a reference to impeach-
ment). In all this it is clear that there is no 'separation of powers', a
term usually employed to describe Montesquieu's theory but which,
in fact, he himself, for good reason, never uses. It is clear from his
text that there is a considerable mingling of powers, and the essential
point he is making is simply that in England no one has a monopoly
of more than one of the three powers.

Montesquieu does not pretend, in this chapter, to have given an
account of the actual working of the British constitution. He describes the letter rather than the spirit, and his description, apart from
a few minor errors, corresponds closely to what one might infer from
such constitutional documents as the Bill of Rights and the Act of
Settlement, which it is difficult to believe he had not studied. It is
only in a later section of the *Esprit des lois* (Book XIX, Chapter 27)
that he examines how the British constitution actually worked, and
here the picture is understandably different, a shrewd account of
how the King placed an 'interest' in parliament, thus bringing about
a struggle between politicians who were 'in' and those who were
'out'. Montesquieu's description of the British constitution can be
considered grossly inaccurate only if it is distorted into a theory of
'separation of powers'.

In Books XIV–XXVI Montesquieu considers the more basic
factors which influence man's social life: climate, geography,
religion, population, and economic factors. Their influence he sees
as a matter of empirical inquiry, and it is in this part of the *Esprit des
lois* that he is often considered a determinist. Critics who maintain
that he claims positive laws to be inevitably fixed by these factors
find it difficult to understand how he can combine such determinism
with his ideas on man's free will and moral responsibility. Montesquieu may seem a strict determinist when he says, for example, that
hot climates make men lazy; but he clearly does not deny freedom
of the will when he goes on to state that in hot countries a wise
legislator will make laws which will incite men to be active. The
importance Montesquieu attributes to such factors is not that they

determine laws mechanically, but that they contribute to what he calls the 'esprit général': 'Plusieurs choses gouvernent les hommes: le climat, la religion, les lois, les maximes du gouvernement, les exemples des choses passées, les mœurs, les manières; d'où il se forme un esprit général qui en résulte' (Book XIX, Chapter 4). The factors enumerated here vary with the stage of man's development. Man being, as shown in Book I, Chapter 2, a physical before he becomes a moral being, it follows that physical factors like climate will be the first, chronologically, to influence him, and it is for this reason that savage peoples are still very much dominated by their physical environment. In less primitive societies, however, men will be less bound by purely physical factors and they will—depending on how enlightened they are—be free to impose their own moral pattern on their social life. A wise legislator can change the 'esprit général', educate public opinion, and, while not aiming at unattainable perfection, prepare the way for gradual reform which will achieve something of the liberty and justice natural to man as a moral being. A good government, far from being blindly determined by factors over which man has no control, is a triumph of man's creative reason:

Pour former un gouvernement modéré, il faut combiner les puissances, les régler, les tempérer, les faire agir; donner, pour ainsi dire, un lest à l'une, pour la mettre en état de résister à une autre; c'est un chef-d'œuvre de législation, que le hasard fait rarement, et que rarement on laisse faire à la prudence. (Book V, Chapter 14)

He sees man as not merely pushed from behind, but led by ideals inherent in his very nature. However, man's nature, though partly rational and moral, is also partly physical and non-moral, and this is the source of much that appears contradictory in his behaviour: 'Ce qui fait la plupart des contradictions de l'homme, c'est que la raison physique et la raison morale ne sont presque jamais d'accord' (*Pensées*, 1208). Among such contradictions Montesquieu notes abuses like despotism, slavery, torture, and religious persecution, which occur when man, untrue to his moral essence, is dominated by his passions and the non-moral side of his nature.

Throughout the *Esprit des lois* Montesquieu believes that his analysis of factors like climate, religion, and customs is alone not sufficient to account for the diversity of positive laws: the underlying principles which constitute the 'esprit des lois' are to be discovered only by analysing the interplay between these factors and man's complex contradictory nature.

Montesquieu's works are an important contribution to a number of specialized disciplines, especially political philosophy, historiography, jurisprudence, and sociology. But he is above all a moralist in the great French tradition. His originality lies partly in his application of the traditional moral analysis of human nature to man's political life, and partly in his understanding of how, depending on man's intellectual and moral development, life in society is influenced by a multitude of interrelated factors. The result is a remarkable awareness of the complexity of man's social life. Some of his theories are antiquated, his analyses are often superficial and his documentation hasty, but he has never been equalled in his vision of how man, while having to contend with his environment and inherited traditions, is in the last resort the artisan of his own destiny, having within his power forces of good and evil.

NOTE

CHARLES-LOUIS DE SECONDAT, BARON DE LA BRÈDE ET DE MONTESQUIEU, 1689–1755, was born at La Brède, near Bordeaux. After studying law at Bordeaux and Paris, he entered the magistrature, inheriting in 1716 the office of *président à mortier* in the Parlement of Bordeaux. His early writings include a number of dissertations on science and philosophy composed for the Académie de Bordeaux. His first important literary work, the *Lettres persanes* (1721), though published anonymously, quickly brought him European fame. In 1726 he sold his legal office and devoted himself more fully to his literary and intellectual pursuits. In 1728 he was elected to the Académie française, and in the same year set out on extensive travels which lasted until 1731 and took him to Austria, Hungary, Italy, Germany, Holland, and England. In 1734 he published the *Considérations sur les causes de la grandeur des Romains et de leur décadence*. The remainder of his active career was devoted mainly to the preparation of his masterpiece, the *Esprit des lois*, published in 1748. Other important works include the *Voyages* and *Pensées*, which were not published until the end of the nineteenth century.

Modern editions. The standard edition of the *Œuvres complètes* is that of André Masson, Les Éditions Nagel, (1950–5: 3 vols.). The Pléiade edition, by Roger Caillois (1949–51: 2 vols.), is more accessible, though less complete, and there is also the less expensive 'Intégrale' edition by G. Vedel and D. Oster. The most useful edition of the *Lettres persanes* is that of Paul Vernière in the Classiques Garnier (1960). There is no good modern edition of the *Considérations*, though the Hachette edition by Camille Jullian is still authoritative. The best edition of the *Esprit des lois* is that of Jean Brethe de La Gressaye, Les Textes Français, (1950–61: 4 vols.).

Criticism. The most useful short general study is that of Joseph Dedieu, *Montesquieu* (1943). Other useful studies include P. Barrière, *Un Grand Provincial: Charles-Louis de Secondat, baron de La Brède et de Montesquieu* (1946), and Jean Starobinski, *Montesquieu par lui-même* (1953). The fullest and most scholarly biography is that of Robert Shackleton: *Montesquieu. A Critical Biography* (1961).

4. Sensibility and the Novel

TOWARDS the end of the seventeenth century, the French novel underwent a revolution in subject-matter and form. The *roman héroïque* of the mid-century was a long, wandering narrative whose characters—often from the world of classical antiquity—embodied lofty standards of nobility, physical courage, and moral strength. These stories were presented as third-person narrative, in a quasi-historical manner, so that the author rarely described in any detail what went on inside the characters' minds.

It is difficult nowadays to understand the popularity of these romances, but they continued to be read and enjoyed well into the eighteenth century. Not, however, to be written. The last decades of the seventeenth century saw the rise of novels which were set in the recent past and were told in autobiographical form. From the 1670s onwards such *Mémoires* became increasingly popular, until by about 1730 this could be considered the normal way of writing a novel. The change entailed two major developments: since the stories were modern, it no longer seemed appropriate to endow their characters with the perfections attributed to personages of a remote and heroic past; and since the narrator was telling his own life-story, he could give a full account of his own motives and reactions. The memoir-novel, in other words, opened the door to realistic and detailed character-portrayal.

The first fictional work in memoir-form to obtain durable success was Lesage's *Histoire de Gil Blas de Santillane* (published in three stages, in 1715, 1724, and 1735). Gil Blas relates his varied experiences from the day he set off for Salamanca as a callow youth, to the time when he is prosperously settled, with a wife and family, on his own estate. In the early days he is often tricked by others. Then he learns to hold his own, and even indulges in trickery himself.

Finally he attains to power and responsibility as secretary to the chief Minister of State. Lesage created, by means of Gil Blas's successive jobs, a lively picture of many facets of French society. (The 'Spanish' setting was a fiction hardly intended to deceive.)

In several ways this novel can be seen as a transitional work, continuing some aspects of seventeenth-century fiction, but also introducing elements which were to be characteristic of the eighteenth century. Lesage looks back to earlier techniques, for instance, in his use of *portraits*, formal descriptions by which fresh characters are presented to the reader; and of interpolated stories, told to Gil Blas by the people he meets on his travels. But Lesage's style—clear, concise, and often ironic—is a way of writing which authors such as Montesquieu and Voltaire were to develop extensively. Similarly, while Lesage mocks and satirizes the society in which his 'hero' lives, he avoids the effects of crude burlesque which earlier satiric novelists had used, and relies instead on an urbanity which again suggests eighteenth-century graces. As for plot, the work might well be envisaged as a series of *contes*, a form of fiction which flourished with particular liveliness under Louis XV. (Lesage has a real talent for the relation of fairly brief episodes, often capped by an unexpected twist of events.) And this episodic narrative is held together by the theme of Gil Blas's gradual rise in social status, a theme which became popular in eighteenth-century France, with its new awareness of social problems. *Gil Blas* therefore typifies certain trends in eighteenth-century fiction. However, since it is a comic novel, we can scarcely expect to find in it the particular development which completed the cycle of change in the French novel, and which gives many works of this period their distinctive tone and mood, the element of sensibility.

In *Manon Lescaut*, Prévost puts into the mouth of Des Grieux a noteworthy description of what it means to be *sensible*:

Le commun des hommes n'est sensible qu'à cinq ou six passions, dans le cercle desquelles leur vie se passe, et où toutes leurs agitations se réduisent... Mais les personnes d'un caractère plus noble peuvent être remuées de mille façons différentes; il semble qu'elles aient plus de cinq sens et qu'elles puissent recevoir des idées et des sensations qui passent les bornes ordinaires de la nature; et, comme elles ont un sentiment de cette grandeur qui les élève au-dessus du vulgaire, il n'y a rien dont elles soient plus jalouses.

Such people are unusually sensitive to every kind of stimulus, and their responses are both more intense and more varied than those of the common run of mankind. Indeed the feelings exhibited by an *âme sensible* often seem, by twentieth-century standards, to exceed what the stimulus might warrant, which explains why *sensibilité* can to some extent be equated with 'sentimentality'.

One might, however, query Prévost's claim concerning the wider range of emotions experienced by the Man of Feeling. In practice, the stress seems to be laid on what one may call the 'softer' emotions: pity, tenderness, generosity, sorrow. (Such reactions as Rabelaisian laughter scarcely come into the domain of sensibility.) And because of this emphasis on a certain range of feelings, the ways of manifesting emotion may also seem limited. Tears are the all too frequent sign of one's own grief or happiness, or of sympathy with other people's sufferings and joys. If the feeling is too strong for tears, one may fall into a stunned passivity which sometimes goes as far as fainting. Marivaux, through Marianne, points out that 'les personnes qui ont du sentiment sont bien plus abattues que d'autres dans de certaines occasions, parce que tout ce qui leur arrive les pénètre; il y a une tristesse stupide qui les prend'.

It might be thought that such acute sensitivity would be considered a curse rather than a blessing, but Prévost sees it as a source of *grandeur*, and as time went on more and more writers came to assume that sensibility was a sign of virtue: to be soft-hearted was necessarily to be good. Sensibility thus becomes an admirable and a desirable quality. And, logically enough, the importance of the emotions is exalted and they are set up as a better guide to conduct than mere reason.

The introduction of sensibility into imaginative literature was of course a gradual process which cannot be dated with any precision. The first clear signs of it occur in the 1690s, in various pseudo-historical *nouvelles* written by women authors. These stories resemble the earlier and more celebrated work of the same kind, *La Princesse de Clèves*, but their characters show a new propensity for emotional outbursts. Fénelon's didactic novel *Télémaque* (1699) also exploits the softer feelings. By the time we come to Marivaux and Prévost, therefore, sensibility is not a startling innovation, but it is safe to say that the popularity of these writers' works helped to establish this vogue in fiction. By the same token, this popularity itself indicates the existence of a reading public which liked its novels to be shot through with sentiment. To what extent the sensibility in such literature either influenced or stimulated behaviour of the same kind in everyday life is a complex question which would take us into the field of social rather than literary history. Only two points need to be made here: firstly, that a number of people certainly did accept the notion of sensibility as an admirable quality, and behaved accordingly; and secondly, that however widespread the vogue of sensibility became, there were always some critics prepared to make fun of it, as mere foolishness, or to attack it more seriously, on the grounds, for instance, that it diminished the role of reason. In life, as in literature, sensibility was only one aspect, albeit an increasingly important one, of contemporary attitudes.

Marivaux's interests were by no means confined to the soft and sentimental. Among the novels he wrote in his late twenties are two parodies—and the laughter of parody is essentially inimical to sensibility. Of his two major novels, the second, *Le Paysan parvenu* (1734–5), has a tone of gay cynicism which allows only rarely for displays of fine feeling. So it is to *La Vie de Marianne* (1731–41) that we must look in order to see how Marivaux exploits sensibility in the novel.

The heroine of this work is supposedly writing her memoirs and sending them, by instalments, to a friend who has asked her to undertake this task. As a baby, Marianne is the only survivor of a group of travellers whose coach is attacked by robbers. She is adopted and brought up by a village curé and his sister, of whom we hear nothing but good. Marianne comes to Paris with the curé's sister, and when the latter dies, the girl is taken by a priest to M. de Climal, a charitable elderly gentleman who agrees to support and protect her. But M. de Climal is a *faux dévot*, a Tartuffe who plans to seduce Marianne. Once his intentions are made clear, Marianne of course rejects his assistance with virtuous indignation. But she is now helpless and alone once more. At this stage she is befriended by

Mme de Miran, who treats her as a daughter. Mme de Miran is all goodness and sensibility; she is even willing to flout public opinion and let her son Valville marry the penniless foundling Marianne with whom he has fallen in love. However, the forces of society react. One of Mme de Miran's relatives, a hard-hearted woman whom Marianne refers to as 'une harpie', has Marianne abducted from the convent where she is staying, and almost manages to frustrate the plans for the marriage.

From this outline of part of the plot, it can be seen that the characters tend to fall fairly clearly into the categories of 'good' or 'bad'. This would seem to be one of the pitfalls of novels which rely largely on sensibility. If the lively feelings and superior standards of the *âme sensible* are to be effectively shown, the novelist must provide, as foils, other characters who are palpably less sensitive and less virtuous. This may well lead to a simplicity of characterization which modern readers find unpalatable. (As an example of how this process was carried to extremes later in the century, one may cite Bernardin de Saint-Pierre's *Paul et Virginie*.) Marivaux, however, usually manages to avoid the monotonous opposition of perfect virtue and unmitigated vice. The 'harpy', for instance, makes only a brief appearance, and is portrayed with a touch of caricature which renders her ridiculous as well as odious. The hypocritical M. de Climal, on the other hand, makes a death-bed repentance. 'Avec des yeux baignés de larmes', he admits to the priest that his charitable actions were only a screen for depravity. The priest exhorts him, weeping the while, to trust in divine mercy; and Marianne adds '... et nous pleurions aussi, Valville et moi'. This scene of edification, so moving to all concerned, makes our final picture of M. de Climal one of villainy redeemed.

Mme de Miran, however, does not falter in her goodness. After our first glimpse of her practical sympathy in befriending Marianne, we are offered a detailed *portrait*, some four pages long, which stresses her generosity and consideration for others. What makes her a more interesting figure is that her kindness is not merely 'une bonté sotte', but shows intelligence and discernment. Marivaux provides a striking example of her perceptiveness. When the end of Marianne's sufferings seems to be in sight and she is on the verge of marrying

Valville, she discovers that he has transferred his affections else-where. With true nobility Marianne tells Mme de Miran that she cannot become Valville's wife, saying that she wishes to spare him the scorn and mockery that such a *mésalliance* would provoke. After a few moments' silence, 'Ma fille, me dit à la fin Mme de Miran, d'un air consterné, est-ce qu'il ne t'aime plus?' Knowing Marianne, she has diagnosed the only reason which could make the girl change her mind and apparently yield to the unworthy prejudices of society. This intuitive understanding of the motives of others makes Mme de Miran more than just a soft-hearted dispenser of charity.

In the matter of evaluating motives, Marianne takes pride of place. She is made to analyse her own reactions—of vanity and *amour-propre*, of virtue and self-sacrifice—with an amplitude never before found in French fiction. And it is precisely these detailed dis-cussions of her feelings which save Marianne, in her turn, from appearing to be merely an innocent prig. For although she never actually does anything overtly reprehensible, she admits to doubts and temptations and discreditable impulses which relieve the per-fection of her conduct.

One admirable aspect of these reflections is the way Marivaux exploits the double time-scale of the memoir-writer. The Marianne who is writing, and who is now a countess of about fifty, both re-calls the motives she then attributed to herself, and also explains in the light of experience the true motives which she did not perceive at the time. One may find a foretaste of Proust in this minute analysis of emotions, helped by the interplay of memory and experience. Inevitably however—and Proust again comes to mind—such de-tailed discussions, which are often expanded into general remarks about human nature, tend to slow up the progress of the story. The eight parts of the book devoted to Marianne cover only a few weeks of her life; and one eventful day occupies some hundred pages.

Was Marivaux daunted by the prospect of covering another thirty years of Marianne's life on this scale? At all events, he interrupted Marianne's narrative so as to begin a subsidiary story, told to her by a nun. Now that Valville has proved faithless, Marianne is thinking of taking the veil, and the nun means to dissuade her from this inten-tion by describing her own experiences. The nun's story takes up three more parts of the novel, and was still unfinished when Marivaux abandoned the work.

One might conclude that while Marivaux was original in his extensive analysis of feelings, he accepted a number of stock devices, such as the *portrait* and the interpolated story, and even such stock characters as the unfortunate heroine and the handsome nobleman who falls in love with her at first sight. This may be true to some extent of *La Vie de Marianne*, but in *Le Paysan parvenu* Marivaux created a hero who is unromantic without either belonging to the tatterdemalion picaresque tradition, or following in the steps of Gil Blas. The young *paysan*, Jacob, is physically attractive and only slightly hampered by moral principles. In Paris he meets a succession of women, of all classes, who are charmed by his handsome face and his zest for life, and he responds sympathetically, in each case, to their advances. Like Marianne, he is made to recount his own adventures, though in a manner which is less refined and reflective than hers. Such a difference may now seem to us 'natural' and predictable, but was by no means commonplace at the time. Writers of memoir-novels did not usually manage to create an individual style for their various narrators; it would be difficult, for instance, to distinguish the heroes of Prévost's three long novels from each other by their style alone. In the case of Marivaux, however, we are reminded that before he came to write his last two novels, he had proved himself as a dramatist,[1] and that in his comedies the characters reveal their personality and their social class by the manner of their remarks as well as by the content.

Marianne and Jacob both use a relatively familiar style which often seems conversational rather than literary. And both of them include, in their accounts, long passages of dialogue. These show far more variety of tone than was common at the time. The conversations include high-minded emotional exchanges between Mme de Miran and Marianne, lively and suggestive flirtatious talk from Jacob and several women, and the celebrated low-life quarrel, in *La Vie de Marianne*, between Mme Dutour and the cab-driver. The last of these provoked disapproving comment from certain contemporary critics because of its so-called vulgarity, though by the standards of

[1] Marivaux's dramatic writings are discussed in Chapter 8, pp. 117–26.

some twentieth-century novels the language of Marivaux's angry cabby is quite restrained. This comic scene, occurring in the course of a day when Marianne traverses heights of happiness and gulfs of despair, illustrates the fact that although sensibility provides the dominant mood of *La Vie de Marianne*, yet Marivaux is always prepared to let laughter break in and lighten the potential monotony of long stretches of intense emotion.

In this respect, as in several others, Marivaux offers a marked contrast to Prévost. The latter is not completely devoid of humour: there are occasional brief satirical scenes in his long novels, and even *Manon Lescaut* has some touches of gaiety. But the prevailing tone of his fiction is serious, even sombre.

With Prévost we move into a world where it is men, even more than women, who are sensitive and suffering souls. The three long memoir-novels he completed all have masculine narrators. In the *Mémoires et aventures d'un homme de qualité* (1728–31) we are offered the experiences both of the Man of Quality himself and of the young nobleman whose guide and companion he becomes. *Le Philosophe anglais ou histoire de M. Cleveland* (1732–9) is the tempestuous life-story of an illegitimate son of Oliver Cromwell. And in *Le Doyen de Killerine* (1735–40), the Dean describes his efforts to help his sister and his two brothers in the course of their complex and harrowing adventures. Since the vicissitudes of love are a recurrent theme in all three works, a number of women characters do appear. But we see them only through the eyes of the narrator, whose chief interest usually lies in his own thoughts and feelings.

This approach is even more striking in the two shorter works, *Manon Lescaut* (1731) and *L'Histoire d'une Grecque moderne* (1741). (*Manon Lescaut* was first published as the seventh and last volume of the *Mémoires d'un homme de qualité*, but can be, and usually is, treated as a separate novel.) In both these works the narrator falls deeply in love, and the object of his passion causes him great suffering. The Greek girl, Théophé, does not return the love of the Frenchman who tells the story, and he is tormented by the suspicion that she may grant her favours to other men while claiming that it is her newly acquired principles of virtue which prevent her yielding to him. The problem is never solved, and Théophé remains an enigma throughout. Prévost here makes a highly effective use of the first-person narrator who can explain his own motives but is harassed by the behaviour of someone else whose intentions he cannot penetrate.

Manon Lescaut resembles this work in some ways, but here the woman's motives are no mystery. Manon is happy only if she can lead a life of comfort with plenty of entertainment: 'C'était du plaisir et des passe-temps qu'il lui fallait.' As long as the Chevalier des Grieux has enough money to supply these needs, she will stay with him, for she does in fact prefer him to other men. But when his funds run low, she accepts the offers of any other man who is willing to keep her. One might be tempted to conclude that while Manon is egotistical, thinking only of her own happiness, the Chevalier is more altruistic in his readiness to make sacrifices and undergo hardships for her sake. But the sacrifices and hardships he faces are always undertaken in order to retain or win back Manon, who is the only source of happiness for him, so that his aims are ultimately no more disinterested than hers. Moreover he is quite ready to exploit other people in his pursuit of Manon, and manages to subdue any qualms of conscience he may feel about his behaviour towards, for instance, his father or his long-suffering friend Tiberge. Beginning with mere lack of consideration for others, he passes on to knavery and crime; he takes to card-sharping as a source of income, and even shoots and kills the servant who is dutifully trying to prevent him escaping from Saint-Lazare.

Such conduct might furnish a racy tale of the contemptuous flouting of conventions. In this case, however, the workings of sensibility completely alter the general effect. The Chevalier presents himself as an unwilling rebel; he acts in unvirtuous and criminal ways only because society does not understand and tolerate his individual needs. Love is a natural impulse. (Within the code of sensibility whatever is 'natural' is also right.) And Des Grieux's love for Manon is irresistible. He explains to Tiberge, in a conversation which has echoes of theological discussions of divine grace, that he is destined to love and follow her, so that appeals to his reason or to the values of religion are useless. It does not even matter that he knows her to be capable of infidelity. This cannot affect his love, which is arbitrary and absolute.

In the opening remarks on sensibility we noted that it was often equated with virtue, and more especially with the sort of kindness shown in acts of charity and compassion for others. But Des Grieux considers no interests but his own. He embodies an exceptional and self-centred form of sensibility. In fact, *Manon Lescaut* presents a realignment of the usual moral values: the people who merit praise are those who sympathize with Des Grieux's passion, while those who thwart or oppose him are blamed. Thus the young M. de T——, who breaks the law by helping to organize Manon's escape from the Hôpital, is approvingly described as 'un homme qui a du monde et des sentiments'. But when M. de G—— M——, already swindled once by Manon and Des Grieux, comes to see them because they have now tricked his son as well, Des Grieux addresses him as 'vieux scélérat', and the reader is clearly expected to share this attitude.

Such a reordering of conventional standards inevitably raises the problem of the supposed moral aim of the book. In the *Avis de l'auteur*, Prévost makes the Man of Quality claim that this story is an exemplary warning of what can happen to anyone who wilfully pursues a guilty passion. 'Outre le plaisir d'une lecture agréable,' he says modestly, 'on y trouvera peu d'événements qui ne puissent servir à l'instruction des mœurs.' Let us not take this too seriously. The novel as a literary genre was held in very low esteem at the time, and in order to circumvent criticism of the pernicious effects of love-stories, novelists frequently claimed that their works provided useful moral lessons. In all probability Prévost realized that the story of Des Grieux and Manon would provoke accusations of immorality, and added the justification of the *Avis* as a form of defence.

Prévost's excuses may be unconvincing, but *Manon Lescaut* has survived, unlike the rest of his novels, because it does carry conviction. This effectiveness is due in part to the brevity of the work. The swift-moving events which become monotonous and incredible as they pile up for volume after volume in his long novels do not go on long enough to pall in *Manon*. Similarly the language, with its frequent hyperboles, superlatives, and exaggerations, does not have time to weary us with its sustained emphasis on the intense emotional stresses of the hero. *Manon*, in itself a kind of digression from the Man of Quality's reminiscences, has no digressions to distract us. It is a compact and concentrated account of one man's tragedy.

Some readers may baulk at the word 'tragedy'. Considering the story critically, one may indeed feel that this tale of an infatuated youth's degradation is not worthy of the term. But Prévost's greatest merit is that he manages to prevent most readers from making such an assessment *while they are reading*. Des Grieux is convinced that Manon is uniquely attractive, that he was fated to love her, and that his experiences arising from that love were tragic. In one sense, there can be no truly objective evaluation of these notions, since there is no witness to the events except the Chevalier himself. (He does not even give us a description of Manon as she might appear to an observer; we can imagine her only through her effect on him and on other men.) We may well decide, in the end, that the Chevalier is too ready to justify his own motives and behaviour, but such a verdict need not affect our acceptance of him as a credible figure, since people of this kind do exist. In view of the lasting popularity of *Manon*, it is clear that in the Chevalier des Grieux, Prévost created a character who can still command the belief of readers living over two centuries later.

The same can hardly be said of the characters in Rousseau's *Julie ou la Nouvelle Héloïse* (1761). Among modern readers few, if any, can accept Julie and Saint-Preux as convincing creations. Yet in its own day this novel was a best-seller, and from the admiring letters which Rousseau received we can see that many of his contemporaries found it both credible and moving. How could so popular and influential a work come to lose its appeal so completely? The answer depends on developments of literary conventions, and of ideas and feelings, during the last two centuries.

The story of *La Nouvelle Héloïse* is told by means of letters, a technique which Richardson had brought into favour not long before—though letter-novels had been written as far back as the sixteenth century. Rousseau was thus using a newly fashionable form. (This may be counted as almost accidental, for we know from the *Confessions* that he had invented the main characters and written some of their letters, simply for his own delectation, before he ever envisaged writing a novel as such.) Nowadays, of course, very few novelists choose to convey their narrative in letters, but the survival of some letter-novels, and notably of *Les Liaisons dangereuses*, indicates that the form alone does not deter modern readers. The difference between Rousseau and Laclos, in this domain, is one of sheer technical efficiency. While Laclos organizes and arranges his letters with great skill and an evident concern for plausibility, Rousseau does not handle the form with comparable mastery. In particular, his characters sometimes write their letters in circumstances, or for reasons, which strain belief. Nowadays it is taken for granted that any competent novelist can arrange such practical details satisfactorily, but this is largely because our expectations are conditioned by the tradition of well-made novels which was established in the nineteenth century. Earlier readers enjoyed the letter-form as such, and were clearly not distracted by Rousseau's technical shortcomings.

If *La Nouvelle Héloïse* followed a current fashion as to form, its content was more original. This is a novel of ideas, perhaps the first French novel which fully merits the description. Other novelists, inevitably, had raised problems of sexual morality; yet others, and notably Prévost, had introduced questions of religion and philosophy. But such concerns were always outweighed by the intrigues and adventures of the plot. Rousseau's plot itself turns on ethical and social problems so that the whole story is at the service of the argument.

Julie and her tutor Saint-Preux fall in love, but her father will not allow them to marry because of Saint-Preux's inferior social status. They have a love-affair. However, Julie finally agrees, out of filial affection, to marry the man of her father's choice, Wolmar. Saint-Preux travels for several years, and the second half of the novel takes up the story when he returns. He finds Julie happily married. It seems that both of them have learnt to master their former passion, and on Wolmar's suggestion Saint-Preux plans to make his home with them and act as tutor to their children. But this plan comes to nothing: after rescuing one of the children from drowning, Julie falls seriously ill. She realizes on her death-bed that she does still love Saint-Preux, and sees death as a mercy, since it will remove her from the dangers of temptation and sin.

Compared with most eighteenth-century novels, this plot is extraordinarily simple and straightforward. It effectively illustrates Rousseau's conviction that romantic love is not necessarily the best basis for marriage; duty to one's parents and to society may exert superior claims. On her wedding-day Julie realizes both the sanctity of the marriage-bond and the importance of religious values, to which she had previously paid little more than lip-service. Her new attitude towards religion pervades the second half of the book—and enables Rousseau to express his own beliefs on the subject.

The fact that *La Nouvelle Héloïse* is a novel of ideas was one reason for its initial success, and should not in itself be a disadvantage nowadays. However, in this particular work most of Rousseau's theories seem to fall into two categories: either they have been so thoroughly accepted that they seem banal; or else they are so out of tune with twentieth-century ideas that they appear to be foolish or impractical. On the first score one may cite his condemnation of duelling. On the second, the major example is his lengthy description of the ideal way to organize and administer a large country estate. The benevolent despotism with which Julie and Wolmar regulate the lives of their employees is now quite outdated. The ideas presented in the novel are therefore liable to bore or antagonize the modern reader.

Furthermore, although Rousseau has built his story around the major questions of love, social duty, and religious responsibility, he has also introduced a number of minor topics which in some cases seem only marginally relevant to the plot. The most obvious instance is a letter in praise of Italian music as compared with French, a subject on which Rousseau felt strongly. And the question of duels, where again he clearly wanted to put forward his own views, is made relevant only by a patently contrived incident in which Saint-Preux feels that it is his duty to defend Julie's honour. Having decided to use the novel as a vehicle for serious ideas, Rousseau did not know where to draw the line, and gave us too much of a good thing.

He justified the digressions in the novel by an argument which appeals to the criteria of realism: since, in everyday life, people put into their letters whatever is occupying their minds at the moment, the apparent irrelevancies of the letters therefore prove how true to life these missives are. And Rousseau went further. He implied, following the conventions of the time, that the letters were authentic and that he himself was merely the editor. Some of his contemporary readers seem to have accepted the suggestion that Saint-Preux, Julie, and Wolmar were real people. Why is it so difficult for us to accord them even the kind of belief required for characters in novels? It is the behaviour of Rousseau's personages and the style of their letters which chiefly act as a barrier.

Both Julie and Saint-Preux are endowed with a high degree of sensibility. (Wolmar is unemotional; one reason for the success of the marriage is that his calm and rational nature is complementary to Julie's lively feelings.) Admittedly, the initial love-affair does involve serious difficulties and sufferings. But Julie and Saint-Preux make high drama of every situation. A case in point is the arrival of Julie's friend Claire, who has agreed, now that she is a widow, to come and live with Julie and Wolmar. She enters unannounced, 'en s'écriant avec un emportement impossible à peindre: "Cousine, toujours, pour toujours, jusqu'à la mort!"' Her small daughter, rushing to meet her, is bowled over. Julie faints from joy, surprise, and shock. Claire, going to help, falls swooning over her. Saint-Preux, 'saisi, transporté, hors de sens', walks round the room 'avec des exclamations interrompues'. The transports of happiness spread through the whole household and last all day. Such heightened treatment of incidents of this kind means that Rousseau has, as it were, no reserves of power for situations we might think more important.

Just as, by modern standards, the characters' behaviour often seems extravagant, so too their language may appear over-emphatic. After he has been allowed to kiss Julie for the first time, Saint-Preux begins a letter to her:

Qu'as-tu fait, ah! qu'as-tu fait, ma Julie? tu voulais me récompenser, et tu m'as perdu. Je suis ivre, ou plutôt insensé. Mes sens sont altérés, toutes mes facultés sont troublées par ce baiser mortel. Tu voulais soulager mes maux! Cruelle! tu les aigris. C'est du poison que j'ai cueilli sur tes lèvres; il fermente, il embrase mon sang, il me tue, et ta pitié me fait mourir.

This passage is characteristic of the more emotional letters in the novel, with its exclamations, interjections, apostrophes, rhetorical questions, and the use of a conventional metaphor such as 'poison'.

Such language often seems too strong for the incidents which give rise to it.

These outpourings tend also to go on for too long. Rousseau's longwindedness, already apparent in some of the early love-letters, becomes even more noticeable in the passages where Julie, 'la belle prêcheuse', lectures Saint-Preux on moral problems and on his conduct. Rousseau is not alone in this prolixity. The portrayal of unrestrained emotions often leads, in eighteenth-century fiction, to a similar lack of restraint over the flow of words. It is as though the novelists felt that to excise anything from what they had written in the first glow of inspiration might make the result less 'natural' and less moving.

Some aspects of Rousseau's approach to sensibility are however individual and deserve special mention. Firstly, he does not make any facile equation between sensibility and virtue. Julie is by nature virtuous, but her true worth is fulfilled only when her sensibility is fortified by religious faith. The unemotional Wolmar is also virtuous, by the light of reason alone, since he is an agnostic. And Saint-Preux is sometimes morally weak because he is too much at the mercy of his emotions, thus demonstrating that sensibility alone is not a reliable guide to virtue. Secondly, unlike Marivaux and Prévost, Rousseau does not assume that sensibility is more or less a prerogative of the upper classes. His simple country-folk are as capable of strong and tender feelings as are Julie and Saint-Preux. And finally, Rousseau extended the scope of sensibility by his appreciation of the beauties of nature. Various outdoor settings—the mountains, the lake, Julie's 'English' garden—are used effectively as a background for crucial incidents in the plot, and Saint-Preux's letters evoking these scenes have a freshness and an almost poetic quality which struck a new note in the novel.

For the most part, however, it must be admitted that the flow of exaggerated feelings, couched in extravagant and rhetorical language, tends to conceal from the modern reader the more admirable aspects of this novel. It is difficult to appreciate the book's real merits of structure and organization, or the quality of Rousseau's thinking, or the attractive rhythmic values of his prose, because sensibility so thoroughly pervades the whole.

This discussion has covered only three of the authors involved in the development of sensibility in fiction. They provide us however with key stages in that development. Many of Marivaux's characters talk and act sentimentally on occasion, but they—or other characters —also introduce notes of unsentimental gaiety and hard common sense. In Prévost the mood of sensibility is dominant, but there is action and adventure to keep the story moving, and the events are often sufficiently unusual to justify strong emotions. With Rousseau and many of his successors the interest has shifted from events to the flow of feelings. The story becomes largely a narrative of emotional reactions, and since these are of a kind which now evoke scant sympathy, such novels have little enjoyment to offer. Indeed one cannot help laughing at the more outstanding manifestations of sensibility, because they appear ridiculous in the light of present-day conventions. It would be rash, however, to assume that our conventions are necessarily superior. Who, in the last resort, can pronounce definitively on the 'right' kind and amount of emotion to feel and show in a given situation? There are still, after all, plenty of people who do openly enjoy sentimentality and relish 'a good cry'. The more sophisticated reader may be reluctant to acknowledge such tendencies in himself, but they often exist none the less.

The sensibility of eighteenth-century literature had its foundations in life. The cult of sympathy, compassion, and *actes de bienfaisance*, moreover, played a significant part in the slow process of social reforms which involved, for instance, the abolition of slavery and of child-labour. This does not mean that we should necessarily, on that account, think more highly of all those works of art which are dominated by sensibility. However, once we realize that we are dealing with something more than a bizarre and ephemeral literary fashion, we may come closer to understanding and appreciating a number of works which gave great pleasure to an earlier public, and which can still afford enjoyment to the reader who is willing to share, for a while, the heightened existence of *l'homme sensible*.

NOTE

ANTOINE-FRANÇOIS PRÉVOST, 1697–1763, known as the Abbé Prévost d'Exiles, led an extremely unsettled life until he was about forty-five. After having been soldier and cleric by turns, he spent the period 1728–34 in England and Holland. On his return to France he became chaplain to the Prince of Conti, and a few years later he finally settled down in the village of Chaillot, where he lived until his death. Prévost's output of fiction was large; he also engaged in journalism, and translated a number of works into French, including two of Richardson's novels.

(Biographical and further bibliographical details for *Marivaux* and *Rousseau* follow Chapters 8 and 9 respectively.)

Modern editions. Marivaux's *La Vie de Marianne* and *Le Paysan parvenu* are available as separate volumes in the Classiques Garnier series, both excellently edited by F. Deloffre (1957 and 1959). These two novels, plus a selection from Marivaux's early fiction, also appear in a single volume, *Romans* (1949), in the Pléiade edition of Marivaux's works prepared by M. Arland.

Editions of *Manon Lescaut* are manifold. There is a critical edition of the original 1731 text by G. Matoré (1953). The text more usually published is that of the 1753 edition, which Prévost had not only corrected, but also amplified by the addition of the 'Italian Prince' episode. This is utilized in M. E. I. Robertson's edition (1943) and the Classiques Garnier edition by F. Deloffre and R. Picard (1965). There have also been two editions of a 1759 text, by C. E. Engel and M. Brun (1960), and C. King (1963). Rousseau's *La Nouvelle Héloïse* appears in the Classiques Garnier series, edited by R. Pomeau (1960), and in vol. ii of the Pléiade edition of the *Œuvres*, edited by B. Guyon and H. Coulet (1961).

Criticism. A useful general work on Prévost is H. Roddier, *L'Abbé Prévost, l'homme et l'œuvre* (1955). Specialized studies include P. Hazard, *Études critiques sur 'Manon Lescaut'* (1929), and E. Lasserre, *'Manon Lescaut' de l'Abbé Prévost* (1930).

On fiction of the period there are relevant chapters in J. Rousset, *Forme et signification* (1962), and V. Mylne, *The Eighteenth-Century French Novel* (1965). The major work on sensibility is P. Trahard, *Les Maîtres de la sensibilité française au XVIIIe siècle* (1931).

5. The Literature of Persuasion

PERSUASION was the aim of the art of rhetoric. The orator was taught to use certain devices, not for their own sake, but to help him to sway his audience, to convince them of the innocence of an accused man, the rightness of a course of action, or the virtues of a dead hero. Thus he might use irony to deflate the claims of his opponent, he might appeal to his audience's passions by the display of his own emotions, and he might please his listeners with his noble, witty, or elegant use of words.

For a long time poetics was very close to rhetoric. At the end of the seventeenth century we find the Abbé Claude Fleury saying: 'Il ne faudrait pas beaucoup de préceptes de poétique à un homme qui saurait ceux de l'éloquence.' Poetry was considered a form of eloquence, admittedly one in which the creator, being divinely inspired, was given greater liberty to indulge his imagination, but nevertheless a form of eloquence which should serve extra-literary ends in the same way as the preacher's eloquence. Horace's praise of the poet 'who has blended profit and pleasure, at once delighting and instructing the reader' was a guiding light for literary theorists of the Renaissance.

Thus in seventeenth-century France, as in many earlier communities, it was difficult to justify literature except as the servant of higher pursuits. In an age when actors were excommunicated and a playwright or a novelist could be described as 'un empoisonneur public', it was natural for theorists and practitioners alike to insist on the utility of literature. Not only critics and moralists such as Boileau and La Bruyère, but writers of comedies and poems, Molière and La Fontaine, assert the usefulness of literature. La Fontaine writes:

> En ces sortes de feintes il faut instruire et plaire,
> Et conter pour conter me semble peu d'affaire.
> ('Le Pâtre et le Lion'.)

The poet should not use his gifts for mere amusement but in order to serve some end comparable to the ends served by traditional oratory. Among other things, literature should devote itself to the glorification of God or the King, or to the instilling of the codes of traditional morality.

All this offers a satisfying picture of the artist as an 'engineer of human souls', subordinating everything else to persuasion. But even rhetoric, as well as being the art of persuasion, was also the art of fine speaking; the besetting temptation of the orator had been to neglect the practical business in hand for the aesthetic pleasures deriving from the use of language, its sounds, rhythms, and so on. The poet too, though he claimed to be pleasing so as to instruct, might also think that, to put it at its simplest,

La grande affaire est le plaisir,

as Molière ends his comedy-ballet *Monsieur de Pourceaugnac*.

Putting it rather less crudely, what we have here is another form of persuasion. Persuasion in literature may mean, as we have seen, the inculcation of views or the popularization of ideas which could equally—though perhaps less effectively—be stated in a non-imaginative form. But persuasion may also mean an alteration of the way in which a spectator or reader apprehends the world, an alteration which is not to be reduced to a set of readily available precepts. Persuasion is perhaps the wrong word here, but whatever it is called, we should notice that this general reshaping of the reader's values is very different from the effect of didactic, instructive, polemic writing. Indeed it may even work against the more limited form of persuasion. Thus sometimes one is aware of a conflict between the stated didactic intention of an author and the way in which his work actually affects an audience.

The seventeenth-century theatre, ostensibly moral in intention, is full of examples of this sort of conflict. Racine writes in his preface to *Phèdre*: 'Les passions n'y sont présentées aux yeux que pour montrer tout le désordre dont elles sont cause. Et le vice y est peint partout avec des couleurs qui en font connaître et haïr la difformité. C'est là proprement le but que tout homme qui travaille pour le public doit se proposer.' We do not know whether these words really express his intentions in writing the play, but they suggest a didactic view of *Phèdre* which is at odds with the way the play acts on the spectator. Although it may be possible to show how *Phèdre* ought to convey the lesson Racine speaks of, any such lesson is subordinate to our emotional response and our pleasure in the beauty of form and language. These hinder rather than help the communication of the lesson; *Phèdre* does not persuade us as a sermon might.

On the whole it is fairly easy in seventeenth-century French literature to tell whether a work persuades in the first or in the second sense, whether it is primarily didactic or imaginative. Even though Pierre Corneille might lace his dramas with *sententiae* and Mademoiselle de Scudéry use her vast novels for all sorts of instructive purposes in passing, the genres of tragedy, comedy, and the novel remained essentially non-didactic. On the other hand the sermons of Bossuet, the *Pensées* of Pascal, and the *Maximes* of La Rochefoucauld, for all their literary merit, are essentially directed towards persuasion. Somewhere close to the border between the two come various forms of verse-writing, particularly satire, the official ode, and the religious poem, where there is an inextricable mixture of persuasion and pleasure, so that it is hard to say which predominates.

In the eighteenth century things are different. True, one can point to *Le Barbier de Séville* and d'Alembert's *Traité de dynamique* as fairly pure examples of the imaginative and the didactic respectively, but between them there is a vast central area containing much of the most valuable writing of the century. Here one does not know if one is dealing with art or with some form of persuasion. The eighteenth century is the century of the popularizer and the writer of polemic, of the *philosophe* who feels it his duty to use every means at his disposal to spread his knowledge and his ideas. In this century ideas are given a literary form and literature is full of ideas.

Although theories of literature in the eighteenth century do not show any radical departure from previous views, there is a significant change of tone. The writer is now invested with the dignity of a religious teacher; he is a moulder of public opinion rather than an amuser. In the words of Duclos: 'De tous les empires, celui des gens d'esprit, sans être visible, est le plus étendu. Le puissant commande, les gens d'esprit gouvernent, parce qu'à la longue ils forment l'opinion publique, qui tôt ou tard subjugue ou renverse toute espèce de fanatisme' (*Considérations sur les mœurs*). Even the actor, still for many Frenchmen an object of reprobation, is given a new status. Diderot, writing with typically gushing enthusiasm, paints a picture of the actor's true role in a Utopian society: 'Ce seront là nos predicateurs... Tous les peuples ont leurs sabbats, et nous aurons aussi les nôtres. Dans ces jours solennels, on représentera une belle tragédie, qui apprenne aux hommes à redouter leurs passions; une bonne comédie, qui les instruise de leurs devoirs et qui leur en inspire le goût' (*Entretiens sur le Fils naturel*). In the world of the *philosophes* the writer could not choose but be a teacher.

Not that everyone (or even every *philosophe*) was totally won over to the subordination of literature to non-literary ends. It was recognized that the twin preoccupation with ideas and moral improvement might be against the interests of art. Voltaire frequently made this point; 'malheur', he said, 'à l'auteur qui veut toujours instruire'. He stigmatized equally the tedious moralizing of the *drame* and an excessive preoccupation with scientific ideas. In the second of these he is joined somewhat unexpectedly by the prosaic d'Alembert who admits: 'Cet esprit philosophique, si à la mode aujourd'hui, qui veut tout voir et ne rien supposer, s'est répandu jusque dans les belles lettres; on prétend même qu'il est nuisible à leur progrès et il est difficile de se le dissimuler' (*Discours préliminaire de l'Encyclopédie*). It is the old complaint, that the eighteenth century is the century of ideas, not of poetry.

Now it is clear that there is a large area of eighteenth-century literature where instruction and the 'esprit philosophique' are not predominant. Although most of the writing of Marivaux, Prévost, and Crébillon *fils* is persuasive in the broader sense, it is not didactic. Nevertheless, in the main, eighteenth-century writers were more concerned to teach than their seventeenth-century predecessors. There was greater cause for their work to be didactic in that the lessons to be learnt had changed. In the previous century, most authors had been content in their role as teachers to put forward venerable ideas in as telling a way as possible. In the eighteenth century on the other hand a vast number of more or less new ideas, many of them subversive ideas, cried out for literary expression. Before going on to discuss the various forms of expression, it may be helpful to indicate what sort of ideas these were.

There were new scientific discoveries, whether it be the new physics or recent advances in the field of biology. Then there were theories concerning the best form of government, the origins and function of religion, the philosophies of Leibniz and Spinoza, the foundations of ethics. At a less elevated level there was the new morality of tolerance, charity, family duty, and the glorification of the repository of these virtues, the commercial middle classes. Dealing with these subjects, persuasion may mean straightforward popularization, sermonizing, exhortation, or polemic. Whatever its area of application, however, there is one thing which is common to all this persuasion. This is that except in rare cases literature cannot be concerned with working out totally new ideas; it must confine itself to the popularization and defence of ideas which have already been thought out. As Condorcet put it: 'Il faut donc choisir ceux de ces résultats qui n'ont besoin ni de développement ni de preuves; éviter à la fois ce qui étant trop abstrait ou trop neuf encore, n'est fait que pour un petit nombre d'esprits. Il faut être philosophe, et ne point le paraître.' One must bear this qualification in mind, but on the whole it is true to say that by comparison with the previous century the literature of the eighteenth century is distinguished by being a literature of ideas.

Of course the majority of didactic works continued to be written in non-imaginative forms. These forms must, however, have recourse to some form of rhetoric—rhetoric is compared by Plato to the cookery which is necessary to prepare raw food for human consumption. But however necessary such preparation may be for the effective communication of information and ideas, it will inevitably involve some adulteration of the raw material. There may come a point where the virtuosity of the rhetoric is seen as an end in itself and ceases to be a tool of communication.

In the eighteenth century the formation of professional, esoteric jargon had hardly yet begun. Most scholars—and *a fortiori* most writers of polemic—made a deliberate attempt to catch the attention and win the respect of the unspecialized *honnête homme* and they did this largely by the literary qualities of their writing. Rather unexpectedly, a contemporary described Montesquieu's heavyweight treatise *De l'esprit des lois* as 'de l'esprit sur les lois', suggesting that the desire to please had in fact marred the usefulness of the work. Rousseau in his political writings sought the arresting formulation ('L'homme est né libre, et partout il est dans les fers'), thereby effectively winning readers and disciples, and confusing those who wished to understand his thought. Voltaire, for all his apparent concern for accuracy and objectivity in history, compares the historian to the writer of tragedy: 'J'ai toujours pensé que l'histoire demande le même art que la tragédie, une exposition, un nœud, un dénouement...'[1]

History and political theory then relied more heavily on literary devices than they do today. An even more striking difference is observable in the field of natural science. Buffon (1707–88), writing a highly serious work on natural history, was very conscious of the need to give his findings the splendours of eloquence. His descriptions of animals, for instance, aim at a presentation which is artistically vivid as well as being technically exact. Take his lion:

> Le cri qu'il fait lorsqu'il est en colère est encore plus terrible que son rugissement; alors il bat les flancs de sa queue, il en bat la terre, il agite sa crinière, fait mouvoir la peau de sa face, remue ses gros sourcils, montre des dents menaçantes et tire une langue armée de pointes si dures qu'elle suffit seule pour écorcher la peau et entamer la chair sans le secours des dents ni des ongles, qui sont, après les dents, ses armes les plus cruelles.
> (*Histoire Naturelle*.)

This passage gives a certain amount of information in an easily accessible form, but it is clearly also aiming to be an impressive piece of description and to give pleasure to the reader through an accumulation of clauses which creates a vivid impression such as we might find in a poem or a novel.

Polemic writing too called for the literary weapons of persuasion. In the *Encyclopédie*, which is both popularization and polemic,

---

[1] Quoted by J. H. Brumfitt, *Voltaire Historian*, p. 161.

Diderot and his colleagues do what they can to make their information and their arguments as entertaining and as telling as possible. In particular they provide excellent plates (essential in popularization), while in the text itself, which naturally enough tends to be dull, they attempt to catch the reader's attention with devices such as the 'renvoi' or cross-reference. In the 'renvoi' the reader is referred at the end of certain mock-serious articles to other articles which 'attaqueront, ébranleront, renverseront secrètement quelques opinions ridicules qu'on n'oserait insulter ouvertement' (*Encyclopédie*: article 'Encyclopédie'). This is seen at its clearest in the satirical 'renvoi'; for instance at the end of the 'éloge pompeux' *Cordelier* we are referred to *Capuchon*, which tells the burlesque tale of the conflict among the Franciscans over the size of their hood. It might be thought that such a humorous device could be effectively used as a means of persuasion, but Diderot had doubts about this sort of game, feeling that it did not really serve the good cause and gave to the *Encyclopédie* the appearance of a 'pasquinade', a piece of buffoonery.

Similar criticism might well be applied to much of Voltaire's polemic, but it would not have worried him. For he in his turn was harsh in his judgement of the *Encyclopédie* as popularization and particularly as polemic. For one thing, in his view, one could not popularize efficiently unless one did it unofficially, preferably from outside France. For another, Voltaire felt that a series of great folio volumes would never bring about any real change, particularly when the greater part of the contents was a tedious and badly written 'fatras'. He preferred to do his persuasion through the clandestine 'petits pâtés', as he called his pamphlets. Against the *Encyclopédie* we should set the *Dictionnaire philosophique*. Here, as he explains in his preface, Voltaire is using a peculiarly literary device, that of leaving most of the work to his reader's imagination. He suggests lightly, insinuates, then moves on to another more or less related topic. The alphabetical method is ideal to Voltaire's purpose; it substitutes for the relentless linear form of the treatise the variety and unpredictability of a ragbag. Few of the articles labour their point (although today we may tire of the over-all repetition), and if occasionally he descends to pomposity, Voltaire constantly redeems himself with paragraphs such as the one beginning: 'Un poulailler est visiblement l'État monarchique parfait' and finishing: 'Enfin Salomon dans son sérail n'approchait pas d'un coq de basse-cour.' Is this irreverent 'pasquinade' or effective persuasion? It is arguable, along the lines suggested by Diderot, that here at least Voltaire is indulging his own and his reader's fantasy to the detriment of any serious communication. Wit is a double-edged weapon.

In their many campaigns, Voltaire and the *philosophes* perfected various other weapons and used all the forms of imaginative literature: the poem, the series of letters, the dialogue, the story, the tragedy. It may be that the censorship, which was theoretically severe, though erratic in its operation, had some influence in channelling subversive ideas into apparently safer, more oblique expression through imaginative literature. Imaginary voyages, such as the one described in Montesquieu's *Lettres persanes*, enabled authors to adopt a falsely naïve critical attitude, which could be excused on the grounds of verisimilitude. Subversive remarks might slip past unnoticed in the two thousand alexandrines of a Voltaire tragedy. But so might they equally in any non-imaginative publication (e.g. the *Encyclopédie*). Moreover many subversive pieces of literature were published without a *privilège*—this was in Voltaire's view the best way of ensuring that they were read. All in all, then, we cannot really ascribe the invasion of literature by persuasion to the censorship, but rather to the desire of proselytizers to use the attractiveness of the novel or the theatre to put across ideas which seemed important to their authors.

Fiction was one of the most obvious literary vehicles for ideas. Fénelon (1651–1715) had given the example when in his *Télémaque* (1699) he had used a continuation of the *Odyssey* to provide lessons for the young Duc de Bourgogne, his pupil. Here we have the most straightforward use of fiction to sugar the pill of instruction for the young, and here first of all we come across the problem facing the reader of so much eighteenth-century literature: is the right way of reading such books to concentrate purely on the content or the lesson, disregarding the vehicle? With *Télémaque* our temptation is to do just this, since the ideas expressed, though often banal, are interesting when set in the historical context of Louis XIV's declining despotism, whereas it is hard to see much literary value in such mellifluous pastiche as: 'Télémaque suivait la déesse accompagnée d'une foule de jeunes nymphes, au-dessus desquelles elle s'élevait de toute la tête, comme un grand chêne dans une forêt élève ses branches épaisses au-dessus de tous les arbres qui l'environnent.' The intention here is that the beauty of presentation should not only give pleasure in its own right, but also lead us on to assimilate the lessons on kingship which fill the book. Most modern readers, being unimpressed or even hindered by the beauty of presentation, will go straight to the lessons, if they read *Télémaque* at all.

Montesquieu's *Lettres persanes* (1721) is a more adult production, but here again we have what looks very like sugaring the pill. It is not quite clear what Montesquieu's intentions were in writing this book. He begins his *Quelques Réflexions sur les Lettres persanes* (1754): 'Rien n'a plu davantage, dans les *Lettres persanes*, que d'y trouver, sans y penser, une espèce de roman', and goes on to outline its qualities as a novel. Montesquieu clearly feels that the mildly pornographic episodes have contributed greatly to his book's success. At the same time, speaking of the advantages of the letter-form, he says: 'l'auteur s'est donné l'avantage de pouvoir joindre de la philosophie, de la politique et de la morale à un roman.'

To most twentieth-century readers the interest of the *Lettres persanes* lies mainly in these 'additions', in the ideas put forward by Montesquieu with a mastery of the well-tried tools of rhetoric which reminds one of La Bruyère. As in *Les Caractères*, well-turned maxims, witty pieces of imaginary dialogue, burlesque and ironical descriptions combine to instruct the reader, this instruction being furthered by the pleasure they give. But sometimes too—and not only in the harem scenes—Montesquieu does something other than simple persuasion. Although at times he abandons all pretence of writing fiction and goes so far as to devote eleven consecutive letters to a discussion of the causes of depopulation, at other times, particularly at the beginning of his novel, he does attempt to create a convincing fictional world. Rica for instance becomes, if only fleetingly, a three-dimensional figure, so that in the letters where he describes his first reactions to Paris, the reader's interest does not bypass the letter-writer, treating him merely as a device, but rests on the relation between Rica and the scene he is describing; thus: 'Je souriais quelquefois d'entendre des gens qui n'étaient presque jamais sortis de leur chambre, qui disaient entre eux: "il faut avouer qu'il a l'air bien persan."' Because Rica is vividly placed in the foreground here, this produces a different effect from La Bruyère's pictures of Paris life. Montesquieu's novel is very effectively instructive, but the fictional element does from time to time attain a sort of autonomy.

It is above all in the *conte philosophique* that the imaginative and the instructive coexist and perhaps even compete. Not always, of course: the *Contes moraux* (1761) of Marmontel (1723–1799) are intended, as their title suggests, to be both entertaining and instructive, and are neither. In some of Voltaire's stories the persuasive so overshadows the artistic as to leave us in no doubt that it is the communication of ideas which is all-important. *L'Histoire de Jenni* (1775), for instance, apart from some pleasant fooling at the beginning, is of interest primarily as a document for the conflict between Voltaire's theism and d'Holbach's atheism in the 1770s. The story here is a concrete, entertaining, and supposedly moving illustration of a thesis.

Stories such as *Candide* (1758) or *L'Ingénu* (1767), in their different ways, take us a long way from this use of a literary form to prove a particular point. It is true that *Candide* appears to centre on the desire to pour scorn on the doctrine of philosophical optimism and perhaps to point in its final pages to an alternative attitude to the existence of evil, incidentally striking blows against the folly and horror of war, the misdeeds of the Jesuits, and so on. In all this it is a piece of persuasion, Voltaire's main persuasive weapon being a sardonic, bitter, oddly detached wit: 'Après le tremblement de terre qui avait détruit les trois quarts de Lisbonne, les sages du pays n'avaient pas trouvé un moyen plus efficace pour prévenir une ruine totale que de donner au peuple un bel Auto-da-fè.' The straight-faced humour here is an excellent means of persuasion, conveying effectively the sheer insanity of superstition.

Yet it could be argued that the main effect of wit (in *Candide* at any rate) is simply to make us laugh, not to make us laugh *at* anything. This is persuasion of the second kind; whether intentionally or not, *Candide*, rather than teaching any particular lessons, suggests a new way of looking at the world, a way of comic detachment which can bring pleasure out of what is most agonizing and horrible. A good example is the dialogue between Candide and Martin:

'Croyez-vous, dit Candide, que les hommes se soient toujours mutuelle-ment massacrés comme ils font aujourd'hui? qu'ils aient toujours été menteurs, fourbes, perfides, ingrats, brigands, faibles, volages, lâches, envieux, gourmands, ivrognes, avares, ambitieux, sanguinaires, calom-niateurs, débauchés, fanatiques, hypocrites et sots? — Croyez-vous, dit Martin, que les éperviers aient toujours mangé des pigeons quand ils en ont trouvé? — Oui, sans doute, dit Candide. — Eh bien! dit Martin, si les éperviers ont toujours eu le même caractère, pourquoi voulez-vous que les hommes aient changé le leur? — Oh! dit Candide, il y a bien de la diffé-rence, car le libre arbitre…' En raisonnant ainsi, ils arrivèrent à Bordeaux.

The subject, moral evil, is one which preoccupied Voltaire and it is put here in a compelling way. But there is no answer to the question and Voltaire, with his Rabelaisian enumeration and the brilliant flat ending which cuts off Candide in full flight, superimposes on the problem the comic realization of the vanity of the argument. Ideas provide the material for pleasure, not pleasure the vehicle for ideas.

Quite how intentional this was we cannot tell, but Diderot's novel *Jacques le fataliste* (1773) is very clearly devoted to just such a reduc-tion of ideas to playthings. *Jacques* was not intended for immediate publication and so had no immediate persuasive end in view. It seems to put forward and illustrate a deterministic view of human life ('Jacques disait que son capitaine disait que tout ce qui nous arrive de bien et de mal ici-bas était écrit là-haut'), but against this it sets the gratuitous freedom of art, which can use ideas as it wishes. Diderot and his reader have the satisfaction of manipulating the story, the characters, and the discussion on determinism at their will: 'Vous concevez, lecteur, jusqu'où je pourrais pousser cette conversation sur un sujet dont on a tant parlé, tant écrit depuis deux mille ans, sans en être d'un pas plus avancé.' And indeed Diderot (in the letter to Landois for instance) did spend a lot of time on this question, but here it is reduced to its proper status as the starting-point for a game.

More agonizingly, in *La Nouvelle Héloïse* (1761), Rousseau found himself torn between his imagination and his persuasive reason, so much so that it is virtually impossible to agree where the novel's centre of interest lies. The first two books are dominated by the passionate love story of Saint-Preux and Julie, the product, as Rousseau tells us in his *Confessions*, of his overheated imagination. But the bulk of the remaining four books shows Rousseau's attempt to integrate this love story into a work which can stand alongside the *Émile* as the work of a teacher of men, an attempt which is not wholly unsuccessful, since the persuasiveness of Rousseau's presentation of the Valais peasants or the idyll of Clarens matches his evocation of unhappy love. Rousseau's position was doubly difficult in that, like Plato, he could find little justification for works of the imagination. He is driven to the excuse that in a corrupt society they may have their place if only to prevent worse disorder: 'J'ai vu les mœurs de mon temps et j'ai publié ces lettres. Que n'ai-je vécu dans un siècle où je dusse les jeter au feu!'

It is no surprise, then, that Rousseau in his *Lettre à d'Alembert sur les spectacles* (1758) concentrates a heavy Platonic fire against the theatre of his time, returning to the attack in the second book of *La Nouvelle Héloïse*. The demand for a more positively virtuous, instructive theatre was not Rousseau's monopoly, however. It is perhaps most cogently put by Beaumarchais in his *Essai sur le genre dramatique sérieux* (1767). Following in the footsteps of Diderot, the pioneer theorist of the *drame*, Beaumarchais attacks tragedy for its remoteness from contemporary concerns and comedy for its shallowness, claiming that 'il est de l'essence du genre sérieux d'offrir un intérêt plus pressant, une moralité plus directe que la tragédie héroïque, et plus profonde que la comédie plaisante'.

Many of the innovations of Diderot's *drame* were directed towards the production of a strong emotional response in the audience. Thus the serious drama would be set in a contemporary middle-class context among characters with whom the members of the audience could readily identify themselves. Great stress was put on the naturalistic depiction of emotion by strangled cries, or at any rate broken tirades (which were supposed to evoke a stronger reaction from the spectator), and on the powerful effects which could be obtained by tableaux and other visual effects.

This stimulation of emotion was not an end in itself. Rightly or wrongly, but quite in accordance with traditional rhetoric theory, the theorists of the *drame* believed that emotional involvement helped persuasion or edification—and it was clear that edification was what the playwright should be aiming at. The two threads, emotion and improvement, are drawn together in Grimm's idealistic picture:

Les hommes sont tous amis au sortir du spectacle. Ils ont haï le vice, aimé la vertu, pleuré de concert, développé les uns à côté des autres ce qu'il y a de bon et de juste dans le cœur humain. Ils se sont trouvés bien meilleurs qu'ils ne croyaient: ils s'embrasseraient volontiers... on ne sort pas d'un sermon aussi heureusement disposé. (*Correspondance littéraire.*)

While the actual lessons to be put across by the *drame* were not earthshakingly new, the *drame* was connected with the philosophical movement, as is suggested by the tirade of Bartholo in *Le Barbier de Séville*: 'Sottises de toutes espèces: la liberté de penser, l'attraction, l'électricité, le tolérantisme, l'inoculation, le quinquina, l'encyclo- pédie et les drames.' Most of the writers of *drames* belonged to the party of the *philosophes* and attempted to propagate through their plays, although in a diluted form, many of the social ideals of their group: tolerance, beneficence, respect for trade and the middle classes, family affection, and so on. Unfortunately this desire to educate often resulted in an eloquence which is not that of the theatre but that of the pulpit. In some cases too, particularly in the *drames* of Diderot, it led to the creation of pasteboard characters and plots which are obviously contrived to allow for the triumph of virtue. Diderot and the others strove for verisimilitude with their broken tirades and realistic sets, but their zeal as teachers led them in precisely the opposite direction. Diderot's *drames* display a com- bination of non-theatrical eloquence and violent surprise and sus- pense which is familiar to the twentieth-century audiences of Sartre and Camus. Even Sedaine's *Le Philosophe sans le savoir* (1765), normally spoken of as the masterpiece of the genre, although it is relatively restrained in dialogue and sober in its presentation of character and situation, is melodramatic in its reliance on coincidence and surprise and its high-flown moralizing tone: 'Préjugé funeste! abus cruel du point d'honneur! tu ne pouvais avoir pris naissance que dans les temps les plus barbares.' It is, moreover, totally lacking in the formal splendour which might redeem these failings or turn them into virtues—as in Corneille.

It is hard to tell how effective this type of play was as persuasion in its own day. Diderot, ironically modifying his earlier enthusiasm, notes in *Le Paradoxe sur le comédien* (1773): 'Le citoyen qui se présente à l'entrée de la comédie y laisse tous ses vices pour ne les reprendre qu'en sortant.' It does indeed seem likely that the copious tears may have been an end in themselves, a source of pleasure in a corrupt society. Emotion, like laughter, may in fact hinder the persuasion which it is supposed to further. In any case these plays no longer persuade in either the narrow or the broad sense, since for all the merits of the theory behind them—which foreshadows nineteenth-century naturalism—they are too often technically weak and, even where the technique is sound, too closely linked to a taste for emotional eloquence which is now almost dead. They are of interest mainly to the historian of bourgeois taste and values in eighteenth-century France.

The *drame* was not the only form of instructive theatre in the eighteenth century, but the other forms were hardly more successful. Voltaire's philosophical tragedies, tirelessly repeating the same lessons of noble republicanism, tolerance, and charity, need not detain us for long, though we might note in passing that Racine's *Athalie* seems paradoxically to be the model for Voltaire's spectacular ideological puppet-shows. The relation between *Athalie* and the *Discours sur l'histoire universelle* of Bossuet is mirrored in that between Voltaire's tragedies and his philosophical world history, the *Essai sur les mœurs* (1756). And just as in *Athalie* there is a balance between the edifying and the entertaining (to use the word in its widest sense), so in Voltaire's earlier tragedies there is an equilibrium between the desire to be useful and the desire to be a great poet. For all his weaknesses as a playwright, which are not unlike those of Diderot, he does go some way in plays such as *Mahomet*

(1742) towards achieving this double ambition. It is only in the later tragedies, *Les Scythes* (1767) and *Les Guèbres* (1769), for instance, written in the period of intense propaganda against fanaticism, that Voltaire appears to abandon all ambition as an imaginative writer and turns the tragedy into a pamphlet whose message is yet further brought home by philosophical introductions and notes. As art these later plays are negligible.

Perhaps the most successful of all the attempts to harness the theatre to the new philosophy is found, oddly enough, in Marivaux's lightweight philosophical comedy *L'Île des esclaves* (1725). Here Marivaux makes more explicit a theme which is latent in many of his comedies, the relation between master and servant. Two pairs of masters and servants—similar to those of *Le Jeu de l'amour et du hasard* (1730)—are cast up on an island which is ruled by ex-slaves. These rulers invert the social positions of the castaways to the immediate despair and ultimate profit of the master and mistress, who are made to see their faults and are sent back to the real world a reformed pair. Marivaux makes his point neatly and almost without the pompous sermonizing which is the great vice of philosophical drama in the eighteenth century. The play has an elegance of construction and dialogue which is a pleasure in itself—but again, as with *Candide*, one can ask whether this pleasure does not in fact get in the way of a serious consideration of the issues raised. Could Beaumarchais be right, perhaps at his own expense, when he claims that 'la moralité du genre plaisant est donc, ou peu profonde, ou nulle, ou même inverse de ce qu'elle devrait être au théâtre'?

It seems likely that some part of the failure of the philosophical theatre of the eighteenth century to achieve any lasting results may be attributed to the demands of theatre audiences. This is borne out by the success achieved by the philosophical dialogue, a form which is in some ways close to the drama, but essentially more private and less dependent on pleasing a given public. It is, of course, as old as Plato and since Plato it has been used in two ways, firstly to provide an attractive exposition of a coherent body of thought, secondly to present a real argument where conflicting opinions can meet on equal terms.

In many of Plato's dialogues the dominant impression is of *mise en scène*, a *mise en scène* which is very attractive, but does not mask the fact that Socrates is right. Roughly the same sort of relation between interlocutors is found in Fontenelle's *Entretiens sur la pluralité des mondes* (1686), published in the seventeenth century but a model for the eighteenth. Written for the ladies, the *Entretiens* move neatly to and fro between evocations of evening in the park of a great house and expositions of Cartesian physics. They have considerable charm, but the instructive prevails—the pill is elegantly sugared, but it remains a pill.

We may pass rapidly over Voltaire's dialogues which, like his *contes*, can be situated on a long scale running from the purely didactic to the more imaginative (e.g. *Le Dîner du Comte de Boulainvilliers*, 1767). None of them ever reaches the artistic autonomy of *Candide*. It is rather in Diderot's dialogues that we find the highest achievement of the literature of ideas in the eighteenth century.

The dialogue form seems to have been natural to Diderot. Frequently, as in the *Promenade du sceptique* (1747) or the *Entretiens sur le Fils naturel* (1757), he uses it mainly as a convenient way of putting across certain clear ideas. In many of his other dialogues, however, Diderot gives greater emphasis to the imaginative element and less to the instructive, particularly in those later ones which were not intended for immediate publication and are not therefore as directly educative in intention as much of the writing we have been considering. In the *Entretien d'un père avec ses enfants* (1770) the question whether a man may be justified in setting himself above the law is debated (quite inconclusively) through a series of anecdotes told and discussed in the vividly depicted family circle of Diderot's Langres home. Diderot's father, his brother the *abbé*, his sister and himself, and one or two chance callers stand before us as real people, more important than the ideas they put forward, ideas which are seen as determined by the temperament and situation of the speakers.

In *Le Rêve de d'Alembert* (1769), the emphasis is mainly on the huge hypotheses of universal sensibility and pre-Lamarckian transformism which are put forward first by Diderot himself and then by the sleeping and semi-delirious d'Alembert. But again the presentation of interlocutors as people is an important element in the dialogue and again we have a domestic interior, this time in the house of a Parisian *philosophe*. More than this, we are left in doubt as to how seriously we should take these 'rêves': are they truths of vital concern to the philosopher or are they ideas which one may simply dream about—or write dialogues about? At one point Mademoiselle de Lespinasse, referring significantly to a passage in Fontenelle's *Entretiens*, asks the doctor Bordeu, who is acting as her Socrates:

Pourquoi vos philosophes ne s'expriment-ils pas avec la grâce de celui-ci? Nous les entendrions.
Bordeu. Franchement, je ne sais si ce ton frivole convient aux sujets graves.
Mlle de Lespinasse. Qu'appelez-vous un sujet grave?
Bordeu. Mais la sensibilité générale, la formation de l'être sentant, son unité, l'origine des animaux, leur durée, et toutes les questions auxquelles cela tient.
Mlle de Lespinasse. Moi, j'appelle cela des folies auxquelles je permets de rêver quand on dort, mais dont un homme de bon sens qui veille ne s'occupera jamais.

But Diderot's highest point comes when he allows his own ideal of the philosopher and of social man to be challenged and mocked in that masterpiece of the literature of ideas, *Le Neveu de Rameau* (1762). Here there is no question of a persuasive Socrates using the conversation to put over a convincing argument; Socrates has met his match in the person of the parasitic sub-genius Rameau, the incarnation of a sort of scruffy, shameful, and shameless Bohemian freedom, the living denial of the ideas of Diderot the man of virtue. As the two talk in the gardens of the Palais-Royal—again a totally convincing setting—they throw in the air all the ideas which matter most to Diderot. Nor do these ideas, and in particular the agonizing doubt of the Enlightenment as to what is truly natural, lose their force, but they are caught up in the strange movement of the dialogue, drowned in the extraordinary verve with which Rameau describes his own pitiful life and the 'pantomime des gueux', which is also, says Rameau, 'le grand branle de la terre'. As Goethe said, 'this explodes like a bomb right in the middle of French literature', and among the things which it blows up is the attempt of the *philosophe* Diderot to preach an idealized bourgeois morality. *Le Neveu de Rameau* is no longer literature of persuasion in the rhetorical sense of the word.

NOTE

Biographical information on the more important writers mentioned in this chapter will be found in the notes following Chapters 1, 3, 4, 7, 8, and 9.

Introductory. On propaganda in the eighteenth century see J. P. Belin, *Le Mouvement philosophique de 1748 à 1789* (1913) and D. Mornet, *Les Origines intellectuelles de la Révolution française* (2nd edn., 1947). More general studies of persuasion include I. A. Richards, *The Philosophy of Rhetoric* (1936), and C. Perelman and L. Olbrechts, *Rhétorique et Philosophie* (1952).

Treatises and polemic. There is an edition of the *Œuvres philosophiques* of Buffon by J. Piveteau (1954). For the *Encyclopédie* see selections by J. Lough (1954) and A. Soboul (1952); the complete original folio edition is in many libraries. Excellent introduction by J. Proust, *L'Encyclopédie* (1965). There is a good edition of Voltaire's *Dictionnaire philosophique* by J. Benda and R. Navès (2nd edn., 1954).

Fiction. There is no good current edition of the *Télémaque* of Fénelon. On the fiction of Montesquieu, Voltaire, Rousseau, and Diderot see notes to Chapters 1, 3, 7, and 9. For examples of uninspired didactic fiction see the *Contes moraux* and the *Bélisaire* of Marmontel (no modern editions).

Théâtre. The most interesting theoretical writing of the period is to be found in Diderot's *Writings on the Theatre* (ed. F. C. Green, 1936). The most important *drames* are Sedaine's *Le Philosophe sans le savoir* (1765, modern edition in Classiques Larousse), Diderot's *Le Fils naturel* (1757) and *Le Père de famille* (1758), and Beaumarchais's *Les deux amis* (1770) and *La Mère coupable* (1792). On the *drame* see the very complete study by F. Gaiffe, *Le Drame au XVIIIᵉ siècle* (1910).

Voltaire's tragedies have been studied by R. S. Ridgeway, 'La Propagande philosophique dans les tragédies de Voltaire' (*Studies in Voltaire and the 18th Century*, xv, 1961). See also R. Niklaus, 'La Propagande philosophique au théâtre au siècle des lumières' (*Studies in Voltaire and the 18th Century*, xxvi, 1963).

Dialogue. The *Entretiens sur la pluralité des mondes* of Fontenelle should be read in the edition of R. Shackleton (1955). For Voltaire see *Dialogues et anecdotes philosophiques* (ed. Navès, 1939). On dialogue in Diderot see H. Dieckmann, *Cinq leçons sur Diderot* (1959).

6. The New Intelligentsia

THERE is little doubt that French intellectuals in the eighteenth century were aware of the specific nature of their occupational roles and often identified themselves with these roles. Cases such as those of Diderot and Rousseau, who had no other stable profession, can easily be multiplied. And there was social awareness too, for the manner in which the men of letters perceived and referred to themselves as an occupational group was to a considerable extent accepted by other members of society. Indeed, the most remarkable thing about them was that their emergence as a socially differentiated group was almost a matter of consensus. Admittedly, there were previous examples, such as that of the Chinese mandarins, who were accepted by their society as a professional intellectualist group. But the mandarins *belonged* to their society. They were interpreters of its tradition and maintained and reinforced its order. The eighteenth-century French intellectuals, by contrast, were ambiguously, if not dialectically, related to their society. They were both within it, as a differentiated group, and outside it, as its most bitter critics. In this respect they invite comparison with the Hebrew prophets of the sixth century B.C., though while the prophets acted as isolated personalities, the French intellectuals gradually emerged into a distinctive status group.

It is true that, in eighteenth-century France, the status of the intellectual was not taken for granted. The attitude of the nobility was ambivalent. On the one hand, they received men of letters in their salons and regarded them as their intellectual equals. Arthur Young, in his *Travels in France* (1792), noticed that 'persons of high rank pay attention to science and literature and emulate the character they confer'. On the other hand, the same nobility closed their ranks whenever this was taken to mean equality in a social sense. Intermarriages between nobility and *roturiers* were still mis-alliances even when the latter were famous intellectuals. The marriage of Diderot's daughter to M. de Vendeul was a rare, if not unique, exception.

Despite all this, the prestige and social status of intellectuals were growing not only rapidly but already higher than ever before in the history of Europe. Though the traditional system of patronage was still alive there were clear signs of the writer's increasing economic independence. The readership market was large and stable enough to allow Diderot to earn his living from his work as a writer and publisher. Sedaine also lived comfortably on the earnings of his plays alone. Economic respectability was, however, only one aspect of the rising status of the intellectual. Knowledge, learning, and talent, even more than money, began to be important determinants of upward mobility in eighteenth-century France. It is a remarkable fact that many men of letters, many dominant personalities in the salons of Paris, were of modest social origins. Diderot's father was a cutler, Rousseau and Beaumarchais were watchmakers' sons, Marmontel and Sedaine were 'fils du peuple', and even Voltaire's claim to nobility is debatable. Besides, many of them came from the provinces. Thus, of all the men of letters living in Paris around the middle (1740-4) and towards the end of the century, only twenty-eight per cent were Parisians. A century earlier this percentage was almost double.

To understand this upward thrust it would not be enough to refer to fashion, or to the taste of the upper class for intellectual entertainment. What the eighteenth-century men of letters had to offer and what their aristocratic hosts expected from them was something more than entertainment. Nor is it enough to connect the prestige of the intellectuals, as has often been done, with a downward spread of literacy and education, unless one is prepared to take the view that the intellectual development of eighteenth-century France was an essentially middle-class phenomenon. The main body of evidence, indeed, leads to the conclusion that the position of men of letters, their roles and status, can be more adequately understood by reference to a general condition of their society which can briefly be referred to as anomie.[1] This emerged in two main ways which became more and more visible in the second half of the century.

There was first of all a lack of confidence in the traditional institutions of society. The nobility had great doubts about the power and indeed the willingness of the monarchy to protect their privileges and maintain the aristocratic order of society. The monarchy's co-operation with and reliance on the middle classes was the main reason for this. Thus, in the second half of the century, and particularly after 1770, one can notice a mounting pressure put by the nobility on the King and on his government to enact new legislation, or to revive old laws by which to bar the members of the middle classes from the positions of high responsibility and prestige. On the other hand, the middle classes mistrusted both the nobility and the monarchy on the account of their anti-bourgeois feeling and lack of political acumen. In a word, doubt and insecurity penetrated to the very foundations of a social order in which the upper classes were defending their position out of fear of losing it, and the middle classes were fighting for a position which they were not supposed to achieve.

Another even more important symptom of anomie consisted in the small measure of agreement regarding basic beliefs, values, attitudes, and expectations. Everything in society could become a matter of dispute, starting from the bottom with the position of each individual member—whether this should be based on the traditional right of birth, or on personal worth—and going up to the right of the King to rule, and indeed to the nature of political authority itself. But the quest for legitimacy was not confined to the political and social order of the time. As will be seen later, the traditional conception of the world as a whole, including religion and God, came under fire. Admittedly, one cannot go as far as to say that the people, bourgeois and peasants, lost their faith. On the other hand, there is little doubt that the climate of opinion dominant in the upper classes—and in a highly hierarchical society this is what counts most—was indifferent if not hostile to the traditional

---

[1] 'Anomie' means an absence of norms. Sociologists use the term to describe that confusion or slackening of social norms which induces in the individual a state of bewilderment regarding what is expected of him as a member of a group.

function of the Church and the traditional image of God. Yet there is evidence for a considerable amount of 'faith' of a kind and of substitutes for God. As de Tocqueville tells us, one of the most symptomatic features of the pre-revolutionary period was the existence of a great number of mystic societies.

It was this state of anomie, this disarticulation of the traditional social order and structure of beliefs, that accounted in large measure for the position of the intellectuals in eighteenth-century France. The novelty of the situation lay neither in the originality of their ideas, nor in their number, which was admittedly impressive, but in the fact that their interests and activities were articulated and indeed determined by a specific social need. Briefly, this was the need felt by many people to understand the changing conditions of their social and cultural environment and, above all, to gain some insight into the future course of events. This must not be taken to mean that the intellectuals simply catered for such public anxiety while being themselves completely free from it. In whatever they did, in their most abstract speculations as well as in their most imaginative writings, they were aware of their social mission. And this mission was not only, as is often believed, to 'enlighten' their contemporaries, to interpret their world, but also to change it. Thus, whatever their field of activity, the intellectuals also played the role of secular exegetes. They were both social analysts and social visionaries.

Returning to the ambivalent relationship between the intellectuals and their society, one can say that they were insiders to the extent to which society was open to change—i.e. ready to accept new ideas, institutions, and ways of life. In other words they were insiders in so far as they were not only approved of, but accepted as a prestige group. But they were also outsiders to the extent to which their society was not open to change, to the extent to which their activities were 'censured'. Now, the point is that French society at the time was both open and closed and this was particularly true in the second half of the century. Consequently the intellectuals were the product of a split society and this fact confers on them a series of unique characteristics, social, cultural, and psychological. They present us with the first example of a modern intellectual élite, or what was later called an 'intelligentsia'. 'Modern' is the key word because they are a prototype of what has since come to be known as a characteristic symptom of the process of modernization in Europe and, more recently still, in many other parts of the world.

This is not the place to embark upon a comparative study of intelligentsia. For the present purpose it would be enough to mention that most societies and historical periods in which such a phenomenon occurred are characterized by intense internal conflicts resulting mainly from an uneven and abrupt cultural development. This was initiated either from within, or from without, either by the rise of a new structure of beliefs and values, or by the encounter between a native and a foreign—adopted or imposed—culture such as took place in nineteenth-century Russia and later in many other countries exposed to an intense process of Westernization. The normal outcome of such situations was not only a struggle between two cultures, but also a polarity of values whose main symptom consisted in a sharp differentiation between the 'new' and the 'old'. The cultural climate of such periods was often dominated by a manichaean view of history according to which the angels of light, the few and the elect, were leading a merciless struggle against the forces of darkness. A strong sense of backwardness and evil existed side by side with a strong sense of progress and perfection.

That the cultural scene in eighteenth-century France contained features similar to those outlined above needs no special demonstration. The growth of science is normally mentioned as the main disturbing factor. It would, however, be more accurate to speak, in this context, of the spectacular growth of the scientific spirit. The most characteristic trait of the period was not concern with science as such, but rather with the implications which a scientific way of thinking had upon man's conceptions, beliefs, and attitudes, and upon his social life in particular. There was more concern with naturalism and materialism than with nature and matter. Even a relatively specialized work, such as Buffon's *Histoire naturelle* (1749–88), was interpreted as a history of the earth which contradicted the Book of Genesis.

The disrupting effect which the scientific spirit had upon the traditional religious culture was considerably enhanced by the fact that it was to a great extent imported from England. Nowhere, and at no other time, were Locke's empirical rationalism and particularly Bacon's and Newton's inductive method taken more seriously —and more naïvely—than in the second half of the century and in France. Newtonian mechanics provided the main pieces out of which a new conceptual model of the world, physical and social, was erected. No less powerful was the impact of England on political ideas and on literature, a phenomenon described in more detail in Chapter 2. To speak in this context about an encounter between two cultures would be somewhat inappropriate. On the other hand, some of the results produced by the enthusiasm for English culture and ways of life were surprisingly similar to those produced by the Westernization of Russia. Without taking this into account it would be difficult to explain the gap between the *philosophes* and the traditional culture of their society.

But this is only one side of the story. If one looks at the situation in a broad historical perspective, nothing seems to be more significant than the cumulative effects of the spirit of secular humanism and rationalism. Clear signs of this were visible at least two centuries earlier. Thus, in the sixteenth century, the clash between the new humanistic and the old traditional culture produced an 'esprit luciférique' like Rabelais, unable to make a definite choice between reason and faith, or between experience and revelation. A century later the same cultural development produced Descartes with his precarious balance between human and divine reason, Pascal with his tragic awareness of the distance between God and the world, and moralists such as La Rochefoucauld or Cardinal de Retz apparently sniggering at traditional religious ethics. The eighteenth century produced a new situation in that not only isolated individuals but relatively well-organized groups became identified with the secular rationalist culture and, from this position, declared war on tradition.

The nature of the situation as well as the mental state of the people involved was aptly summed up by Diderot when he defined the purpose of the *Encyclopédie*: 'Il faut tout examiner, tout remuer sans exception et sans ménagement. Il faut fouler aux pieds toutes ces vieilles puérilités, renverser les barrières que la raison n'aura point posées, rendre aux sciences et aux arts une liberté qui leur est si précieuse. Mais ce siècle s'est fait attendre si longtemps... ' This amounts to a *manifesto* on the part of the French intelligentsia. They were conscious in a high degree of their unity as a group, and so 'conspiratorial' and 'cohesive' in their activities that they were often compared to a religious sect. Two of their common traits are closely related to this—their radicalism and totalism. As an illustration of the former it is enough to mention that they, and the *philosophes* in particular, went as far in their desire to change the world as to believe that anything which contradicted their ideas was false, inferior, and corrupt. Moreover, they acquired a new *sense of the natural*, invested their ideas with it, and denounced as unnatural anything which did not correspond to this.

Since what has just been said indicates a 'revolutionary' frame of mind, it is necessary to add that the eighteenth-century intellectuals believed in reason and conceived rationality as a natural condition of human life. Oppression and terror were so closely associated in their minds with the society in which they lived that it would hardly be possible to imagine them in the position of a Robespierre forcing people to be free, or of a Lenin building up a political party with the purpose of accelerating the work of reason within society and history.

As for their totalism, one can say that it was a natural outcome of their high sense of mission. Their commitment to a cause pervaded their activities in all spheres of life—political, civic, and cultural. It is thus not surprising to see Diderot, for example, fighting *the same* battle in all his philosophical, scientific, or literary writings. It seems that his main interest lay not in ideas as such but in what one can *do* with ideas. This is a characteristic trait of many social movements and it will be taken up at a later stage. For the moment it is necessary to discuss briefly the main ideas held by the eighteenth-century intelligentsia.

As has often been said, there is not much that is strikingly new in the philosophy of the Enlightenment. The historian of ideas would have little trouble in tracing its origins back to Descartes's rationalism, Bayle's scepticism, Locke's sensualism, and Bacon's and Newton's scientific empiricism. The *philosophes* borrowed heavily and sometimes uncritically. And yet this does not preclude altogether a series of questions regarding the more specific nature of their intellectual orientation: why did they choose these sources? why were they eclectic in this particular sense? or even more pertinently, what did they do with such a great variety of borrowed ideas? Whatever the final answer to these questions may be, one thing has to be emphatically stated: the *philosophes* made an attempt to bring together into a coherent structure of thought the main body of ideas of seventeenth-century French rationalism and of English empiricism, and assigned to it new emotional and social connotations. What follows is an attempt to illustrate this.

According to d'Alembert, the main qualities of Descartes were 'une imagination forte, un esprit très conséquent, des connaissances puisées dans lui-même plus que dans les livres, beaucoup de courage pour combattre les préjugés les plus généralement reçus et aucune espèce de dépendance qui le forçât à les ménager'. It is, therefore, Descartes's critical attitude of mind that the *philosophes* appreciated most. Moreover, the emphasis was put on the negative aspect of such an attitude, on methodological doubt and freedom from any received truth. For them Descartes was a 'rebel leader' ('chef de conjurés') and they consequently accepted his critical method and rejected the more positive side of his philosophy as sheer metaphysics. In this respect the *philosophes* stood closer to the late seventeenth-century rationalists than to Descartes, that is, to *libertins* and cynics such as Saint-Évremond, Bayle, and Fontenelle, who declared war against religion on behalf of intellectual and moral freedom. The influence of Bayle was particularly important in that he supplied the *philosophes* with a method for the rational analysis of tradition, and with an early model of the *Encyclopédie*, i.e. a compilation of all rationally examined knowledge with the manifest purpose of destroying the prestige of dogma and prejudice. But above all the *libertins* provided the *philosophes* with a dichotomic intellectual outlook in which religion and tradition stood over against freedom and even nature.

At this point a characteristic aspect of their rationalism must be mentioned. Though hostile to any metaphysics the *philosophes*, or most of them, assumed that human nature was essentially rational.

Some of them, Rousseau and Diderot, for instance, were inclined to believe that what was natural was also rational, and the idea of a basically rational universe was very much in the centre of their thought. If this is so, how can one account for these quasi-metaphysical effusions? Can one say, as some of their interpreters have done, that the *philosophes* worked out a clear concept of reason and of rationality and constructed their image of the world around it, inspiring in this way a series of later philosophical enterprises such as those of Kant and Hegel? Can one assume further that their intention was to extend the Newtonian concept of nature (i.e. a model of rational explanation) to human behaviour, to society, and to history? The answer is 'yes' and 'no' for the very obvious reason that, as a group, the *philosophes* were neither homogeneous nor consistent enough in their conceptualization of the world. They were considerably disturbed by two opposing traditions of thought— classical rationalism and scientific empiricism—and most of them shifted, at one time or another, between two radically different sets of suppositions regarding the origins and the organization of our knowledge of the universe. In this context, Mornet speaks of an important breaking-point being reached around 1750 when the Cartesian concept of 'mathesis universalis' began to go out of fashion, and when Diderot predicted a great revolution in science which was to usurp the throne of geometry. The throne of geometry, but not the throne of reason, for without the belief in a basic human rationality, in a set of principles and norms applicable to the human condition in general, the *philosophes* would never have embarked on the gigantic enterprise of the *Encyclopédie*. Nor would they have assumed the existence of a 'natural' religion, society, and morality, i.e. a religion, a society, and a morality based on the universal principles of human reason.

This has, however, to be seen in a broader context. Though Mornet may exaggerate when he maintains that 'the eighteenth century learned quite quickly how to mistrust the Cartesian principles of universal reason', it is nevertheless true that they took a lively interest in the development of the natural sciences and that this had in time tempered and deflated their hankering for universality. Some of them went so far as to consider philosophy as a branch of science, as a body of empirical generalizations about the structure and function of the human mind derived mainly from physiology, natural sciences, and medicine. Their concern with the method and spirit of empirical science had undoubtedly a great deal to do with the well-known materialistic and quasi-naturalistic tenets of their thought. But much more relevant is the fact that the same preoccupation with science lies at the origins of two other general traits of their thought which for lack of more suitable words can be called positivism and the sense of historical reality. Emphasis on empirical observation led the *philosophes* to two main ideas about, or rather attitudes towards, man and his environment. They acquired, first, a sense of differentiation and diversity and, secondly, a sense of development and progressive realization of human knowledge and nature in general. Thus, Montesquieu makes a geographic and ethnographic study of laws, Voltaire insists on the historical and ethnic character of morality, Condillac and Rousseau use observation and a great deal of personal insight to demonstrate the development of human reason. Similarly, Condorcet outlines in a grand theory the stages of human progress, mental and social. But, needless to say, the intention was not to deny the existence of reason with a capital 'R', but rather to reveal its multiple aspects and stages. In this respect, the *philosophes* foreshadowed the Romantic concept of a concrete and particularized universality.

One should not look, however, for too much unity of conception, for the *philosophes* were neither philosophers nor scientists. They were concerned more with the attitudinal implications than the internal consistency of their ideas; most of them developed a strong aversion to 'systems' of any sort. Reason and rationality were for them programme-ideas rather than analytical tools. And so were their materialism, naturalism, theism, and atheism. This should not mean that they picked their ideas by chance as one would pick a handy and solid stick before starting a fight. It simply means that they did not manage to elucidate the more cognitive aspects of such concepts. Hence, obscurity of meaning and even contradictory connotations were inevitable. Take, for instance, the concepts of reason and nature. At one level, the two concepts are closely associated: this was a theoretical position which the *philosophes* adopted as the solid basis for their attack against the political and religious order of their society which, in their view, was neither rational nor natural. But when they came to elucidate the formula 'rational nature and natural reason', they became involved in serious difficulties and contradictions. As P. Hazard aptly puts it:

Nature was too rich in its composition, too complex in its attributes, too potent in its effects to be imprisoned in a formula and the formula gave way under the strain. Despite all their efforts to elucidate it by analysis, to get possession of it through science, to reduce it to some easily intelligible concept, those same wise and learned men who should have been basking in the warmth of certitude, still went on giving the world all manner of different and sometimes directly contradictory interpretations. Conscious of all this, they began to behold in Nature the reappearance of that Mystery which they were bent on banishing from the world.

There is a sense, however, in which the *philosophes* may be called rationalists. As one of their admirers writes: 'They argued that knowledge is superior to ignorance; that social problems can be solved only through reasonable action based on research and analysis rather than through prayer, renunciation, reliance on all-wise authority, or patient waiting for God.' Yet this interpretation insists too much on the epistemological side of their rationalism. In fact they were not altogether free from an ontological and quasi-Hegelian concept of reason according to which the world possessed intrinsic tendencies to become more and more rational. Moreover, reason and rationality were for them action projects used by man to make the world more and more rational. They were constantly associated with primary impulses and feelings such as freedom, equality, brotherhood and, at least in Diderot's writings, with a more concrete meaning of liberation and love. But above all, reason constituted the foundation of an eschatological vision operating, as any myth does, within a circular movement of human history: there was reason at the beginning, reason at the end, and any stage in between was both a re-enactment of a primeval state and a fulfilment of a prophecy. It was in this way that the cult of reason was born.

We can now look more closely at the idea repeatedly mentioned so far that the eighteenth-century intellectuals were the spearhead

of a social movement. This is all the more necessary as, according to
de Tocqueville and many others who followed suit, they were anything but socially representative; they were Utopians, dreamers,
'raisonneurs de cabinet et architectes de nuées'. Unlike the eighteenth-
century political thinkers in England, the *philosophes* had little
knowledge and even less practice of social affairs.

One can, of course, submit such a thesis to the test of facts. Thus,
after referring to the administrative functions and talents of Fénelon,
Vauban, Montesquieu, Voltaire, Helvétius, Turgot, and many
others, Mornet exclaims 'mais c'est de Tocqueville ou Taine qui
furent des gens de cabinet'. This is certainly relevant, but statistics
alone can seldom be decisive in matters of historical interpretation.
More relevant is de Tocqueville's unawareness of the multiple
ways in which an intellectual can be related to his society. On this
point he is a narrow political empiricist, inclined to deny an adequate
knowledge of social affairs to anyone who is not directly involved in
administration.

No one seriously interested in the relationship between these
eighteenth-century intellectuals and their society can fail to notice
the following points: first, many of them were concerned not only
with society in general terms but also with some specific aspects of
social life such as education, laws, customs, beliefs, government, to
mention only a few. Secondly, their approach and method cannot
simply be labelled speculative and impressionistic. Even Rousseau
conceived of his *Contrat social* as an aspect of a larger and more
empirically oriented work on political institutions. Thirdly, many
of them were keen travellers and keen observers, and as a result of
this came very near to a systematic comparative approach to social
phenomena. Furthermore, it would not be difficult to detect in the
works of Diderot and Montesquieu elements of what may be called
structural analysis, i.e. an explicit awareness of the interconnection
between the various aspects, institutional and behavioural, of a given
society.

But the intellectuals' relationship with their own society cannot
and should not be judged by their objective and systematic knowledge of it. They were part of their society, seriously involved in its
making and unmaking in a cultural and psychological sense, and as

such they had reliable sources of information. To doubt this would mean to ignore, among other things, the role played by the salons in eighteenth-century France. That membership of the salons was confined to a pre-selected social group, i.e. aristocrats with intellectual habits, should be seen as a favourable condition from this point of view. To this one should add the fact that owing to their social origins many intellectuals had a wide range of social contacts and social awareness. To understand this one should bear in mind that we are dealing with people like Diderot, Rousseau, Marmontel, and many others who, in a psychological sense, were true products of social mobility (i.e. they had personal experience of social life at all levels).

This is a crucial point regarding the relationship between these intellectuals and their society. If one can single out one mental trait which most of them possessed in abundance, this would certainly be *social sensibility*. Quite contrary to de Tocqueville's view, they were in a sense too much involved in their society, too open to and affected by the waves of public opinion and feelings. They not only knew their society, but they worked on it by totalizing and reinforcing feelings and thoughts shared by many of its members— in other words, by performing a sort of social maeutics. In this sense they can be seen as an *elitic group* in a broad social process.

As previously mentioned, our contention is that this was the process of modernization or, more precisely, an early stage in the modernization of French society. First of all knowledge, education, in a word, enlightenment defined both the position and the social function of the elitic group. They may have been naïve, but they certainly believed that stupidity lay at the very root of a social order based on political absolutism and legitimated by religious beliefs and institutions. Moreover, ignorance was the mainspring of superstition, barbarity, extravagance, slavery, and many other evils which they considered characteristic of traditional society. When Condorcet divided mankind into superstitious and enlightened he had in mind two types of society.

But this is not all. The intellectuals used knowledge, or rather the spread of knowledge, in a more positive way. Briefly speaking, they fought systematically for the promotion of knowledge, intelligence, and education to the rank of social values and criteria of social differentiation. It is at this point that they made solid contact with tendencies operating diffusely within their society and consequently established themselves as the first modernizing élite in Europe. This point requires some elaboration.

Officially, eighteenth-century French society was divided into two classes, the nobles and the non-nobles ('les roturiers'). In reality, however, it had a more complex hierarchical organization, and the main reason for this was the emergence of the middle strata of the bourgeoisie. As this is largely a matter of common knowledge, it is enough to mention only those points which have particular relevance in the present context.

To start with, the eighteenth-century French bourgeoisie was a heterogeneous social group which included two large and hierarchically organized occupational categories, business and the professions. The former consisted of financiers, *négociants*, industrialists, and merchants. The latter included the intellectuals, lawyers, doctors, lower clergy, law clerks, and assistants. However, the specific feature of the bourgeoisie as a social group was not its hierarchical organization, but rather its mobility, its inherent tendency to form an open society. The occupational categories just mentioned were to a large extent open categories, that is, social positions which the individual achieved on the basis of his interests and abilities. For instance, it was customary for the best talents in the business families to go to liberal professions since the latter enjoyed higher status. Even more significant was the tendency of the bourgeoisie to form an open society outside itself or, to put it more cautiously, to break down the resistance of the nobility to the upward mobility of the prosperous middle strata of society. The bourgeoisie had behind it a relatively long tradition of achievement and upward mobility. The practice of buying offices and titles and even sons-in-law of noble origin is well known. But the point is that this met with an increasing resistance from the nobility which gathered momentum in the second half of the century when the King was forced to revive the old legislation restricting the access of the bourgeoisie to high positions. Even the prices paid for sons-in-law of noble origin went up considerably. All this resulted in a difficult and ambiguous situation for the bourgeoisie. As one writer puts it, the late eighteenth-century French bourgeoisie became a 'cramped group', a group severely frustrated in those aspirations which were hitherto considered achievable and legitimate.

We can turn now to the intelligentsia. Could one simply say, as has often been said, that they were the representatives or, more precisely, the ideological defenders of the bourgeoisie? One thing seems to be as clear as daylight, namely, that the bourgeoisie and the intellectuals were the main agents of, and the main fighters for, an open society. This is obviously important, but not enough.

The two groups differed considerably in their attitudes towards the traditional order of society, let alone in their vision of the future society. There is hardly any evidence that the eighteenth-century bourgeoisie had any revolutionary or reformist aspirations—at any rate before 1770. They were anxious to be differentiated from the lower ranks by exemption from taxes and military service, and even more anxious to join the upper ranks. Towards the nobility they had an ambivalent attitude in the sense that they wanted it to be open before they arrived there, and closed after. In a word, the bourgeoisie believed and fought for mobility, but only within the existing social order. This is aptly summarized by Elinor Barber when she writes: 'Although the bourgeois of the eighteenth century built his aspirations of social mobility on implicitly universalist values, there is little, or no, expression of equalitarianism. Careers should be open to talent, but these successful careers were only means to the end of nobility, not ends in themselves.'

Now, it would be only fair to mention that the author just quoted finds little if any difference between such views and those held by the intelligentsia before 1770. As an illustration she refers to Voltaire's and Montesquieu's 'traditional faith in aristocracy', and to their support for 'enlightened absolutism and constitutional monarchy'. It is obvious, however, that such a view is rooted in too narrow an approach to the social and political ideas of the intelligentsia. More precisely, it confuses the conservatism of Voltaire and Montesquieu with the image of society implicit in the attitudes of the intelligentsia as a group. If this is taken into account it will easily become apparent that the intelligentsia did not only criticize the traditional social order but that they made a systematic effort to legitimize a new social order based on universalist values such as freedom and equality. Thus the main difference between the two groups consisted in the degree to which they were alienated from the traditional order. While the bourgeoisie perceived itself as a marginal group because it was not accepted, the intellectuals perceived themselves as an alienated group because they belonged to another society.

Despite its glaring inconsistencies, it is not difficult to find some important points of convergence in the political thought of the Enlightenment. To start with, it was commonly maintained that the only legitimate political authority was the authority of the law. Admittedly, the argument was not original. Most of it consisted in paraphrasing Locke's and Montesquieu's ideas on the consensual and contractual nature of political power. But in doing so the *philosophes* hammered home the general idea that 'no man has received from nature the right to rule others', that 'the prince derives from his subjects the authority he holds over them and this authority is limited by the laws of nature and of state', and finally that 'liberty is the right to do what the laws permit'. Thus, in their attitudes and opinions, they went a long way towards a conception of a social order based on rational authority or, to use Max Weber's words, towards the concept of 'a rational–legal legitimacy of power'.

Though generally speaking they were concerned with the limitation rather than the elimination of the traditional power of monarchy, Rousseau at least made an important step forward with his concept of a society in which men are free not only because the government is checked by laws but because these laws are assented to by each man individually. One may, of course, point to the danger involved in a formula which brings so closely together authority and liberty, society and the individual, but there is little doubt that the kind of freedom Rousseau has in mind is not the freedom of the bourgeoisie to enjoy equally and fully the advantages offered by eighteenth-century French society. What he has in mind is freedom as a basic condition of political society, freedom as a universalist value. It is precisely because of this that he has sometimes been labelled as the advocate of anarchic individualism.

This takes us to another modern trait of the intelligentsia: their concern with the individual as a value in himself. In the case of Rousseau this is so obvious that it can easily be considered as a dominant motif in his writings. It also appears as a dominant motif in his life, prompting descriptions of him as a paranoid personality, i.e. a person displaying both compulsive needs for self-assertion and obsessional fears of being prevented from doing so. The individual-istic motif in Rousseau has two distinctive though interdependent aspects expressed in *Émile* and *Les Confessions* respectively. The former asserts the individual as a moral value, as an autonomous personality, while the latter goes a step further by stressing the value of the individual as sheer inwardness and subjectivity. It is this latter aspect that made Starobinski speak about the 'safe-guarding or the restitution of transparence' as a common motif of Rousseau's writings. His autobiographical urge, his desire to reveal his uniqueness, are obvious manifestations of this. But there is also a social side to it, i.e. the marginality of his condition in the society of his time and the desire to find another society open to indi-vidualistic values.

Rousseau's relentless effort to establish his authentic self may be a personality trait. This is not, however, the case with Diderot. His concern with the authenticity of the individual's inner life is so rational and almost scientific that it often reminds one of contem-porary depth psychology. A quick glance at his literary writing illustrates this. Consider, for instance, his reaction to his own por-trait by Michel van Loo: 'Mais que diront mes petits enfants, lorsqu'ils viendront à comparer mes tristes ouvrages avec ce riant, mignon, efféminé, vieux coquet-là? Mes enfants, je vous préviens que ce n'est pas moi. J'avais en une journée cent physionomies diverses selon la chose dont j'étais affecté... J'ai un masque qui trompe l'artiste.'

It is not easy to summarize this surprisingly modern, almost Pirandellian, aspect of Diderot. He is undoubtedly aware of the dynamic relationship between the social environment and the mani-festation as well as the realization of the individual's inner self. There is first of all the presence of and the relationship with others. As Diderot writes in his *Essais sur la peinture* (written 1765):

Un homme fait une lecture intéressante à un autre. Sans qu'ils y pensent l'un et l'autre, le lecteur se disposera de la manière la plus commode pour lui: l'auditeur en fera autant...

Ajouter un troisième personnage à la scène, il subira la loi des deux premiers; c'est un système combiné de trois intérêts. Qu'il en survienne cent, deux cents, mille: la même loi s'observera.

It would not be too rash to infer from this and from many other passages in his works that communication, or to put it in more technical language, existence for the other, is an important component of personal identity; and not only the other as a specific human being, but the other as totality, as society, culture, and institutions, for all of them have a direct impact on the individual's perception of himself, on his sense of identity. In dealing with this, Diderot reveals himself as a remarkable social and cultural analyst, and certainly as one of the greatest iconoclasts of all times. He is in this sense a rare if not unique prefiguration both of Marx and Freud. Thus, a century ahead of Marx, he started his war against society for the liberation of the individual; i.e. his campaign of denunciation and demolition in order to create the conditions for an authentic, or 'honest', existence. And though his conception of society is different, his campaign is not less systematic and radical than that of Marx. Starting from religion and the Church he gradually broadens his attack to all institutions, political, economic, educational, and finally to art, philosophy, and the other aspects of culture. He sees his society as an organized whole and consequently only a radical change can produce the desired liberation.

But the war goes beyond society into the minds of its individual members. Almost a century and a half before Freud, Diderot explores the deep motivational sources of human behaviour, and seems to become aware of the existence of the Oedipus Complex. What is certain, however, is the fact that he is acutely aware of a basic duality and contradiction between the depth and the surface of the individual's mind. Furthermore, he is aware that the latter changes according to the situation in which the individual finds himself and that this creates an infinite capacity for disguise and self-deception. This makes it necessary to carry the war inside the mind, to pierce the surface, to pull off the mask and thus allow the individual to establish direct and natural contact with himself and with others. Here too, Diderot's tactics are based on surprise and shock, his main aim being to disarm the enemy by sudden exposure to the naked reality of his own mind. This explains Diderot's preoccupation as an author and a critic with *la littérature licencieuse*. There is little doubt that he appreciated as well as wrote it, and used it in his war of liberation. Whenever he sees someone, and particularly a member of the upper classes, buying his *Bijoux indiscrets*, he has the feeling that he has caught him red-handed, the feeling that, in dropping the mask of conventional sexual morality, the purchaser is on the way to dropping all masks and becoming a man like others. Michel Butor makes this point very clearly when he insists on the close connection between the *Encyclopédie* and Diderot's literary works, especially *Les Bijoux indiscrets*, the *Supplément au Voyage de Bougainville*, and the *Correspondance littéraire*. The connection is, obviously, an ideological one and in order to understand it one has to bear in mind the two senses and sources of liberation, social and psychological. Diderot sees them together. Consequently, his battle against the institutions of traditional society and his criticism of conventional sexual morality are inspired by the same desire to increase freedom. Moreover, the principal means for achieving this are the same, knowledge, education—in a word, enlightenment.

NOTE

Listed below are some of the most relevant primary and secondary sources which throw further light on the ideas and attitudes discussed in the above chapter:

Basic texts. D'Alembert, *Discours préliminaire* (to the *Encyclopédie*) (1751); Bayle, *Dictionnaire historique et critique* (1697); Condorcet, *Esquisse d'un tableau historique des progrès de l'esprit humain* (written 1793-4); Diderot, see note to Chapter 7: the most directly relevant works are: *Lettre sur les aveugles, Le Rêve de d'Alembert, Éloge de Richardson, Supplément au Voyage de Bougainville, Observations sur le Nakaz, Essais sur la peinture* (posthumously published 1795), and 'Salon de 1767' (in *Correspondance littéraire* of 1767); the novels and plays are also relevant; Helvétius, *De l'esprit* (1758); d'Holbach, *Le Christianisme dévoilé* (1761); Montesquieu, *L'Esprit des lois* (1748); Rousseau, *Lettre à d'Alembert sur les spectacles* (1758), *Du contrat social* (1762), *Émile* (1762), *Confessions* (1764-70); Toussaint, *Les Mœurs* (1748); Voltaire, *Lettres philosophiques* (1734), *Essai sur les mœurs* (1756).

Criticism. E. G. Barber, *The Bourgeoisie in 18th Century France* (1955); I. Berlin, *The Age of Enlightenment* (1956); M. Butor, 'Diderot le fataliste et ses maîtres' in *Critique*, nos. 228 and 230 (1966); E. Cassirer, *The Philosophy of the Enlightenment* (1951); R. Escarpit, *Sociologie de la littérature* (1964); P. Gay, *The Party of Humanity* (1964); J. Guéhenno, *Jean Jacques* (3 vols.): vol. i, *En marge des 'Confessions': 1712–1750* (1948); P. Hazard, *European Thought in the Eighteenth Century* (1965); J. F. Lively (ed.), *The Enlightenment* (1966); R. Mandrou, *La France aux XVIIᵉ et XVIIIᵉ siècles* (1967); D. Mornet, *Les Origines intellectuelles de la Révolution française* (5th edn., 1954); D. Mornet, *La Pensée française au XVIIIᵉ siècle* (10th edn., 1962); J. Proust, *Diderot et l'Encyclopédie* (1962); J. Starobinski, *Jean-Jacques Rousseau: la transparence et l'obstacle* (1957); J. L. Talmon, *The Origins of Totalitarian Democracy* (1952); A. de Tocqueville, *L'Ancien Régime et la Révolution française* (1856).

7. Diderot

'NOUS sommes l'univers entier' (*Corresp*. vi. 376), Diderot once exclaimed. It is in the light of this intuitive truth that he elaborated his original philosophical ideas. Eighteenth-century French philosophy which, until quite recently, it was customary to decry, is held in increasingly high esteem. It certainly examined, in the wake of Locke rather than of Descartes, some of the great questions of the age and of modern society. Montesquieu, Voltaire, Rousseau, d'Alembert, Condillac, and d'Holbach, with their encyclopedic knowledge and unparalleled range of interests, made outstanding contributions in many fields, but it was perhaps Diderot whose thought showed the greatest depth as well as breadth, who was best able to interpret and synthesize the data at his disposal, to evolve the new methodology required for the study of Nature, and to foreshadow some of the scientific discoveries of the following century. Whatever the problem with which he was concerned—the universe, life, man and human destiny, religion, the origin and government of the world, society, ethics or aesthetics—Diderot never oversimplified the issues. He accepted the diversity of fact for which he sought to account and with great intellectual integrity never tried to make the fact fit in with his theories. His approach was undogmatic, empirical, and dialectical. Hence many of the difficulties he had to face and some of the real or apparent contradictions in his thought. 'Tout se tient dans la nature' (ii. 111),[1] he wrote, and again, 'Tout ce qui est ne peut être ni contre nature ni hors de nature' (ii. 187). He is always aware of the 'grande chaîne qui lie toutes choses' which in the *Encyclopédie* is defined as 'l'enchaînement des connaissances'. If the world is one it

---

[1] References to the Assézat–Tourneux edition of the *Œuvres complètes* (see Note) are referred to throughout in this way by volume and page-number.

will be reflected in the microcosm of man as well as the macrocosm
which is the universe. He wrote in the *Éléments de physiologie*:

> Je suis porté à croire que tout ce que nous avons vu, connu, aperçu,
> entendu; jusqu'aux arbres d'une longue forêt, que dis-je jusqu'à la dis-
> position des branches, à la forme des feuilles et à la variété des couleurs,
> des verts et des lumières; jusqu'à l'aspect des grains de sable du rivage de
> la mer, aux inégalités de la surface des flots soit agités par un souffle léger,
> soit écumeux et soulevés par les vents de la tempête; jusqu'à la multitude
> des voix humaines, des cris animaux et des bruits physiques, à la mélodie
> et à l'harmonie de tous les airs, de toutes les pièces de musique, de tous
> les concerts que nous avons entendus, tout cela existe en nous à notre
> insu. (ix. 366–7)

Moreover the link between us and the world is not purely material.
There was for Diderot, who believed in the objective reality of
Nature, a close parallel between the laws of the universe and those
that govern the working of the mind. 'Le type de nos raisonnements
les plus étendus, leur liaison, leur conséquence, est nécessaire dans
notre entendement comme l'enchaînement, la liaison des effets, des
causes, des objets, des qualités des objets l'est dans la nature' (ix.
372). The reasoning is by analogy and it leads to an awareness of
the link between the physical and the spiritual worlds and of a good
reason for the validity of our thinking whenever it is soundly based
on fact. It is the awareness of this link, but refusal to accept that
the determinism of the physical world could be translated without
modification into the spiritual world, which made him recoil from
the views of the mechanical materialism of La Mettrie as expressed
in such works as *L'Homme machine* (1748) and *L'Homme plante*
(1751).

Nevertheless, he did move rapidly from deism to a belief in
natural religion, thence to a monistic materialism; his *Pensées
philosophiques* (1746), his *Promenade du Sceptique* (1747, publ. 1830),
his *Lettre sur les aveugles* (1749), and his *Pensées sur l'interprétation
de la nature* (1754) providing the significant landmarks.

In 1745 Diderot was approached by the publisher Le Breton with
a view to bringing out an encyclopedia. It was originally to have
been a French translation of Chambers's *Cyclopædia*, but Diderot

soon changed the nature of the undertaking which under his direction and that of his coeditor d'Alembert became an important mouthpiece of radical thought. He gathered around him a team of active *littérateurs* and scientists who shared his passion for knowledge and reform and his opposition to the reactionary forces of Church and State. He outlined his programme in a *Prospectus* (1750) which d'Alembert expanded into a brilliant *Discours préliminaire* (1751). The *Encyclopédie* is a magnificent testament of the age of Enlightenment and marks one of the three or four great intellectual landmarks of the eighteenth century. It is important for its conception and its realization. It was intended, firstly, to present knowledge as an organized whole, stressing the interconnections between the sciences; and, secondly, as a *dictionnaire raisonné* to bring out the essential principles and applications of every art and science. Its underlying philosophy was rationalism and faith in the progress of the human mind. It is, therefore, more than a compendium of past and present knowledge; it is rather the mirror of advanced thought, embodying needed social and political reforms and pointing the way to a scientific and technological revolution. The publication of the *Encyclopédie* with its seventeen volumes of text and eleven volumes of plates[1] (1751–72) was the greatest publishing venture of the century. It provided Diderot with his chief occupation and source of income. His work as coeditor, and as sole editor following on d'Alembert's resignation in 1758, was rendered most difficult by the cabals of enemies and the defection of friends, the opposition of the Parlement and the Church, coupled with the vacillating policy of the government and the censorship. As author or part-author he contributed innumerable articles, particularly on the history of philosophy, social theory, aesthetics, and the mechanical arts. His range of knowledge and experience, already great before he assumed his life-work, was further extended in all possible directions so that it became truly encyclopedic. He was certainly better able than most of his contemporaries to synthesize intelligently all the newest discoveries of science and progress realized in different fields.

It is Diderot's rejection of Christianity and the deepening of his materialist philosophy that provides the key to all his writing and led

[1] These are of exceptional practical and historical interest.

him to the expression of some of his most interesting ideas. In the
Lettre sur les aveugles, which led to his arrest and detention for three
months in the prison of Vincennes, he detailed his proposal to teach
the blind to read through developing their sense of touch, stressing
our dependence on our senses for our ideas, adumbrating an evolutionary theory of survival by superior adaptation, and challenging
the existence of an intelligent God. The order we see in the universe
is nothing more than our apprehension of the laws of motion of
matter. These ideas he developed in the *Pensées sur l'interprétation de
la nature* which is the *discours de la méthode* of the eighteenth century,
with its emphasis on empiricism and the inductive form of reasoning
linked with the name of Bacon, and offers examples of the kind of
scientific results obtainable by scientific investigations and well-
founded conjectures. His emphasis on experimentation points to the
failure of Cartesianism to account for reality, his recourse to hypotheses brings out the inadequacy of current scientific knowledge.
His monistic materialism was no doubt most brilliantly expressed in
the *Entretien entre d'Alembert et Diderot* and in the *Rêve de d'Alembert* (both written in 1769 and published in 1830), in which he evolved
the first modern theory of the cellular structure of matter. Starting
from sensationalist premises, and following in the steps of Maupertuis, he gave a positive content to Leibniz's idealistic monad and tried
to show that the passage from the inorganic to the organic may be
achieved in stages. He saw matter as a whole lending itself to many
forms and invariably endowed with *sensibilité*, active or kinetic. His
molecular theory of the universe hinged on his non-cartesian conception of motion inherent in matter (which he shared with Toland):
'Le mouvement est également et dans le corps transféré et dans le
corps immobile. Le repos est un concept abstrait qui n'existe point
en nature' (ii. 106). Nature is a product of matter in motion. Time is
seen as the factor underlying all changes, and therefore an essential
part of evolutionary processes. He discarded the theory of pre-
formation, which would in fact lead to a mechanical and static
conception of the universe, in favour of epigenesis, which explained
organic formation in terms of juxtaposition and contiguity. Whilst
Buffon and Needham, who had discovered infusoria, believed in
spontaneous generation, Diderot could not, for this hypothesis did

not resolve the problem of the special sensitivity of living organisms. His medical knowledge led him to stress increasingly the importance of *organisation*—molecular combination endowed with specialized functions—and to see in the autonomous working of the brain the kingpin of a neural mechanism, a kind of sixth sense of extraordinary power.

His ideas on embryology are astonishingly modern. Whilst his contemporaries were still arguing against bi-parental heredity, he expounded his own theory to account for birth and heredity, foreshadowing the present scientific theory of genes and chromosomes, accounting for the phenomenon of recessive genes, indicating the fundamental role of chromosomes, and explaining monsters or abnormality by the impairing of one or other of the pair of 'threads' at the moment of generation. He was, of course, handicapped by lack of a suitable and well-defined vocabulary and had to anticipate scientific verification. Moreover, there seems to have been some confusion in his mind between a cellular organization and a nervous system. But the discovery of organic cells and the principle of cell-division came to confirm the broad lines and the details of his hypotheses, and the soundness of his methodology. We cannot here retrace the evolution of Diderot's transformist or near-transformist theories. But in attempting to break down the barrier between inorganic and organic nature, Diderot was successful in arriving close to the modern molecular theory, and if we substitute for his living molecule the modern cell and for his dead molecule the atom, we have a complete chain from the molecule to the universe which is as all-embracing as that of any modern materialist philosophy. 'Le prodige, c'est la vie, c'est la sensibilité; et ce prodige n'en est plus un... Lorsque j'ai vu la matière inerte passer à l'état sensible, rien ne doit plus m'étonner' (ii. 133–4). He proceeds to adumbrate the chief theories of Lamarck and Darwin; the principles governing heredity and natural selection, the necessary link between organs, functions, and needs, or, as he states concisely in the *Éléments de physiologie* (1774–80): 'L'organisation détermine les fonctions et les besoins' (ix. 336). Man is a living part of a living world, only to be understood in his cosmological context. The detailed exposition of Diderot's genetic theory is particularly impressive, and we are taken well beyond the sensationalist doctrine of Locke, Condillac, and Helvétius, even if the passage from sensitivity to judgement, intellectual activity, and by extension creativity, is left unexplored, and if his genetic theory of understanding remains too summary to be convincing. In the *Suite de l'Entretien*, which serves as a post-script to the *Rêve de d'Alembert*, he deals with the problem of abnormality with striking insight. The so-called monstrous and perverted is not outside the scope of nature, for 'Tout ce qui est ne peut être ni contre nature, ni hors de nature'. It may be accounted for genetically, or by a peculiar reaction to a given environment. The very large number of monsters thrown up by Nature, of abor-tive species, argues against divine design. Throughout the *Rêve* Diderot is much concerned with physiology. Is not man the monster of woman and vice versa? And have not hybrids as well as peculiarly formed creatures to be accepted since they exist and can be ac-counted for within the terms of nature? He stresses, as he had done in the *Lettre sur les aveugles*, the close connection between physiology and what we know as psychology, showing how the physiological sometimes determines the psychological response, and how some-times the head determines the response of the body; as for example in his explanation of dreams which was so to impress Freud. In later works he increasingly stressed the power of the brain to determine life and events, always within the framework of his monistic and energetistic materialism.

How, in the absence of scientific proof, was Diderot able to advance such accurate theories? In the first place he was well informed of the most recent results of science. He knew of Need-ham's experiments and of those of Malpighi. He had read and annotated Haller's great work on physiology, the writings of Charles Bonnet, Bordeu, Robert Whytt, and above all Buffon. We have the reading list he drew up as part of his preparation for his *Éléments de physiologie* which confirms this. We know too of his many personal contacts with scientists and medical men. He accepted their evi-dence and only had recourse to hypotheses when these were necessary to account for the facts, whilst always bearing in mind the need to preserve the essential unity of matter. 'La sensibilité, propriété générale de la matière' (ii. 116) was such a hypothesis. By deepening it he came to see that this *sensibilité* was latent and significant only in living matter. This led him to examine the organization of matter with sensitivity concentrated in specific organs and to establish the special role of the brain in relation to the nerve centres. Thus, a full yet simple explanation of the universe can be made to include the mental processes of man. He envisaged an ever-changing world without God in which forms are born of chance and are then indefinitely and necessarily subject to change. Hence our limitations in ever apprehending nature which must be ultimately unknowable. As he had already written in 1753: 'Si l'état des êtres est dans une vicissitude perpétuelle; si la nature est encore à l'ouvrage, malgré la chaîne qui lie les phénomènes, il n'y a point de philosophie. Toute notre science naturelle devient aussi transitoire que les mots' (ii. 48). Diderot certainly had the power to select significant data, synthesize known facts, and interpret them. He used inductive as well as deductive reasoning and carefully chosen analogies. His mind seized upon hidden connections and correspondences. He also made use of his faculty of intuition and unfolded step by step his new and majestic vision of life, building up a grandiose picture which he expressed with appropriate eloquence, bordering on lyrical ecstasy. In the *Rêve* there are mature passages which echo the new cosmic revelation of the blind Saunderson, and he conveyed a deep, almost mystical communion with the very processes of nature. The excitement of gradual discovery is conveyed through the ebb and flow of discussion. Thought as well as life has its organic complexity. It becomes creative when, without ever denying the authenticity of facts, it goes beyond them to reach a cosmic understanding of the universe. In an age of destructive criticism, Diderot's ability to synthesize appears extraordinary. He knew that experimental philosophy was destined to take the place of rational speculation and that the question *how* and not the question *why* was the key to intellectual progress. And since the one who knows and knowable facts are of the same substance, conjectures that are well founded have validity.

The question whether the *Rêve* in particular should be considered as a set of speculative essays or a reflection of Diderot's definitive opinion focuses attention on the wrong point. On 2 September 1769 Diderot wrote to Mlle Volland, referring to the *Rêve*: 'Il n'est pas

possible d'être plus profond et plus fou' (*Corresp*. ix. 140). And again,
'Cela est de la plus haute extravagance, et tout à la fois de la philosophie la plus profonde' (ibid. ix. 126). It is scarcely possible to
better this final comment by Diderot. Certainly he was particularly
attached to this work in which he took a special delight. The peculiar
quality lies not only in the merit of the scientific theory or the new
and viable philosophy propounded, but in the author's ability to
convey his satisfaction at having fulfilled an intellectual need and
in his conviction that the literary form adopted matched the quality of
the thought. He realized that following in the footsteps of Fontenelle
he had enlarged even further the realm of literature. In some ways
the *Éléments de physiologie* take us further than the *Rêve*, but they
do not have the same interest or vitality because they lack the same
artistic power, nor do they carry the same conviction. But whether
wholly successful or not Diderot always has a proper respect for
literary values, concentrating on discovering the form of expression
ideally suited for his thought. So philosophy and science become the
subject of stylized dialogues, scenes from plays with an element of
marivaudage. He broke down the idea of narrow genres and evolved
new and more embracing literary forms. His theatre includes moral
sermons and his novels have disquisitions on ethics and aesthetics.

The determinist materialism which he had evolved had grave
bearing on the moral issues which were never far from his mind.
If it is true that 'les êtres ne sont jamais ni dans leur génération, ni
dans leur conformation, ni dans leur usage que ce que les résis-
tances, les lois du mouvement et l'ordre universel les déterminent à
être', there can be no liberty. Virtue must spring from a felicitous
natural disposition, and *bienfaisance* and *malfaisance* must take the
place of good and evil. At the time he wrote the *Lettre sur les
aveugles* he saw the world as one in which morality was almost
entirely dependent on the senses, yet he was inwardly convinced of
the need for morality, and in the absence of God he was unable to
find a basis for virtue. Starting from Shaftesbury's standpoint in the
Essai sur le mérite et la vertu, which he freely translates 'Point de
vertu sans croire en Dieu, point de bonheur sans vertu', he vacillates,
trapped with most contemporary thinkers into the self-deception of

believing, because he wanted to, that virtue necessarily produces happiness. This is a point of view which he underlines in his two major plays, *Le Fils naturel* (1757) and *Le Père de famille* (1758), and which lies behind his theory of the *drame*, the serious, bourgeois drama of real life, half-way between comedy and tragedy, the presentation of which was to uplift the spectators and attract them to the theatre to listen to moral sermons of greater emotional appeal than those delivered from the pulpit. In the preface to *Le Père de famille*, and in other writings on the theatre, Diderot states that education holds the key to moral progress. From the standpoint of philosophic propaganda, this ethic reinforces the cause of the encyclopedic movement. But this ethic was more for the unthinking crowd than for the honest thinker. Diderot soon came to believe that the only thing to do with the *méchant*, that is the man born bad whom nothing can modify, was to destroy him, a view he expressed as late as the *Neveu de Rameau* where, however, his admiration for genius as such leads him to wonder whether genius, which must take its course, does not carry its own justification. He now thinks increasingly in terms of the individual and not solely in social terms. It is Moi (i.e. Diderot) and not Lui (i.e. Le Neveu de Rameau) who is thankful for the genius of Racine and is ready to put up with his alleged wickedness. His consideration of genius, of the nature of man in his social context, and his dissatisfaction with common, bourgeois, prejudiced morality prompt him to say: 'Il n'y a point de lois pour les sages' (v. 307); and to proclaim: 'Il est une doctrine spéculative qui n'est ni pour la multitude, ni pour la pratique et que si sans être fat on n'écrit pas tout ce qu'on fait, sans être inconséquent on ne fait pas tout ce qu'on écrit.'

This being so, the problems posed by the *doctrine spéculative* remain. How in an immoral society can one establish a moral law? This dichotomy was clearly shown in the *Neveu de Rameau*. The dialogue between Diderot and Rameau's Nephew is spontaneous and witty, and the comments are pungent, bitter, and ironic. In essence, this satirical work challenges the cant of contemporary society and the hypocrisy of conventional morality. It offers a vigorous dramatic sketch of a parasite and an eccentric, a musician who is gifted yet unable to make his mark through insufficient talent,

and who is shamelessly selfish and amoral. He is challenged up to
a point by Diderot and each protagonist scores in turn, each,
however, remaining basically faithful to his views and to himself;
the debate is certainly inconclusive. This brilliantly conceived,
highly original, and entertaining *divertissement* cuts deep. It has
authenticity and reveals the complexity of Diderot's nature and of
his philosophical ideas. Man outside the context of society may be
devoid of meaning. He must subordinate himself to the society of
which he is an integral part. Yet man is unique whether he be
a genius or a *génie manqué*, a great creative artist or an interpretative
artist with still something of the great creative power, thereby
transcending the whole determinist concept of man. But perhaps the
Neveu in his freedom from social convention and from unques-
tioned belief in absolutes may well owe his disposition to the
maudite fibre paternelle, as he himself alleges, and to a predictable
reaction, given his nature, to the corrupt society in which he has to
survive. From the philosophical standpoint the work may be reconciled with determinism. It is the ethics that are ambivalent.

Diderot's dichotomy reached crisis point by 1773. Only a new
work of fiction, superimposing on reality an imaginary story closely
connected with but not determined by reality, could crystallize his
new attitude. *Jacques le fataliste* (1773, publ. 1796) which owes
something to Laurence Sterne and has been considered as a kind of
'anti-Candide', is in the tradition of the picaresque novel and of the
conte philosophique. All Diderot's important late literary works may
be seen as investigations of the psycho-physiological condition of
man, his moral behaviour, his relative independence, with a view to
confirming or modifying his materialist philosophy. Jacques, who
believes in Fate, is involved in an endless argument with his master,
who does not. As they journey along they retell the story of their
lives and loves and listen to that of others whom they chance to
meet. The novel has authenticity, perhaps partly because of its
complexity. It has been claimed that Jacques and his Master in-
carnate two aspects of Diderot, yet Jacques's popular fatalism has
little in common with Diderot's scientific determinism, and his sardonic interest in others differs greatly from Diderot's normal attitude of profound interest in the value of other people as individuals.

It is possible that Diderot underwent a kind of catharsis in writing this novel. Certainly he does not reject determinism, but he perceives that it cannot be made to apply indiscriminately to every action in life, as Jacques so ridiculously asserts. The moral world is not wholly and obviously dependent on the physical, as Jacques believes, and we are made to laugh at his expense. Man in his actions is incalculable. But the Master's championship of free will is equally ridiculous. Man's understanding is seen as limited, so that he can only partially discover the truth. If we all share the limitations of Jacques and his Master, how then is it possible to establish philosophical and ethical codes?

In *La Religieuse* (1760, publ. 1798), a profoundly moving novel of the horrific experiences of a nun immured without vocation, Diderot had not directly attacked the Church, but a man-made system running counter to Nature, and he had shown some of the dangers of celibacy and sexual repression. In the *Supplément au Voyage de Bougainville* (1772, publ. 1796) Diderot unfolded in far-off Tahiti his dream of a free society based on tolerance and on sexual liberty without, however, indulging in Rousseau's form of primitivism or wishing to bring Tahiti to Paris. But in *Jacques*, as in many of his *Contes* (*Les Deux Amis de Bourbonne, Ceci n'est pas un conte, Mme de La Carlière*) he examines individual cases without the same propensity for seeing things in black and white. Jacques and his Master are mimes posturing just like the Neveu, and offer us pasteboard parodies. Their stories with countless but always significant digressions seem nevertheless real to us; but they don't in fact illustrate the views of either the Master or Jacques. The examination of one very long and constantly interrupted episode in the book—that of Mme de La Pommeraye—is enough to show the curious juxtaposition of psychological truth based on the facts of life and of the ratiocination of would-be philosophers. Mme de La Pommeraye can scarcely be held to have been biologically determined to good or evil, since her feelings can change from love to hate and revenge. Her transformation, like the change of heart of the prostitute d'Aisnon, is not pre-determined but comes within the range of the possible. Side by side with such surprising transformations, the childish disputation of Jacques and his Master forms a strange and

seemingly irrelevant counterpoint. There is therefore no strict moral
code even for ordinary people. Man fitted into a code of virtue is not
necessarily happier. Punishment does not necessarily discourage
wrong-doing. The easy morality Diderot had so emotionally stressed
in the *drames* was founded upon unrealistic precepts. Each individual
case has its *raison d'être*, for 'chacun apprécie l'injure et le bienfait à
sa manière'. All of us, like the characters in the book, tell our own
story which is an artistic distortion of the truth, a simplification
based on selection which demonstrates our creative force. When
Jacques causes his master's saddle-strap to break and his master
proceeds to fall, he thinks he is proving the link of cause and effect
at the expense of free will, whilst in fact he is simply demonstrating
his own power. However, it can, and should, be argued that Diderot
at no point invalidates his scientific determinism or closes the door
on psychological determinism since, unlike Condillac, he believes
that the brain acts as a sixth sense. Unlike Helvétius, he holds
heredity to be stronger than environment in determining aptitudes
and shaping a destiny (and unlike modern behaviourists he believed
in the inheritance of acquired characteristics). In the *Réfutation de
l'ouvrage d'Helvétius intitulé l'Homme* (publ. 1875) and in the *Essai
sur les règnes de Claude et de Néron* (1779), known as *Essai sur Sénèque*
(which may be regarded as a late apologia), he reveals his new
philosophical preoccupations, dissociating himself from the simpler
theories held by his contemporaries and modifying his own in the
light of experience. At the personal level he opts for a stoicism in
which virtue has its own reward. At the philosophical level it is the
behaviour of man in his unpredictable creative life, whether it be
ultimately determined or not, that keeps him fascinated. His moral
attitude, a 'recherche du bonheur', is founded on his monistic conception of the universe; so that society is seen as the union of mankind, and the solitary man stands condemned as he was in the *Essai
sur le mérite et la vertu*, as well as in the *Entretien sur le fils naturel*.
Yet Diderot, whose life and works constantly show a deep-seated
desire to belong, shows awareness of being an outsider; hence his
interest in the genius, who is an exceptional creature striving to live
among ordinary men, and in individual man who also, after his
fashion, partakes of genius. Faced with an apparently insoluble

philosophical problem, and one which he does not intend to solve—
for how in any case could it be solved in a novel, however realistic,
of which the author determines the terms of reference?—he con-
trives to by-pass both the problem and the whole of his cherished
philosophy, since he now finds them of no practical consequence
from the humanist standpoint, which he has discovered to be the
only one truly based on an observation of reality. Hence the
humorous and ironic tone of his writing. Neither science nor
philosophy can provide the total explanation of man who in some
measure shares the creative power commonly attributed to God.
Man, alone in the universe, can seemingly make time itself stand
still, as happens in moments of ecstasy and emotional stress. The
apparent waywardness of Diderot's thought, if not of his reasoning,
serves to prove the complexity of the exterior world it mirrors. His
method is not now simply the one he favoured in his *Pensées sur
l'interprétation de la nature*, not one that can be applied indiscriminately. It is the development of a personal form of apprehension and expression of reality. The dialogue form which he made his
own can serve, as in the *Rêve de d'Alembert*, the linear exposition of
a thought, allowing for pauses for purposes of clarification, or as
a springboard for a further development; it can also, as in *Jacques le
fataliste*, prove even more exciting when a large number of characters, and we must include the author and the reader among them,
bring out in lively conversation the strange complexity of human
nature, the *pantomime des gueux* which is the substance of the novel
and the very epitome of mankind.

Diderot clearly had the makings of a playwright and sought the
glory of the dramatist. His major plays were not truly successful and
are only of importance in the history of drama, but he did write one
delightful play—*Est-il bon? Est-il méchant?*—which has only recently
been produced at the Comédie Française. But his best play is undoubtedly the *Neveu de Rameau*, successfully presented by P. Fresnay
and J. Bertheau on the stage of the Michodière in 1963, and his
finest scenes are to be found in *Jacques le fataliste* or in his correspondence or his *Salons*. His dramatic theories are of importance
since they influenced the type of play performed in France up to the

French Revolution and even the romantic *drame* as well as the later theatre of Scribe and Sardou. Perhaps even more significant was their determining influence on Lessing, whose *Hamburgische Dramaturgie* appeared in 1767-8. Diderot stressed the need for greater realism on the stage and favoured the serious, dramatic, bourgeois drama of real life. Characters should be presented against their milieu and belong to specific professions, so that the moral and social implications of the play, which he considered to be of primary importance, should have greater impact. He urged modifications in stagecraft and décor and was convinced that *tableaux vivants*, reminiscent of canvases by Greuze, would deeply move the audience. Certain of his suggestions were adopted on the French stage by such playwrights as Augier and Dumas *fils*. But all these innovations, however interesting, are incidental, not fundamental. His *Réflexions sur Térence* (1762), his *Entretien entre Dorval et Moi*, his *Essais sur la poésie dramatique*, throw light on questions of aesthetics and ethics as well as on the *drame*, whilst his better-known *Paradoxe sur le comédien* (1773-8, publ. 1830), which is in dialogue form, and in which he argues that great actors like great poets are insensitive for they need judgement and a cool appraisal of their part if their interpretation is not to be impeded, deals with philosophical and psychological issues transcending the immediate subject of his discussion; in particular the creative force in man. Characteristically he uses the word *poète dramatique* for playwright.

By covering the *salons* or annual art exhibitions in Paris, he was able to gain an insight into the minds and techniques of painters and cultivate his natural good taste. The *Salons* have set a standard for all subsequent art criticism although Diderot's approach is a literary one. It is the subject of the canvas, its meaning or message, which he regards as being of outstanding importance. At times he transcends the contemporary, grappling with the fundamentals of art. Sometimes the aesthetic implied in his comments on particular works is at variance with his theories. Observation and association with artists made him realize the inadequacy of the current theory of 'le beau idéal'. He admired Greuze for his bourgeois pathos, but also the realism and colour of Chardin, and the art of Vernet. He condemned the artificial style or rococo associated with Boucher. The catholicity of his taste, his understanding of technical matters, and his instinct prompted him to make illuminating remarks which were taken up by the impressionists and even to some extent by the surrealists.

Diderot's *Encyclopédie* article 'Beau', based as it is on a careful perusal of the works of French and English writers on the subject, develops a theory of beauty defined as the perception of relationships in accordance with sensationalist philosophy and the relativity of all things. The great artist is the man who seizes on significant relationships and analogies. He needs to be fired with enthusiasm and to be able to communicate his vision through sounds, colours, lines, or words. The importance of gesture and expression in communication he stressed in the *Lettre sur les sourds et muets* (1759) which deals with words as signs and symbols, abstractions not to be confused with reality, and at some length with the problem of language, especially inversion. The need for the close association of word and gesture, of sound and rhythm in the case of the poet, he stressed in the *Paradoxe sur le comédien*. Beauty springs from an awareness of harmonies of sound, colour, sense, rhythm, and structure, the numerous 'correspondances', to borrow Baudelaire's term, between sense impressions, and the quality of a work will depend on the adequacy of the artist's power of expression. Art mirrors life but cannot be equated with life. It is like the 'clavecin oculaire' of le Père Castel which Diderot found so fascinating. This clavichord had coloured ribbons so that, when it was played, a 'symphony' of colour resulted.

In his later years, Diderot held more radical political views than was believed. The *Encyclopédie* was a major instrument in the war on existing social and political institutions. The articles such as *autorité politique* which stated that sovereignty rested with the people and that on *droit naturel* are of equal importance with those specifically aimed at abuses from which the people suffered and in which he developed economic theories, discussing luxury, taxation, population problems, as well as the principle of equality. Diderot stressed the need to divorce the powers of State and Church, refusing to subordinate political institutions to religious sanction. In *Observations sur les instructions de Catherine II à ses députés* he went even further in identifying sovereignty with the nation, which was invested with legislative power, and in voicing criticism of a benevolent despotism as well as of tyranny. But, although Diderot's political theories after 1765 are particularly interesting, it is the earlier ones that exercised some influence in shaping political opinion prior to 1789. These were not as conservative as has sometimes been stated. His suggested curbs on absolute power may appear Utopian, but they are absent from Rousseau's politics: they include natural law and the inalienable civil liberty of the individual in society, the right to free speech which transcends any reason of public security, and individual fulfilment in an open society. But he has little to say on structures of government or constitutional fundamental law. His theories are not always consistent and at times he is drawn to the idea that social controls are necessary, at others he comes near to the position of the anarchist.

Apocryphally, Diderot's last words were: 'Le premier pas vers la philosophie, c'est l'incrédulité', a ghostly reiteration of a statement made in the early *Pensées philosophiques*. His open-minded scepticism, always present, is also always provisional. Scepticism is an avenue to truth and should never lead to mere negativism. He thus rejoins Montaigne and takes up a position of great consequence within the tradition of humanism. A new definition of the philosopher emerges from Diderot's deceptively simple statement: 'Si l'on voit la chose comme elle est en nature, on est philosophe.'

NOTE

DENIS DIDEROT, 1713–84, was born at Langres. He was educated by the Jesuits there and tonsured in 1726. From 1729 to 1732 he studied in Paris and, having been articled to Me Clément de Ris from 1732 to 1734, he gave up the law and led a hand-to-mouth existence for ten years. He struck up a friendship with Rousseau in 1741, which was to last till 1757. In 1745 the 'libraire' Le Breton entrusted Diderot with the direction of the *Encyclopédie* for which he drafted a Prospectus in 1750. In 1751 the first volume appeared, but publication was suspended in 1752. It was resumed in 1753, again suspended in 1759, and not completed till 1772. In 1759 Diderot's father died and in the same year he met Sophie Volland. 1761 saw the first performance on the stage of the Comédie Française of the *Père de famille*. Catherine the Great of Russia purchased his library in 1765 and at her invitation he went to Russia in 1773. His health suffered from his long journey, but he continued to write and to revise earlier works until his death in Paris.

Modern editions. The four volumes of Diderot's works in the Classiques Garnier include all essential texts and will be found adequate for general purposes. The *Œuvres complètes*, ed. Assézat–Tourneux, (1875–7: 20 vols.) should be used in conjunction with the following critical editions: *Pensées philosophiques* (ed. Niklaus, 1950); *Lettre sur les aveugles* (ed. Niklaus, 1951); *Lettre sur les sourds et muets* (ed. Meyer, 1966); *Le Rêve de d'Alembert*, etc. (ed. Vernière, 1951; ed. Varloot, 1962; ed. Roger, 1965); *Le Neveu de Rameau* (ed. Fabre, 1950); *Le Supplément au Voyage de Bougainville* (ed. Dieckmann, 1955); *Contes* (ed. Dieckmann, 1963); *Quatre Contes* (ed. Proust, 1964); *Est-il bon? Est-il méchant?* (ed. Undank, 1961); *La Religieuse* (ed. Parrish, 1963); *Éléments de Physiologie* (ed. Mayer, 1964); *Les Salons* (ed. Seznec and Adhémar, 1957–67: 4 vols.); *Correspondance de Diderot* (ed. Roth, 1955–65: 12 vols.).

Criticism. J. Thomas, *L'Humanisme de Diderot* (1932, rev. 1938, 1942); H. Dieckmann, *Cinq leçons sur Diderot* (1959); J. Proust, *Diderot et l'Encyclopédie* (1962); R. Kempf, *Diderot et le roman* (1964); *Cahiers de l'Association Internationale des Études Françaises*, vol. xiii (1961); *Europe*, nos. 405–6, Jan.–Feb., 1963. L. G. Crocker, *The Embattled Philosopher* (1954), provides a good general introduction to the life and the works; M. Wilson, *Diderot, the Testing Years* (*1713–1759*) is the best biography up to 1759 (a further volume will follow). *Diderot Studies*, 1949–65, vols. i–viii, ed. Otis E. Fellows *et al.*, is still in process of publication. It includes critical essays, monographs, and critical editions of texts in English and in French.

8. The Comic Theatre: Marivaux and Beaumarchais

As might have been expected, it was not until a playwright of genius appeared who was prepared to 'forget' Molière that France once again achieved great eminence in the comic theatre, though Marivaux's high reputation was late in coming. In the years following Molière's death the theatre was more and more frequented precisely by that society which increasingly saw itself depicted on the stage. In the last three decades of the seventeenth and possibly the first three of the eighteenth centuries the theatre appears as the core of an essentially narcissistic phenomenon. If the expression 'comédie de mœurs' means anything at all, it means plays such as *Le Chevalier à la mode* (1687) and *Les Bourgeoises à la mode* (1692), by Dancourt and Saint-Yon.

The expression 'à la mode' is of great importance and points to something applicable to far more than these two plays. To call either them or their companions 'satire' is somewhat excessive: professional seduction or (for the sake of the *bienséances* only) near-seduction, adultery or near-adultery, girls whose virginity weighs heavily upon them, gambling, swindling, and many other peccadiloes, are modish, and presented as such. It is a whole society laughing at its own decadence, but with no thought of the seventeenth-century 'castigat ridendo mores'. On the contrary, this is the laughter of condonement. Everything is permitted save slowness of wit, and there is never a one to cry 'bienheureux les pauvres d'esprit'.

The modishness of excessive gambling, the *chic* of adultery, or of being a kept man, or a complacently horned husband: these things are relatively new, contemporary. As attitudes, they are also relatively unenduring, unlike the basic flaws around which Molière constructed his comedies. The moralizing reaction embodied in the comedies of Destouches, the 'black' comedy of Lesage's *Turcaret* (1709), further exhaust the seam of comic possibility.

In following none of these paths, Marivaux was to prove brilliantly original. Not that his early works bore the slightest promise of this, though two early parodies are of some importance to us: *L'Iliade travestie* (1717) and *Le Télémaque travesti* (1717). These are the products of a writer completely *engagé* in the quarrel of Ancients and Moderns, for both works are an attack on the Homeric cult of the time. They are a virtually irretrievable *prise de position* not merely in general terms in the quarrel of Ancients and Moderns, but in all the implications of that. The writing of the *Iliade travestie* meant that, by his natural taste and, as it were, as a matter of record, Marivaux held the epic, heroic style in some contempt. His *Télémaque*, although not published until much later, has yet another implication. An obvious parody of Fénelon's *Télémaque* (1699), it may thus be held to be a parody of the excessive role of sentimentality in the evolution and formation of the individual, for in Fénelon's work the young hero is so often guided down the path of virtue in a flood of tears. *Télémaque travesti* may thus be regarded as a form of self-inoculation without which Marivaux might possibly, a little later, have listened to the siren voices of *le larmoyant*.

Did Marivaux require any other self-persuasion as to the way he was to go, he was to provide it for himself in rich measure in his first, and last, tragedy, *Annibal* (1720). Marcel Arland and other critics have pointed out that *Annibal* proved to the writer that he was neither a dramatic poet nor a tragedian. We may be even more thankful that by the time *Annibal* was produced, the singularly untragic figure of the Bergamasque rogue Arlequin had already beckoned to him from the wings.

Apart from his own literary efforts, the salon society of this time was to exert a tremendous influence upon his development. For better or worse, the ecology of Marivaux's growth is to be studied in the salon, and notably that of Mme de Lambert. The salon, in the eighteenth century, together with the coffee-house, is among the more remarkable *foyers de culture* of French evolution. In contradistinction to the official *foyers* represented by the various Academies then in existence, salons had the advantage of being eclectic in recruitment and unhampered by any tinge of 'establishment'. Immediately on arrival in Paris it would seem that Marivaux had access to that of Mme la Marquise de Lambert, at the Hôtel Colbert. Here he would find discussed every contemporary issue: social, moral, psychological, scientific, or aesthetic. He would meet Fontenelle, Pierre Corneille's nephew and pioneer of objective scientific thought, famous for his *Entretiens sur la pluralité des mondes* (1686) which, we should remember, represent the polite purveying, in elegant language and dialogue form, of scientific facts to a lady. He would meet La Motte, advocate of the Moderns against the Ancients, La Motte whose theory that poetry can well be expressed in prose prepares us for the remark of a latter-day critic: 'Toute la poésie de la première moitié du XVIIIe siècle est dans Marivaux, comme toute la poésie de la seconde moitié est dans Jean-Jacques Rousseau' (Jules Lemaître). Marivaux would meet Montesquieu, whose implied indictment of French society in the *Lettres persanes* (1721) the salon found a little savage, and he might even have experienced the fulsome charm of Fénelon. The occasions at the Hôtel Colbert represent *préciosité* in a final and brilliant phase, the art of urbane politeness at its highest point of expression in manners and conversation, and the cultivation of an essentially female-orientated human commerce, stimulated not least by the Marquise herself, whose analyses of the feminine heart are not without distinction. Mme de Lambert died in 1733, and thereafter Marivaux frequented two other salons, that of Mme de Tencin and, from 1749, that of Mme Geoffrin. But there is no doubt that the Hôtel Colbert was the major influence.

Against this social background we can see a Marivaux learning to talk elliptically and urbanely of the tender passion, but before we pass to a consideration of his drama it is necessary to fill in an important feature of his temperament: Marivaux the observer, or even spy. 'Dans tout le cours de mes aventures, j'ai été mon propre spectateur, comme le spectateur des autres.' This perhaps gives us a key to Marivaux's knowledge of human nature: a retiring spirit who combines, from that retirement, an observation of others with a continual introspection. It is the passage of these habits into the *structure* of the plays that goes far to creating the special quality of his comedy. The much recounted story of 'l'ingénue au miroir' seals for ever the detachment of the observer: as far as the observation of woman goes, he will never again be *engagé*. He was in love with a beautiful girl, 'belle sans y prendre garde', as he youthfully imagined. All her graces seemed to him utterly unstudied. And then, returning one day to pick up a forgotten glove, he found his beloved rehearsing at the mirror the 'spontaneous' gestures and expressions that had charmed him. The figure that, according to himself, he employed to express his chagrin was already theatrical: 'Je viens de voir, Mademoiselle, les Machines de l'Opéra; il me divertira toujours, mais il me touchera moins.' Thus, Dorante and Silvia in *Le Jeu de l'amour et du hasard* (1730) will wish, from the safety of their disguises, to observe the person they each imagine to be their intended; and many a Marivaux character will wish to observe or test the partner-to-be before becoming sentimentally involved. The transfer of this structure to the theatre, the delegation of function of author-spectator or narrator-witness to certain dramatic characters, and frequently to the valet, has been the object of recent critical attention. In dramatic terms it results in the constant complicity of the audience, who frequently know more of what is happening in the mind of a character than does the character himself. It was the predestined role of the valet, play-maker within the play, spinner of intrigue since Plautus and Terence, to take over the role of actor-witness, in this sublimation of his historical function.

This structure was new in French comedy, and naturally demanded a novelty of interpretation. This was to be supplied in large measure by the Comédie Italienne. If it be true that genius is a long patience, it is equally true that in the living theatre it is sometimes a brief coincidence. It is difficult, and possibly otiose, to speculate as to the fate of Marivaux's plays had not the Regent in 1716 recalled the *Italiens* to France, whence they had been excluded in 1697 for ridiculing Mme de Maintenon in a play called *La Fausse Prude*. Such evidence as there is suggests that whenever a Marivaux comedy was given to the *comédiens français* there was always the danger that the reticence, the modesty of the feminine roles would be submerged in the self-expression of an actress trained in a tradition of outspoken, declamatory rhetoric. That part of the actress's role which, in Marivaux's comedies, is unsaid or half-said, possibly suffered.

It is in this last area of the implied, the half-expressed, that the Italians were so well qualified by the history of their development. In the dramatic work of Marivaux the pause, the silence, the remark made at once at a conscious and at a sub-conscious level of meaning, are of vital importance. The Italian players, trained in the tradition of the *commedia dell'arte* (popular comedy in which the actor, rather than learning a text by heart, improvised from a rough scenario), pitchforked into a foreign country when Ganassa first brought his players to France in 1570, were admirably suited to the task. By the time that Marivaux's plays were being staged, the Italians were already playing in French, and their difficulty with the language would clearly lead the players to rely heavily on facial mime to reinforce a point. When one inserts in the middle of such a picture the actress Zanetta Rosa Benozzi, called Silvia, the idea of coincidence in the fortunes of Marivaux takes on its full meaning. Perhaps the real greatness of Silvia was that she could act the acting which is in all our behaviour, and which is, paradoxically, natural. Silvia's *jeu naturel* was natural for this reason; and in many scenes Marivaux shows us a character who acts the surface dialogue while her heart is saying something else, either to herself or to the man opposite. The genius of Marivaux lay in part in his ability to write such a *monologue sous-jacent*, and that of Silvia in signalling it to an audience, without—as often as not—betraying it to her partner on stage. Her performance must have been a major confidence-trick of communication.

For a writer so uniform in general idiom, the subject-matter of Marivaux's comedies, and the different sub-species of comedy to be found in his complete dramatic works, are surprising in their range and might remain unsuspected by the reader who confines himself to those plays which have achieved greatest popularity, say, *Le Jeu de l'amour et du hasard*, *Les fausses confidences* (1737), *L'Épreuve* (1740), *Le Legs* (1736), and *La (Première) Surprise de l'amour* (1722). Fleury, Larroumet, Fournier and Bastide, and Marcel Arland have all made attempts at classification. The last of these distinguishes (though he admits that they interpenetrate) *comédies d'intrigue* (e.g. *La fausse suivante*), *comédies héroïques* (e.g. *Le Prince travesti*), *comédies morales* (a) *de caractère* (e.g. *Le Legs*), (b) *de mœurs* (e.g. *Le Petit-maître corrigé*), (c) *sociales ou philosophiques* (e.g. *L'Île des esclaves*), (d) *allégoriques* (e.g. *L'Amour et la vérité*), (e) *fantaisie exemplaire* (e.g. *Les Acteurs de bonne foi*), *drames bourgeois* (e.g. *La Mère confidente*), and the numerous *comédies d'amour*, starting with *Arlequin poli par l'amour*.

Granted that love remains the staple interest, this attempt at classification none the less reveals the richness of subject-matter treated in the comedies. McKee has ventured to suggest as the predominant theme the 'innate goodness of man and the necessity of being kindly disposed towards one's fellows'. Marivaux's stage fathers are a singular example of this. 'Marivaux', says the same author, 'places greater value on character than birth.' The plays, when all the accusations of frivolity, flippancy, and Voltaire's gibe that Marivaux spent his time weighing flies' eggs in a spider's web, have been heard, remain morally and socially responsible, and innately optimistic. The *Île des esclaves* (1725) reverses the social order, the former slaves who inhabit it enslaving those *seigneurs* who stumble upon the island, making their slaves their masters. At first blush this might appear to be a revolutionary situation, but Trivelin, the leader of the islanders, soon reveals all the *bonhomie* of his creator:

Quand nos pères, irrités de la cruauté de leurs maîtres, quittèrent la Grèce et vinrent s'établir ici, dans le ressentiment des outrages qu'ils avaient reçus de leurs patrons, la première loi qu'ils y firent fut d'ôter la vie à tous les maîtres que le hasard ou le naufrage conduirait dans leur île, et conséquemment de rendre la liberté à tous les esclaves; la vengeance avait dicté cette loi; vingt ans après la raison l'abolit, et en dicta une plus douce. Nous ne nous vengeons plus de vous, nous vous corrigeons.

The Revolution, in short, without the Terror, and Trivelin makes it quite clear that those who are the perpetrators of social injustice are sick men who can be cured, and indeed at the end, in an atmosphere of beatitude, Arlequin's master Iphicrate *is* cured.

The island theme is used again in *L'Île de la raison* (1727), and owes something to the contemporary vogue of *Gulliver's Travels* in translation. On the island, only the truly *raisonnables*—the natives— are of normal, or 'reasonable', size. Eight Europeans who have chanced upon the island have turned into midgets, and in the measure in which they acquire *la raison* under the tutelage of the islanders, return to normal size. Only six of them manage to do so, the odd men out being the Philosopher and the Poet. *La Colonie* (1750) is a plea for social equality and an early statement of the case for women's votes. One critic has remarked that there is no instance in Marivaux's theatre where 'birth triumphs over personal merit', and if we make the reservation that birth and merit frequently coincide, this is true.

However, the stock-in-trade of the comedies is, of course, love. Not the egotistical pleasure-seeking which would escape involvement and which so frequently passed for love in comedy between 1685 and the death of Louis XIV, nor the more maudlin excess of the *larmoyant*, but a love in its incipient stages, born under the assumption that, once shared, it represents happiness. It is an end in itself. If, as frequently happens, there is any initial reluctance to become involved, it is not because the characters wish to avoid involvement as a matter of principle, but because they wish to spy, to observe the partner before commitment. They do not shrink back in the name of freedom so much as in the name of the *finality* of love itself. This explains the structure and the movement of many of the plays, the most noteworthy example being the quadruple disguise of *Le Jeu de l'amour et du hasard*. When the final word is uttered, there is a general state of bliss, often underlined by the author in the closing lines. 'Allons, saute Marquis!' says Arlequin at the end of *Le Jeu*, borrowing a remark from a character who actually does jump for joy in Regnard's *Le Joueur* (1696), and the Arlequin of *Les fausses confidences* brings down the curtain to 'Pardi, nous nous soucions bien de ton tableau à présent! L'original nous fournira bien d'autres copies'. The original of the portrait, Araminte, is thus promised a life of productive happiness with Dorante.

It has often been said that all Marivaux's plays are in a sense 'la surprise de l'amour', and this is true of many of them if we merely take *surprise* as meaning the ultimate admission, whether to oneself or to another, of a love that had not in the first instance been admitted, or had been ignored. It is tantamount to saying that Marivaux concerned himself with 'la naissance de l'amour', another

much-quoted truth. And between them, they make nonsense of
Voltaire's stricture that 'il a connu tous les sentiers du cœur sans
trouver la grande route'. Apart from the perfidious assumption that
comedy is at all concerned with *la grande route*, Marivaux's very
greatness lies in the fact that he evolved a language and a dramatic
structure which gave expression and analysis, for the first time in
French comedy, to precisely those *sentiers* which do lead to the
grande route, at which point the comedy stops.

Much has been said about the 'cruelty' of Marivaux, exhibited
where one character examines or tests the other's love, and particularly in *L'Épreuve* in which Lucidor pretends to arrange an
advantageous marriage with somebody else although Angélique
loves Lucidor and is loved by him. He even sets the local chaw-bacon
Blaise to wooing her as well. The suffering of the deceived Angélique
is obvious. In any consideration of this topic it is as well to remember
that Marivaux is writing within the general convention of comedy,
one of the main and inalienable features of which remains a happy
ending, and another, historically speaking, the passage of the protagonist through possible disaster to happiness. The audience of a
Marivaux comedy is the most informed of audiences: it knows
perfectly well that the suffering Dorante, the suffering Araminte,
the suffering Angélique are in no danger of dying for love. They are
protected by convention and they are protected by the obvious
euphoria in which the play is set, as Marivaux leads us through the
sentiers to the *grande route*.

The dramatic language of Marivaux is essentially the language of
this love, or rather the communication (and sometimes the sub-
conscious signalling) of it. It is inseparable from a study of the
situation which seems created precisely in order to allow this sort of
communication to operate. Since the researches of Deloffre,[1] we
cannot claim that the language is some sort of verbal transposition
of salon conversation, though it is no doubt partly inspired by it and
is strictly oral: Marivaux the dramatist does not write literature.
His language may be regarded as the stylization and refinement of
this type of conversation, submitted to the exigencies of a dramatic
situation favouring the *surprise de l'amour*.

[1] See page 132.

'Il y a des manières', says Damis in *Les Serments indiscrets* (1732), 'qui valent des paroles; on dit "je vous aime" avec un regard, et on le dit bien.' In this observation is to be found the major qualification for interpreters of Marivaux. The semantic evolution of the term *marivaudage*, more often than not pejorative, has somewhat obscured its basically theatrical nature. For Diderot it is 'disserter à perte de vue sur de menus problèmes'. In its moral aspect it can connote an over-refined form of moral analysis. La Harpe's definition is stylistic: '... le mélange le plus bizarre de métaphysique subtile et de locutions triviales, de sentiments alambiqués et de dictions populaires'. Sainte-Beuve talks of 'badinage à froid, espièglerie compassée et prolongée, pétillement redoublé et prétentieux, enfin une sorte de pédantisme sémillant et joli'. Only between 1850 and 1860, Deloffre observes, does the term acquire a content of grace and subtle tenderness, coinciding with a return to favour of the painters Watteau and Lancret, with whom Marivaux has so much in common.

In so far as theatrical *marivaudage* (at least by Marivaux!) may not profitably be considered outside the dramatic situation which permits of it, it is as well to consider a typical example of it from one of his most popular plays: *Les fausses confidences*. In Act I, scene xv, Dorante has been introduced by his former valet Dubois into the household of Araminte, with whom he is in love. Araminte has been deliberately informed by Dubois of Dorante's love, Dorante knows that Dubois has told her, but Araminte does not know that Dorante has this information. The audience is fully informed, and knows that Araminte should sack this forward fellow who, from the relative lowliness of his status of *intendant*, presumes to love her. The dialogue that follows is a highly talented construction in two layers. Araminte is superficially consulting Dorante as *intendant* about a possible lawsuit with the count, who is also a suitor. That is the superficial stratum of communication. The superficial commerce between the two therefore remains staid, polite, and official. If Araminte decides not to pursue the case, that means that she is prepared to accept the count, but if she tells Dorante to examine it, then she has not made up her mind and there is hope for him. The word *examiner*, amongst others, takes on a breathless intensity below its superficial meaning, and the whole passage is a piece of running, disciplined symbolism which achieves the impossible by remaining natural, oral, conversational, and true. An analysis of the passage in this light will reveal the true heart of theatrical *marivaudage*, which is only in part linguistic, but is always a brilliant exposition of affective human communication—among the most brilliant in world theatre. Only actors and *a fortiori* actresses who can play the dotted lines and the white spaces on the page should be allowed near it.

No one can trace effectively the mark left by Marivaux on French comedy. If we think of him in terms of comedy of euphoria, of lightness of touch, Musset comes near to him on occasion, provided we remember that *On ne badine pas avec l'amour* (1834) is in theme at least the obverse of anything that Marivaux wrote, with the hilarious exception of *Annibal*. If we consider the line of euphoria a little further, we inevitably see a latter-day brother in Jean Giraudoux. But if we regard Marivaux as the master of the semi-expressed, the unexpressed, and indeed of the contra-suggested, then we have to recognize a late descendant in the drama of Jean-Jacques Bernard and, to a lesser extent, in the entire between-the-wars drama of the unexpressed.

To cross the distance which separates Marivaux from Beaumarchais is to cross one of the two singular deserts (the other is lyric poetry) in the incredibly fertile French eighteenth century. Yet this distance is hardly greater than that which separates dramatic theory from practice during this period. The greatest achievement of the period is the theoretical elaboration of the *drame bourgeois*, though its exemplars in the drama are on the whole boring, whether they be Diderot's *Père de famille* (1758), or Beaumarchais's *Eugénie* (1767), *Les deux amis* (1770, 'par un auteur qui n'en a aucun', wrote some wag on a playbill), or *La Mère coupable* (1792). Sedaine, in *Le Philosophe sans le savoir* (1765), is a better practitioner than either. The basic point that, by implication, they attempt to make is that the affairs and emotions of the bourgeois, of the man of business, are a fit subject for artistic treatment. Situated between comedy and tragedy, the *drame* is *sérieux* because its characters are deemed worthy of serious attention, of taking and holding the centre of the stage, and it is thus a cultural facet of the advancing bourgeois revolution.

One of the first significant acts in the adult life of Beaumarchais contains most of the features of later ones: invention, promotion of the invention, the inventor attacked, a brilliant counter-attack turned into self-publicity, ultimate triumph. It helps to understand the man when we reflect that this applies equally well to his invention of a new escapement for watches in 1753 and to his invention of Figaro. In that year he had revealed his discovery to the royal clockmaker Lepaute, who had claimed it as his own. His *Mémoire* to the Académie des Sciences bears many marks of his later *Mémoires*. Beaumarchais is upheld by the Académie, the watch reaches the King, and the author becomes *horloger du roi*. His visit to Spain (1764–6) illustrates the point even more cogently. His eldest sister, Marie-Louise, in addition to his second eldest sister, Marie-Josèphe, was living in Spain and was affianced to one Clavijo, who had retracted after the bans of marriage were published. Beaumarchais extracted from him a new promise of marriage, and when Clavijo disappeared, had him dismissed from his post of Crown Archivist. The incident not only has the stuff of a *drame sérieux* but was actually turned into a play by Goethe, and it is hard to say to what extent that intrigue happened to Beaumarchais, or to what extent he is the author of it. On his death in 1770, Pâris-Duverney leaves in his will a statement of debt of 15,000 *livres* to the author, and this is immediately attacked by the financier's great-nephew, the Comte de la Blache. Beaumarchais wins the first hearing in 1772, and La Blache appeals. In the meanwhile, Beaumarchais is busy with the mistress of a friend, the Duc de Chaulnes—an affair which ends in a brawl and the imprisonment of the author—during which La Blache wins his appeal, thanks to the intervention of Counsellor Goëzmann. Released during the day in order to visit the judge, Beaumarchais wastes no time in leaving money with Mme Goëzmann, on several occasions, to secure an audience with the judge—which was perfectly normal practice. Nevertheless, Goëzmann attacks Beaumarchais in law for corruption; Beaumarchais is publicly censured, but Goëzmann loses his job. As public censure means the burning of the *Mémoires* written in support of his case, the loss of civil rights, and the loss of his magistrature, Beaumarchais has both won and lost. No matter, it is all grist to the dramatic mill and will appear, transmuted, in Act III, scene xv, of the *Mariage de Figaro*:

> *Le Comte*: Que nous répond le défendeur? Qu'il veut garder sa personne, à lui permis.
>
> *Figaro* (avec joie): J'ai gagné.
>
> *Le Comte*: Mais comme le texte dit: *laquelle somme* je payerai à la première réquisition, ou bien j'épouserai, ... la Cour condamne le défendeur à payer deux milles piastres fortes à la demanderesse; ou bien à l'épouser dans ce jour. (*Il se lève.*)
>
> *Figaro* (stupéfait): J'ai perdu.

Dramatic intrigue, dramatic action, are movement, and in the writing of the *drame* of his own life Beaumarchais surely cannot be accused of failing to cover the ground. Even the pavilion scenes of the *Mariage de Figaro* have a trial run in real life before they reach the stage. While in Spain, the author meets the King's *valet de chambre*, a crafty Italian called Pini, whom later the King sends to ask if Beaumarchais cannot provide him with a mistress. Beaumarchais, nothing loath, offers his own, and the meeting takes place in conditions of the strictest clandestinity in a little pavilion near the Palace, with Beaumarchais bringing his mistress, and Pini the King.

Beaumarchais's disgrace-in-victory, after the first round of the *affaire Goëzmann*, had induced him to offer himself as a secret agent in London for Louis XV, and he went to London to secure the suppression of a scandalous pamphlet attacking Mme du Barry. As he returned to France to report on his mission, the King died, so that mission and Mme du Barry were suddenly without interest: when Beaumarchais neglects to supply a *coup de théâtre* in an episode of his life (and he was, at his best, essentially a man of episodes), Fate has an ingratiating manner of stepping into the breach, much as chance will operate rather better than Figaro in the *Mariage*. A second mission sends him to England to suppress a pamphlet regarding the rights of Spain to the French throne, involving him in the chase of a Jew—who may even have existed— named Angelucci, or sometimes Atkinson, from London to Amsterdam, to Nuremberg, and to Austria. Fact and fiction are here so

fused that they have never been unscrambled, and the more colourful incidents of the account could slide unnoticed into *Gil Blas*. His
involvement with d'Éon, a man masquerading successfully as a
woman, is the obvious inspiration for Chérubin's disguise, while his
trips to England, together with his stake in the destinies of the
English colonies in America, both politically and commercially,
explain Figaro's previous presence in London and his 'knowledge' of
English, just as the formation of a society to protect dramatic
authors' rights is announced by Figaro's lament about the money
which he failed to make out of his play: on the *Barbier de Séville*, the
Comédie Française only paid Beaumarchais his share of the seat
money, neglecting anything due to him from season tickets.

Fate itself continues to supply appropriately dramatic colour to
his life, supplementing that which he invents for himself. During
the polemic following the playing of the *Mariage*, it ensures that
a card-playing Louis XVI shall write out the warrant for his arrest
on the back of the seven of diamonds. It ensures too that when he is
arrested on 23 August 1792, imprisoned and awaiting death, thanks
to the attentions of Marat, it should be the Procurator of the Commune, Manuel, his worst enemy, who gives him his release, to his
tearful astonishment. This is the very structure of the *comédie
larmoyante*, but Fate still has an ironic twist *à la Beaumarchais*, for it
was his own mistress Amélie who had secured that release, being the
mistress also of Manuel. Neither Manuel nor Beaumarchais was
aware of her double role.

The events of his life are such as to demand polemical support,
and this provides us with a rich *basso continuo* of defensive literature,
which, in the case of the *Mémoires* against Goëzmann, is also highly
dramatic literature. It certainly appeared so to the Parisian public,
who saw Beaumarchais as its champion against the detested Maupeou
Parlement. The *Mémoires* are highly successful, and part of their
success is due to the fact that, in addition to their wit, they display
a rich sense of comic situation. They have all the fascination of the
trial-on-the-stage: it is not surprising that la Du Barry should have
the scene with Mme Goëzmann played for her, or that Voltaire
should say of the *Quatrième Mémoire* (the opening pages of which
are a monumental parody of petitionary prayer): 'Il n'y a point de

comédie plus plaisante, point de tragédie plus attendrissante.' And as the rogues' gallery gathers round Goëzmann, they are all brought on stage, *seriatim*, and ridiculed to death. In this diverting procession we cannot but foresee the trial scene of the *Mariage*.

Discounting *Tarare* (1787) and the *parades*, the dramatic work of Beaumarchais is a sandwich with the meat in its proper position: in the middle. Before the *Barbier*, before the *Mariage*, there is the practitioner and theorist of the *drame bourgeois*, exemplified in *Eugénie* (1767), preceded in the first edition by the *Essai sur le genre dramatique sérieux*. In the latter, Beaumarchais takes up the ideas of Diderot and in so doing unhappily convinces himself of their truth, and actually manages to write a *drame sérieux* in which there is not a smile, let alone a laugh. He wishes (although at this time wealthy and successful in other domains) to have himself talked of as a dramatic innovator. If *Eugénie* was a moderate success, the same cannot be said of his next play, *Les deux amis* (1770)—*drame commercial*, as it has been called—which was a definite failure. One view of the reason for this is that the pathos fails to emanate naturally from the situation, but the matter is really one of natural genius rather than technique. His *drames* failed for two reasons. Firstly, they were *sérieux*: the natural verve and gaiety of Beaumarchais, his main attributes, had to be suppressed out of fidelity to the *genre*, as did his own particular instinct for using the play as a form of publicity for himself. Secondly, they were *bourgeois*: in the rocket-like ascension of his career, Beaumarchais proceeds directly from the launching-pad of the artisan's condition to the stratosphere of *noblesse*, and the bourgeoisie are perhaps not quite his line of country, whatever his effect on the Revolution (considered as a bourgeois revolution) may have been. In *Les deux amis*, he seems to know too much commerce, and not enough bourgeois, and in *Eugénie* the main characters are hardly bourgeois at all.

Of the wit, verve, sunshine, and dynamism of *Le Barbier de Séville* (1775) and *Le Mariage de Figaro* (1784), there is little left to say that has not already been well said, except perhaps that to have a natural flair for intrigue is not necessarily to be able to construct a play. It has often been said that after *Les deux amis*, and with the *Barbier*, Beaumarchais returned to the good old comedy of intrigue, but it has been plausibly argued[1] that 'the mechanical defects of the *Barbier* have been as much underplayed as the mechanical virtues of *Les deux amis*', and it would indeed be otiose to suppose that the success of the two masterpieces is due to a return to 'la bonne vieille comédie'. They are successes, essentially, because they display a Beaumarchais stepping back into his own skin. They are not the structures of a self-appointed dramatist forcing himself to be *à la page*: they are both a case of spontaneous combustion. Neither in *Eugénie* nor in *Les deux amis* is there a character into whom Beaumarchais can pour his own spirit. There is no Figaro. The *Barbier*, on the other hand, and the *Mariage* more so, are the perfect playground for the author being himself; thus, the episodes which are the basic units of both plays seem to grow and explode in a series of sympathetic detonations. The 'situations'—the Count, Suzanne, Chérubin, and the armchair and the pavilion scene at the end of the same play, are a crystallization around chance, and are not particularly significant as incidents in a linear plot. Both plays, further, demonstrate a basic truth about Beaumarchais, explaining their own success and the relative failure of his first two plays, and his last. It is this: he was incapable of saying anything serious *by solemnity*. In the *Mariage* and the *Barbier* many important things are said in the very avoidance of solemnity. Beaumarchais, who was clearly his own hero, wrote masterpieces when he himself, filtered through Figaro, was the dramatic embodiment of that intrigue which he used throughout his life to further his own career. Bereft of that embodiment, he failed, and when, in *La Mère coupable* (the third of his Figaro trilogy), he makes a double-dyed villain the embodiment of intrigue, he fails badly.

If, placing him in the history of the French theatre, we attempt to link him with Marivaux, across the desert, it must be in his habit of not making his characters necessarily or fully explicit. He is a master of the hint, the dotted line, the ellipsis. In *La Mère coupable* he may even be the fore-runner of Scribe and 'la pièce bien faite'. Jack-of-all-trades, master of a considerable number from watch-making to making harps to gun-running (he was less successful with muskets), Beaumarchais went through life being a professional

[1] By A. Pugh in the *Modern Language Review*, lxi, no. 3.

Beaumarchais. He was the auto-adman of the century. Oddly enough, that is almost a definition of the Sartrian *salaud*; and the hypothesis that Beaumarchais was a *salaud* is so palpably absurd that Sartre's definition may possibly be in need of adjustment.

NOTE

PIERRE CARLET DE CHAMBLAIN DE MARIVAUX, 1688–1763, was born in Paris, into the *noblesse de robe*. His first theatrical success, *Arlequin poli par l'amour*, was produced at the Comédie Italienne in 1720. He frequented the salons of Mme de Lambert, Mme de Tencin, and Mme Geoffrin, and the first of these in particular had a considerable influence on him. The remainder of his dramatic works were played at either the Comédie Italienne or the Comédie Française, with more success at the former. His two major novels, *La Vie de Marianne* and *Le Paysan parvenu*, were published between 1731–41 and 1734–5 respectively (see Note to Chapter 4).

Modern editions. The standard complete edition of the plays is that published by Fournier and Bastide (1946–7: 2 vols.). Other readily available editions are by Marcel Arland (Pléiade, 1955) and by Schérer and Dort (Intégrale, 1964). Editions of single plays include *Arlequin poli par l'amour* (ed. R. Niklaus, 1959) and *Le Jeu de l'amour et du hasard* (ed. M. Shackleton, 1954). Mme Sylvie Chevalley's edition of a lost play, *La Commère*, rediscovered by herself, appeared in 1966.

Criticism. The best general study is still that of G. Larroumet, *Marivaux* (new edn., 1894), and the authoritative work on the language is F. Deloffre, *Marivaux et le marivaudage* (1955). A complete review of all the plays in chronological order is given by Kenneth McKee, *The Theatre of Marivaux* (1958). See also M. Arland, *Marivaux* (1950), and Marie-Jeanne Durry, *A propos de Marivaux* (1960), embodying *Quelques nouveautés sur Marivaux* (1939). An article by J. Rousset ('Marivaux et la structure du double registre', *Studi Francesi*, January–April 1957) is important for any study of the presence of the author within the play.

PIERRE-AUGUSTIN CARON DE BEAUMARCHAIS, 1732–99, was the son of a watchmaker. His life, with its mixture of litigation and picaresque imbroglio, defies summary. It includes the waxing and waning of his standing in court circles; his business relationships with the financier Pâris-Duverney; the *affaire La Blache* and, involved in it, the *affaire Goëzmann*; his visits to Spain and England; his 'affairs of State'; the mock-heroic Angelucci episode, and the supply of arms to the American colonies in revolt. Among his plays (including *drames bourgeois*, *parades*, and opera) the most famous are, of course, *Le Barbier de Séville* (1775) and *Le Mariage de Figaro* (1784). His *Mémoires* on the *affaire Goëzmann* (1773–4) should also be mentioned.

Modern editions. E. Fournier edited the *Œuvres complètes* (1876). The complete dramatic works are edited by M. Allem (Pléiade, 1934) and R. d'Hermiès (1952). There are single editions of *Le Barbier de Séville* and *Le Mariage de Figaro* by E. J. Arnould (1963 and 1952) and L. Allen (1951 and 1952). M. Roulleaux-Dugage has discovered an opera libretto to the *Mariage de Figaro*, partly in the hand of the author, from which it might appear that Beaumarchais is the real inventor of Chérubin's aria 'Mon cœur soupire' ('Voi che sapete').

Biographies. R. Dalsème, *La Vie de Beaumarchais* (1928), can be completed by P. Richard, *La Vie de Beaumarchais* (1951), and the very readable Cynthia Cox, *The Real Figaro* (1962).

Criticism. Standard works are L. de Loménie, *Beaumarchais et son temps* (1856), and E. Lintilhac, *Beaumarchais et ses œuvres* (1887). Technique: J. Schérer, *La Dramaturgie de Beaumarchais* (1954). Language: G. von Proschwitz, *Introduction à l'étude du vocabulaire de Beaumarchais* (1956). Comedy: J. B. Ratermanis and W. R. Irwin, *The Comic Style of Beaumarchais* (1961). For further bibliographical guidance see J. Hampton, 'Research on the *Mariage de Figaro*', in *French Studies* (January 1962), E. J. Arnould, 'Le "Barbier de Séville" et la critique' (ibid., October 1962), and E. J. Arnould, *La Genèse du 'Barbier de Séville'* (1965).

9. Rousseau

ROUSSEAU is able to fascinate and disturb in a way that very few writers in the eighteenth century manage to do. Not only are his writings still provocative and challenging in themselves, but they are animated in a particularly dramatic way by the inescapable presence, behind the written word, of the personality of the author in all its complexity and richness. As a controversial figure, Rousseau reaches across two hundred years to communicate directly with the twentieth century on many relevant levels—as an artist, as a philosopher, as a moralist, as a political theorist, and, perhaps most notably and interestingly of all, as a human being with recognizable human problems. He stood apart from his contemporaries; his profound sense of apartness forms one of the more dramatic themes of his *Confessions* (written 1764–70) and other autobiographical writings, and is implicit in his philosophical works: 'Je ne suis fait comme aucun de ceux que j'ai vus; j'ose croire n'être fait comme aucun de ceux qui existent. Si je ne vaux pas mieux, au moins je suis autre.' His 'otherness', reinforced by his sense of personal isolation in what he considered to be a vindictive society, activates much of his thought, and although Rousseau himself tended to separate his self-revelations from his 'vrais écrits'—the *Discours sur les sciences et les arts*; the *Discours sur l'origine de l'inégalité*; *Du contrat social*; *Julie, ou la nouvelle Héloïse*; *Émile, ou de l'éducation*; and the *Lettre à d'Alembert sur les spectacles*—the points of contact between the personal problems of adjustment to life and the wider moral and philosophical issues concerning the place and fate of modern man in a hostile and unauthentic social environment are always apparent and always illuminating.

By the side of Rousseau the great protagonists of eighteenth-century Enlightenment become figures of respectability, conformers almost, with an aloofness and lack of emotional involvement which have no place in Rousseau's mentality. His work records the struggle for personal survival of a man in revolt against the menacing dehumanizing edifice of the modern state. One of the basic issues to be raised in his work, namely the degree to which society is responsible for the individual's loss of happiness and moral integrity, is always intimately linked to the experiences of a watchmaker's son, cast out of society at the age of sixteen, or so it appeared to him in retrospect, with the untimely closing of the gates of his native city. It is this element of impassioned, and at times unbalanced, personal commitment, imparting a life-or-death urgency to his most abstract arguments, that lies at the heart of the long controversy surrounding Rousseau's reputation as a writer and his claim to be considered as a constructive thinker airing problems of real public relevance. The barrier between objective thought and subjective feeling is at times too obviously fragile, but the fact that personal difficulties and philosophic problems interlock in a variety of contexts need not in itself invalidate his general conclusions. In some respects, on the contrary, the interplay between these two aspects can lend a measure of coherence and clarification to his ideas.

One of the more persistent psychological ripples to run across the surface of his thought concerns precisely this sense of being 'autre', recorded with mixed feelings of pride and horror in the *Confessions*, the *Dialogues* (1782), and the *Rêveries du promeneur solitaire* (written 1776–8). His hypersensitive awareness of processes of dislocation and depersonalization operating in his own life gives way very easily to the more general, but never academic, issues of the fragmentation of the individual in the face of pressures emanating from an amorphous and corrosive society. From what was originally an emotional position springs a whole complex of moral and political attitudes. Thus it is that in a century of gross inequality Rousseau pleads for the rights of the ordinary underprivileged citizen, a lower-class voice from Voltaire's 'canaille', asserting in an age of rationalism the rights of natural feeling, and proclaiming in a society still ruled by the divine right of kings the indivisible and inalienable sovereignty of the people. The sense of disorientation, the quest for a lost harmony and a lost happiness, the lack of an authentic, coherent identity, the corruption of moral truth, these are the themes in Rousseau's own life that have immense moral and political repercussions in his works of doctrine. The problem is always to separate the 'true' self from the mask which society has imposed. In the *Confessions* the problem of identification both of self and of others, of penetrating the mask and answering the question 'Que suis-je moi-même?', is for Rousseau central to the structure of experience, and underscores all the events and crises recorded. The feeling of dislocation, of acting out an unauthentic role, is frequently illustrated in the *Confessions*. One of the early crucial incidents concerns the celebrated affair of Mlle de Lambercier's comb which the young Rousseau is accused of breaking. He is punished, whilst protesting his innocence. The end of childhood is marked by Rousseau's realization that the inner knowledge of innocence is powerless against the outward appearance of guilt. 'Ce qui se voit n'est que la moindre partie de ce qui est.' At all moments of crisis, communication of the truth about himself is difficult, and Rousseau describes the consequences of such incidents in terms which closely resemble those in the *Discours sur les sciences et les arts*, in which he depicts 'le cortège des vices' emerging 'dès qu'on n'ose plus paraître ce qu'on est'. The pattern of innocence unjustly accused and punished, epitomized in the childhood incident of the comb, repeats itself throughout the various defensive positions that Rousseau adopts in his autobiographical works. All these analyse in extreme personal terms the effects of the resulting state of alienation from self. The two *Discours*, *Julie, ou la nouvelle Héloïse*, (1761), *Du contrat social* (1762), and *Émile* (1762), argue the social and historical origins of this condition, and explore possible solutions.

In all aspects of his work Rousseau describes a human condition, even more familiar to the age of Freud and Kafka, in which the social structure confronts man as a destructive and malevolent force. In Rousseau's view it is in the social world that the individual loses his coherence and becomes 'étranger à soi-même'. Time and again he will re-examine in his personal writings situations in which the actor is another Rousseau, an unrecognizable extension of himself pursuing a line of conduct in contradiction to the natural behaviour of the 'real' Rousseau. Relationships with others, the need to conform and the need to dissimulate, trespass inevitably upon the individual's

integrity and freedom of action. The natural, instinctive basis to
human action undergoes in society a vicious transformation from
'amour de soi' to 'amour propre'. These two notions, fundamental
to Rousseau's arguments concerning the depravation of modern
man, relate very closely to his investigation into the essential
dichotomy between the state of nature and the state of society,
between 'être' and 'paraître'. They apply in a variety of contexts
and are manifested at all levels of human activity and experience.
Only 'amour de soi' is authentic and legitimate, as it is related to
natural instincts of self-preservation, and as such to the state of
nature and the will of God. The second motivating force in human
affairs, 'amour propre', arises only with men in society as a development of purely rational processes. From 'amour propre' springs the
growth of a competitive social environment in which each individual,
encouraged partly by the socially based impulses of ambition and
acquisitiveness, and partly by the need to define himself, seeks his
own advantage at the expense of others. This lack of self-sufficiency
places man at war with his neighbour. It was with a view to controlling this state of hostilities that the idea of a social contract or
truce between the strong and the weak first arose, and the whole
condition of government becomes in Rousseau's thought a skilful
manœuvre on the part of those who have, to deceive those who have
not into acquiescing to the inequalities inherent in social organization. The central driving force is no longer the 'amour de soi' of
natural self-sufficient man, but the 'amour propre' of civilized man,
expressing itself in the sanctification of property, the urge for esteem,
the loss of moral independence and, ultimately, in the loss of happiness. This awareness of a lost happiness and a lost virtue in contemporary society, and the pursuit of these two ideals in a future
society, form the horizons to Rousseau's thought.

With the *Discours sur les sciences et les arts* (1750) and the *Discours sur
l'origine de l'inégalité* (1754), Rousseau formulated his first philosophical inquiries into the origins of the human situation as he saw it. The
conviction that the whole structure of the human personality has
been distorted by the various processes of depersonalization, which
social existence imposes upon individuals as one of its inescapable conditions, is present throughout Rousseau's analyses both of

himself and of man in the social setting. The authority for his conclusions is ultimately his personal experience as martyr-victim of
society's iniquities. The underlying corollary to the philosophic
investigation is always the personal issue: 'Comment serais-je devenu
méchant?' The cultural and sociological arguments of the two early
Discours provide the basic historical perspective out of which evolve
many of Rousseau's later themes and attitudes. In the first *Discours*
he points with extraordinary eloquence to the arts and the sciences,
symbols of the civilizing process, and in the second *Discours* to the
concept of property, the symbol of social organization, as integral
factors in the loss of man's virtue and liberty:

Voilà comment le luxe, la dissolution et l'esclavage ont été de tout temps
le châtiment des efforts orgueilleux que nous avons faits pour sortir de
l'heureuse ignorance où la sagesse éternelle nous avait placés. Le voile
épais dont elle a couvert toutes ses opérations semblait nous avertir assez
qu'elle ne nous a point destinés à de vaines recherches... Je sais que notre
philosophie, toujours féconde en maximes singulières, prétend, contre
l'expérience de tous les siècles, que le luxe fait la splendeur des états; mais
après avoir oublié la nécessité des lois somptuaires, osera-t-elle nier
encore que les bonnes mœurs ne soient essentielles à la durée des empires,
et que le luxe ne soit diamétralement opposé aux mœurs?

Le premier qui ayant enclos un terrain s'avisa de dire: 'Ceci est à moi',
et trouva des gens assez simples pour le croire, fut le vrai fondateur de la
société civile.

It is in the light of the circumstances attached to the development
of modern man in the two *Discours* that the major doctrinal works,
Du contrat social, *Julie, ou la nouvelle Héloïse*, and *Émile*, as well as
other more minor but equally interesting works like the *Lettre à
d'Alembert sur les spectacles* (1758), fall into place and compose a related
body of thought. The common factor between them is the question,
posed and answered in different and, at times, contradictory ways, of
the possibility for action in the face of modern man's irrevocable
divorce from the state of nature, and the consequent depravities
incurred through the workings of the historical process of civilization. Moral and political questions consistently interlock: 'Il faut
étudier la société par les hommes et les hommes par la société; ceux

qui voudront traiter séparément la politique et la morale n'entendront jamais rien à aucune des deux.' In the political context the problem is to translate the liberty which man enjoyed in the state of nature to the circumstances of modern conditions. The problem is redefined in *Émile* in terms of a contrast between 'l'homme naturel' and 'l'homme civile':

> L'homme naturel est tout pour lui; il est l'unité numérique, l'entier absolu, qui n'a de rapport qu'à lui-même ou à son semblable. L'homme civile n'est qu'une unité fractionnaire qui tient au dénominateur, et dont la valeur est dans son rapport avec l'entier, qui est le corps social. Les bonnes institutions sociales sont celles qui savent le mieux dénaturer l'homme, lui ôter son existence absolue pour lui en donner une relative, et transporter le moi dans l'unité commune; en sorte que chaque particulier ne se croie plus un, mais partie de l'unité, et ne soit plus sensible que dans le tout.

Rousseau's vision for man's future lies not in a retrogressive re-creation of the long-past state of nature, but in imitating as closely as possible the virtues of that state by the creation of a suitable moral–political environment. The ultimate test for the authentic political institution lies in its effectiveness as an instrument for restoring the individual to himself. All the practical measures he proposes in his three major works of doctrine are aimed at encouraging the individual to rediscover his natural impulses and motivations, the 'amour de soi', and, by the destruction of the artifice of 'amour propre', to shed the mask of society's pressures and prejudices. As the savage acted naturally to survive physically, modern man must act naturally to survive morally. As a moralist, Rousseau contemplates in *Du contrat social* the conditions which would exist ideally in a just society which, whilst enabling men to live together, would at the same time guarantee their equality, their liberty, and their moral integrity, counteracting thereby the trends analysed in the two *Discours*.

The prevailing situation was for Rousseau one of profound injustice: 'L'homme est né libre, et partout il est dans les fers.' The new social contract is therefore a keystone in his scheme for the redemption of modern man: 'Trouver une forme d'association qui défende et protège de toute la force commune la personne et les biens de chaque associé, et par laquelle chacun, s'unissant à tous, n'obéisse pourtant qu'à lui-même, et reste aussi libre qu'auparavant.' By this total, but freely undertaken, surrender of the individual's will to that of the community, liberty and equality are preserved, since a surrender to the community does not involve a surrender of rights to other individuals as implied in the present state of affairs, 'car l'impulsion du seul appétit est esclavage, et l'obéissance à la loi qu'on s'est prescrite est liberté'. An authentic society is created in which the destinies of its members are dissociated from the despotic and capricious will of a privileged individual or group of individuals. The law itself becomes the executive expression of the sovereign collective conscience of the whole community, which Rousseau terms the 'volonté générale'. Here for Rousseau lay the political basis for the creation of conditions of equality and moral liberty essential to man's recapture of the happiness that he enjoyed in the pre-social state of nature.

Du contrat social is concerned throughout all the issues it debates, from the legitimacy of government to the place of religion within the State, with the defence of human potential and human dignity in the political context. The pattern for the new society presupposed, however, the existence of the new citizen. In *Émile, ou de l'éducation* Rousseau confronts the problem of moral regeneration on the individual level, and creates his model pupil–citizen Émile, who is to emerge from the educational processes described in the treatise free from the malaise of alienation from self and others that plagues man in the present social set-up, and possessing the necessary moral strength and natural virtues to participate fully in the creation of the society of the new social contract. As with the emotional problems described in *Julie, ou la nouvelle Héloïse*, the educational principles of *Émile* do not exist in a vacuum; they are clearly related to the broader context of Rousseau's moral, philosophical, and political ideas: 'Notre véritable étude est celle de la condition humaine.' The child learns, not through the arbitrary exertion of authority and discipline, which would lead only to the donning of the mask of dissimulation and conformity, but through the impersonal law of necessity—a law rooted in nature which the child is made to perceive through the various 'leçons pratiques' devised by the tutor.

Authority is not therefore seen to spring from the will of another individual, from which the child would learn only the vicious principle of the effectiveness of tyranny. Here lies the formal core of Rousseau's 'education through experience' method applied to Émile during the critical moments of childhood of the first three books of the treatise. Through the five main phases of Rousseau's educational scheme, coinciding with the five 'ages' in the child's growth to physical maturity, the direction of the argument is towards the re-creation of natural man destined to live eventually in the natural society but who, meanwhile, will be invulnerable to the pernicious practices and pressures of society as it is:

> Dans l'ordre naturel, les hommes étant tous égaux, leur vocation commune est l'état d'homme; et quiconque est bien élevé pour celui-là ne peut mal remplir ceux qui s'y rapportent... Vivre est le métier que je lui veux apprendre. En sortant de mes mains il ne sera, j'en conviens, ni magistrat, ni soldat, ni prêtre; il sera premièrement homme... on doit lui apprendre à se conserver étant homme, à supporter les coups du sort, à braver l'opulence et la misère... Il s'agit moins de l'empêcher de mourir que de le faire vivre. Vivre, ce n'est pas respirer, c'est agir; c'est faire usage de nos organes, de nos sens, de nos facultés, de toutes les parties de nous-mêmes qui nous donnent le sentiment de notre existence.

This purpose lies beyond the scope of a purely pedagogical treatise, and the broader philosophical bases to the work become visible in Book IV, a vital phase in Émile's development, when he is brought into contact with the world, and his attention is directed towards problems of a moral, social, and religious nature.

The second section, entitled the *Profession de foi du vicaire savoyard*, upon which a great deal of contemporary criticism centred, and which Rousseau himself considered to be 'le morceau principal' of the whole work, contains Rousseau's views on 'natural religion', which, as a firm basis to natural morality, is offered as an alternative to the supernaturally based structures of revealed religion, which had already been denounced in *Julie, ou la nouvelle Héloïse*. Émile is now conducted from the physical to the moral environment, and thereby to a spontaneous acquisition of the idea of God as a reasonable explanation for these phenomena. Through the observations that he is encouraged to make about himself and his place in the world as a part of nature's design, Émile is led to an awareness of God's presence and purpose irrespective of the teaching of sects and the sanctions and traditions of societies. The 'vicaire savoyard', in his search for truth, dismisses existing religious institutions as social perversions of the natural religious consciousness of primitive man, awed and dazzled by the spectacle of God as manifested in the beauties of nature. God's presence in human affairs, as civilization developed and moved away from direct contact with nature, degenerated from a spontaneous, instinctively perceived phenomenon into a man-made fabrication, an idea—or rather a series of conflicting and mutually intolerant ideas—resulting in a breakdown of the natural, instinctive awareness of the Deity common to the primitive community. This man-made religion thus becomes an extension of the general state of fragmentation involved in the process of socialization, with political and social ramifications all based upon 'amour propre'.

In proposing a return to natural religion, Rousseau does not, however, envisage a naïve discarding of man's intellectual development and achievement. The *Profession de foi* is much more than a sentimental defence of primitive piety. Rousseau does not seek to escape from the Enlightenment, and the first stage in the regeneration of man's religious consciousness will involve the resources of reason: 'Les plus grandes idées de la divinité nous viennent par la raison seule. Voyez le spectacle de la nature, écoutez la voix intérieure.' Only the misuses of reason, epitomized in the pernicious jargon of the metaphysicians and the obscurantism of the theologians, are attacked. Reason itself remains intact in Rousseau's religious thought as an important component of the 'voix intérieure', his guide to action in which there is no conflict between rational perception and instinctive feeling. Rousseau's concern is, as always, with the disintegration and internal strife within the human personality under the pressures of modern life, and his appeal to reason is in some measure based upon its power as a unifying and ordering force: 'La foi s'assure et s'affermit par l'entendement; la meilleure de toutes les religions est infailliblement la plus claire... Le Dieu que j'adore n'est point un Dieu des ténèbres; il ne m'a point doué d'un entendement pour m'en interdire l'usage; me dire de soumettre ma raison, c'est outrager son auteur.'

From this point of view the *Profession de foi* remains an intensely rational document, a confrontation of mysticism with logic. In its rejection of 'la fantaisie des révélations' it proclaims strong rationalist convictions as well. as the more celebrated notions concerning the intuitive certainty of feeling and the voice of the heart. The emphasis throughout Rousseau's exposition of natural religion, both in the *Profession de foi* and in the relevant sections of his novel, is upon the practical steps which can be taken to carry out God's purpose in this life. The basis to moral conduct is found, by a process of rational argument, to lie in certain patterns of behaviour inscribed by nature within the human heart, and summarized by Rousseau in one of his characteristically disarming maxims: 'Tout ce que je sens être bien est bien; tout ce que je sens être mal est mal.' The implication of the existence of an instinctive guide to action has invoked charges of moral anarchy and irrational subjectivity. Rousseau's vision, however, involved the re-creation of a universal moral consciousness which would function on a basis of universal consent in much the same way as the 'volonté générale' would function with intuitive infallibility in the political sphere. In the well-known theories of conscience and of the pre-eminent rightness of unpremeditated feeling, Rousseau's natural morality is given a divinely inspired basis of universal consent, transcending the narrowness of orthodox religious dogma, yet adding nevertheless a spiritual ratification to the natural promptings of instinct which lie behind the actions of the natural man:

Il est donc au fond des âmes un principe inné de justice et de vertu, sur lequel, malgré nos propres maximes, nous jugeons nos actions et celles d'autrui comme bonnes ou mauvaises, et c'est à ce principe que je donne le nom de conscience... Conscience! conscience! instinct divin, immortelle et céleste voix; guide assuré d'un être ignorant et borné, mais intelligent et libre; juge infaillible du bien et du mal, qui rend l'homme semblable à Dieu, c'est toi qui fais l'excellence de sa nature et la moralité des actions; sans toi je ne sens rien en moi qui m'élève au-dessus des bêtes, que le triste privilège de m'égarer d'erreurs en erreurs à l'aide d'un entendement sans règle et d'une raison sans principe.

In *Émile* the themes of self-knowledge, of the recapture of lost virtue and lost happiness, drawn from all areas of Rousseau's thought and personal revelations, re-emerge in his confrontation of the problem of how man is to remain in harmony with himself, and at the same time contribute positively to the creation of the new society, involving the paradox, never totally resolved in practical terms, of the achievement of liberty through the surrender of liberty.

Rousseau's glorification of natural man, and of the innocence and happiness to be found in the state of nature, was interpreted by contemporaries as a naïve appeal for a literal return to the primitive, and ridiculed as such. Rousseau's reasoning on this issue was not, however, simple-minded or escapist in a trivial sense. He saw the corruption of modern civilization as part of an inevitable historical process in man's evolution, which was still unfolding. The self-divided man of modern times was at an interim stage in his development, unhappy in his present state certainly, but unable to return to his original position, however desirable that might be. Rousseau never really contemplated a literal recreation of a primitive way of life. The natural society of Rousseau's vision lay in the future, not in the past, and was conceived in terms of a fulfilment of human nature—not a retrogression. Man has a social destiny to follow to which he is called by the processes of evolution, by his conscience, and ultimately by God. Outside society, as the themes of *Julie, ou la nouvelle Héloïse* indicate, there is innocence but not virtue, since virtue is definable only as a victory of the will in the exercise of a moral choice which did not confront primitive man. 'Chère amie, ne savez-vous pas', Saint-Preux asks Julie, 'que la vertu est un état de guerre, et que, pour y vivre, on a toujours quelque combat à rendre contre soi?'

The purpose of Émile's education was ultimately to provide him with 'the art of living with his fellows'. As far as Rousseau himself was concerned, the art was never acquired. It remained an unfulfilled dream which he abandoned only at the last moment. In his own experience, society for Rousseau meant rejection, persecution, accusation. The achievement of Julie, the achievement of Émile, the achievement of the 'good' Jean-Jacques emerge, in the personal context, as dream achievements which mirrored the failure of the real

Rousseau to find an effective basis for reconciliation with his environment and fate. The desperation of his personal position in the face of society's 'plot' to destroy him is reflected dramatically in the celebrated 'réforme morale et intellectuelle' of the eighth book of the *Confessions*, and in the pathologically disturbed writings of the *Dialogues*. During the latter part of his life the personal quest for stability and happiness was pursued for the most part in voluntary isolation from social contact, and from the destructive forces of urban life. The intellectual search for a solution to the problem of human unhappiness had resulted in the composition of works which were to affect deeply the movement of European thought for many decades after Rousseau's death, and whose repercussions can still be felt today. Taken together, *Du contrat social*, *Julie, ou la nouvelle Héloïse*, and *Émile* represent a dense and wordy body of ideas. The personal search, developed throughout the *Confessions* and other autobiographical works, culminated in Rousseau's last, unfinished composition: the *Rêveries du promeneur solitaire*, a 'formless journal' recording his thoughts during the last few years of his life, and ending only a few months before his death.

The *Rêveries du promeneur solitaire* remains, perhaps, Rousseau's most outstanding performance from a literary point of view. In its lyrical absorption with the exploration of the inner landscapes of feeling and imagination, of the tortured labyrinth of self, the work marks one of the great turning-points in the art of autobiographical literature, and its techniques of self-revelation established a most suggestive pattern for later Romantic attitudes. Here Rousseau mounts a final defence of his integrity, and a final attempt to find happiness 'en dépit des hommes'. The superb musical balance of phrase and poetic eloquence of vocabulary, characteristic of Rousseau's prose at its best, reach the climax of their effect in the evocative description of the Île de Saint-Pierre, and of Rousseau himself in a state of mystical reverie, at one with nature, with God, and, most important of all, with himself:

Mais s'il est un état où l'âme trouve une assiette assez solide pour s'y reposer tout entière et rassembler là tout son être, sans avoir besoin de rappeler le passé ni d'enjamber sur l'avenir; où le temps ne soit rien pour elle, où le présent dure toujours sans néanmoins marquer sa durée et sans aucune trace de succession, sans aucun autre sentiment de privation ni de jouissance, de plaisir ni de peine, de désir ni de crainte que celui seul de notre existence, et que ce sentiment seul puisse la remplir tout entière; tant que cet état dure celui qui s'y trouve peut s'appeler heureux, non d'un bonheur imparfait, pauvre et relatif tel que celui qu'on trouve dans les plaisirs de la vie mais d'un bonheur suffisant, parfait et plein, qui ne laisse dans l'âme aucun vide qu'elle sente le besoin de remplir. Tel est l'état où je me suis trouvé à l'île de Saint-Pierre dans mes rêveries solitaires, soit couché dans mon bateau que je laissais dériver au gré de l'eau, soit assis sur les rives du lac agité, soit ailleurs au bord d'une belle rivière ou d'un ruisseau murmurant sur le gravier. De quoi jouit-on dans une pareille situation? De rien d'extérieur à soi, de rien sinon de soi-même et de sa propre existence, tant que cet état dure on se suffit à soi-même comme Dieu.

Even in these circumstances, however, happiness eluded Rousseau. As subsequent 'promenades' show, the serenity of the Île de Saint-Pierre was a contrived serenity, a fragile and temporary moment of escape into 'le pays des chimères... le seul digne d'être habité', which was to founder on the more persistent themes of guilt and the desperate urge to self-justification in the face of his crimes and accusers, real and imaginary. The shield of indifference to society's opinion, essential to Émile's armoury, and behind which Rousseau himself attempts to hide, was too easily penetrated. The solitary wanderer, retreating into a state of rapturous and timeless fusion with the natural beauty of the Swiss landscape, 'delivré de toutes passions terrestres qu'engendre le tumulte de la vie sociale', was apart from society but still vulnerable. Society's accusations were to remain to torment him and to pose a continual question mark over the carefully nourished image of his own essential goodness and innocence.

NOTE

JEAN-JACQUES ROUSSEAU, 1712–78, son of a Genevan watchmaker, abandoned
Geneva and protestantism in early youth to lead an unsettled existence in provincial France. The year 1742 found him in Paris where, apart from a brief
interval in Venice as an embassy secretary, he passed ten uncomfortable years.
In 1751 he renounced society and took up music copying. The controversy
surrounding *Émile* forced his departure from France, and he spent 1766 in
England with David Hume. Acute persecution mania dominated his last years.

Works. Following the publication of the prize-winning *Discours sur les sciences
et les arts* (1750), and its by-product the *Discours sur l'origine de l'inégalité*, the
main philosophical compositions succeeded each other rapidly: the *Lettre à
d'Alembert sur les spectacles* (1758), *Julie, ou la nouvelle Héloïse* (1761), *Émile*
(1762), condemned by the Paris Parlement, and *Du contrat social* (1762). The
autobiographical works, published posthumously, include the *Confessions* (in two
parts, 1782 and 1789), the *Dialogues* (1782), and the *Rêveries du promeneur
solitaire* (1782). Rousseau engaged in several musical and theatrical enterprises,
and is also remembered for the *Lettres écrites de la montagne* and the *Considérations sur le gouvernement de Pologne* (1772).

Editions. The thirteen-volume *Œuvres complètes*, edited by Ch. Lahure (1865),
is still the most accessible 'vulgate', although inaccuracies abound. The Pléiade
edition, by B. Gagnebin and M. Raymond (1959–   ), is in progress (vols. 1
and 2 have appeared). *La Nouvelle Héloïse, Émile, Les Rêveries*, and *Du contrat
social* (including the *Discours* and *Lettre à d'Alembert*) are available as Classiques
Garnier. D. Mornet's scholarly four-volume edition of *La Nouvelle Héloïse* (1925)
is particularly useful. Four volumes of a very full modern edition of the correspondence, edited by R. A. Leigh (1965–   ), have been published. Pending the
completion of this work, the twenty-volume *Correspondance générale*, edited by
Th. Dufour and P. Plan (1924–34), is satisfactory.

Criticism. D. Mornet, *Rousseau: l'homme et l'œuvre* (1950), and J. Broome,
Rousseau: a study of his thought (1963), provide informative general surveys.
Useful specialized treatments include R. Grimsley, *Jean-Jacques Rousseau* (1961),
J. Starobinski, *Jean-Jacques Rousseau: la transparence et l'obstacle* (1957), and M.
Raymond, *La Quête de soi et la rêverie* (1962). Important research material is
presented in H. de Saussure's *Rousseau et les manuscrits des* Confessions (1958),
and P. Jimack, *La Genèse et la rédaction de l'*Émile *de Jean-Jacques Rousseau* (1960).

10. Libertinism and the Novel

IN the eighteenth century libertinism, while it necessarily maintained a free-thinking attitude towards religion, had also extended its influence to affect social behaviour and, in particular, the relationship of the sexes. That it was a most significant intellectual and social phenomenon is beyond question. Indeed it provided the subject-matter of a considerable body of literature from the publication of Crébillon's first novel in the 1730s to that of the novels of Sade in the last decade of the century. Perhaps more important is the fact that libertinism developed from a social game of love into a desperate and cruel battle of the sexes in which mental and physical domination—usually of the female by the male—was the outcome of a desire for self-assertion. Since the basic assumptions of even the libertine game reflect an attitude to love which is markedly different from that of the seventeenth century, a brief consideration of these differences is essential.

In reaction to the coarse behaviour of the Court at the beginning of the seventeenth century, a desire for a more civilized way of life led to the popularity of pastoral novels such as d'Urfé's *L'Astrée* and to the establishment of salons in which the hostess, surrounded by a group of friends, cultivated good taste, polite behaviour, and polished conversation. Though the resulting 'préciosité' was sometimes excessive, it also introduced a certain style and control, and society witnessed the rebirth of gallantry in which the man showed complete devotion and respect to his lady and was 'complaisant, soigneux, soumis'. The vulgar and disruptive qualities of physical pleasure were tempered by the somewhat superficial but socially acceptable pleasures of the mind, and though passion might still erupt, a combination of 'coquetterie' and 'pruderie' largely preserved a balance of head and heart. The positive desire for refinement reflected a deeper need for a fuller and richer society, and even a certain superficial wit and elegance could not entirely stifle the generosity and warmth of feelings.

It is in her depiction of the intensity and range of feelings which the characters have for each other in *La Princesse de Clèves* that Mme de Lafayette conveys the complexity and depth of the triangular relationship. Husband and wife show trust and respect though their marriage is torn apart. And it is Mme de Clèves's qualities which inspire love and fidelity in Nemours. If duty and guilt prove fragile arguments against her passion, it is also because of her fears that she refuses Nemours after her husband's death. Mme de Clèves's most profound insight is that passion alone is insufficient for a full and lasting relationship, and this she could only have enjoyed in her marriage had it been allied with her deep respect for Clèves. Nowhere in the libertine novel does one have such a full and complex presentation of human feelings, and the noticeable impoverishment may be largely attributed to changed social attitudes.

In its definition of 'libertinage' the *Encyclopédie* says: 'il tient le milieu entre la volupté et la débauche', but makes no mention of love. And in their nineteenth-century study, *La Femme au XVIIIe siècle*, the Goncourt brothers draw attention to this significant change in emphasis: 'L'idéal de l'amour au temps de Louis XV n'est plus que le désir, et l'amour est la volupté.' They go on to describe the pervasive influence of 'la volupté', stressing its effect on clothes, make-up, and general deportment. In ornaments and furnishings as well as in paintings, engravings, and sculpted decorations, scenes of love abounded. And the atmosphere of ease and sensual gratification was maintained in the variety of sofas and ottomans and even in clocks which depicted the victory of love over time. One is hardly surprised that love became, in the words of the Goncourts: '… liaisons où l'on s'engage sans grand goût, où l'on se contente du peu d'amour qu'on apporte, unions dont on prévoit le dernier jour au premier jour, et dont on écarte les inquiétudes, la jalousie, tout ennui, tout chagrin, tout sérieux, tout engagement de pensée ou de temps.' Love was capricious; it wore a mask and set traps, and sincerity was lost 'sous la risée suprême de la parodie'.

The salons remained an important feature of the social fabric of the eighteenth century, but in the questioning of attitudes and values in which religion, law, and statecraft were all considered critically, the upheaval in beliefs was reflected in the behaviour of the leisured classes who frequented these salons. The idea of fixed laws and values was swept away in the upsurge of scientific examination but, in a predominant atmosphere of frivolity, stylishness and scandal were encouraged at the expense of serious discussion. Subtlety and politeness introduced a brittle elegance into conversation which allowed momentary contacts without any real involvement. In his *Considérations sur les mœurs* (1750) Duclos, whilst pointing to a better society in which he optimistically believed, commented on people's indifference to each other, their delight in passing pleasures, and their general dissipation which reflected, he thought, an absence of sensitivity. If 'l'homme aimable', a social butterfly, attempted to win recognition to satisfy his self-esteem, it was through the cultivation of wit and the intellect that many tried to impose themselves on others. 'L'homme d'esprit' believed he could see through the other person's mask and thereby demonstrate his own mental superiority. And language was both the mask for his own weaknesses and his weapon of attack.

The male sought success in the libertine game as if seduction were itself a career. In his desire to seize the momentary opportunity, he lost respect for the woman. As the game developed, mental domination added another dimension to easy victory on the sofa. The Goncourts again describe this succinctly: 'Refuser dans l'amour, ou dans l'à peu près de l'amour, jusqu'au mot qui est sa dernière illusion et sa dernière pudeur, là est la satisfaction suprême de l'amour propre et de la fantaisie de l'homme du temps.'

The life of the society woman of the century was largely devoted to pleasure. At her public levée, surrounded by flattering admirers, she gave her daily orders before going out to visit the shops and show herself off in the Tuileries and the Palais-Royal. After an evening meal she would attend the opera or a party and retire in the early hours of the morning. Caught up in the frenzy of intellectual questioning, she discussed the topics of the day which included her own modesty, virtue, and duties. She was subjected to considerable pressures and often capitulated to the light-hearted cheapening of her own behaviour. Once degraded she enjoyed the general amusement which accompanied the downfall of other virtuous women.

It would be wrong to assume that everyone's behaviour was debased, but as women apparently became freer, went out alone, and received their own visitors, family and personal ties were loosened. This new female freedom was in fact largely illusory, since women became more vulnerable to unscrupulous men. And the novels, which we can now discuss in the light of this background, present in general a picture of empty, fragile relationships in which the female was trapped, a prisoner of the male.

The most striking feature of Crébillon's novels is that, though they were published over a period of forty years, they reflect no marked development in either ideas or technique. He portrays relations between the sexes in a stylized and hollow social framework and makes extensive use of witty euphemism to avoid vulgarity in his descriptions of the discussions and antics which take place on and around the sofa. He is, however, principally concerned with the mental reactions of his characters as they confront each other. If, in his book *An Essay on Crébillon fils*, Clifton Cherpack rightly emphasizes Crébillon's interest in the complexity and texture of thoughts and feelings, he does not examine the underlying conception of human relations which determines this analytical approach. And he largely accepts Crébillon's involved style as the necessary literary extension of his detailed analysis. Although Crébillon's reputation largely rests on his psychological penetration, it is perhaps also the source of his weakness, since the minute details of feelings, motives, gestures, and actions often result in little more than a string of disembodied insights into the strategy of seduction, loosely contained in a weak narrative framework. But what detracts most of all from his novels is the fact that his world rests on a fixed conception of behaviour in which man is a machine to be studied, understood, and manipulated. Thus every affair is predictable and the eventual capitulation of woman is a constant. The only variety in the over-all pattern of events occurs in the skill and method of attack and defence. The game takes place, therefore, in an enclosed system which reflects a behaviourist view of psychology.

Crébillon's characters, living in an easy, permissive society for which love is dead, are quickly bored by the pleasures which they still seek in the satisfaction of their basic desires. Given to analysing their own and other people's behaviour, they undermine the spontaneity of their feelings and reduce mutual love and respect, in their philosophical system, to a shadow of its former self. Since constancy is no longer fashionable, excitement is sought in the proliferation of affairs rather than in lasting relationships. And one character even comments that natural love was corrupted by those who originally introduced the idea of feelings developing in time, failing to understand it as a momentary physical need which could be quickly satisfied: 'On sait aujourd'hui que le goût seul existe; et si l'on se dit encore qu'on s'aime, c'est bien moins parce qu'on le croit, que parce que c'est une façon plus polie de se demander réciproquement ce dont on sent qu'on a besoin' (*La Nuit et le moment*, 1755).

Because the game is stylized, vulgarity is tempered and yet success is still ensured to the satisfaction of both personal vanity and public opinion. The impersonal traffic of affairs is controlled by gossip, fashion, and rumour, and no one is sufficiently powerful to discount social pressure. Once a man's reputation is created by society, women like to be associated with him. It is essentially a society of professionals who demonstrate their linguistic skill in persuasion and self-defence, and always seize the opportunity if someone's guard drops. Indeed, much of their time is spent in the verbal fencing which Crébillon describes at such length, and it is only at moments of intense desire that the level of consciousness and language is broken.

Woman is a piece of machinery for Crébillon's male character. He claims that he knows her better than she knows herself, can manipulate her as he wishes, and can enjoy her painful fluctuations between love and duty. He is not, however, coldly cruel and avoids, if he can, the scandal and shame of a bad technique or a clumsy break-up. Not only does he predict her emotions and anticipate her capitulation; he also establishes the rules of her conduct. For it is the male who values woman's virtue as he destroys it, demanding physical satisfaction from her and, at the same time, that she should yield gracefully and with nobility. The more she struggles and resists the more he will admire her, and yet if she insists on preserving her virtue, he will try to ruin her socially. It is in the complexity of this situation that the complexity of the woman's role and her complete subservience to the male are clearly seen. He enjoys conquering her virtue as it allows him to prove himself, and even the coquette, the most skilful female opponent, displays false modesty and virtue to add piquancy to the affair. The virtuous woman's actions are limited, for she must never reveal her feelings first or take the initiative, and when she yields to a man's confession of love she is frequently disillusioned. Since she seeks more than sexual satisfaction but rarely finds it, she is the constant loser and, once engaged in battle, her only initiative is in keeping the man's desire and interest alive by refusing to satisfy him fully. The same pattern occurs time and time again in the novels which stress the man's cynical delight in his mastery of woman's every feeling and argument: 'Plaire, être même passionnément aimé: me voir l'objet des vœux, et des désirs de toutes les femmes: jouir tour-à-tour de leur ivresse, et de leur désespoir; les sacrifier perpétuellement l'une à l'autre, et les trouver enfin, malgré leur orgueil, et même de leurs projets, soumises à tous les mouvements qu'il me plaît de leur donner' (*Lettres athéniennes*).

Crébillon chose a variety of fictional forms—letters, first and third person narrative, the *conte*. He even developed the fairy-tale to extend his exploration of libertine behaviour. To some extent all his novels lack order and cohesion. The novels in the form of letters are written basically by one female character whose conceptual analysis of her behaviour allows little action and development. But various characters contribute to *Lettres athéniennes* (1771) and in this novel, as in *Les heureux orphelins* (1754), Crébillon introduces political ideas, adventures, and secondary stories with little regard for continuity and artistic form. It is within the restricted form of the *conte* that Crébillon's incisive wit is best displayed, and in *Les Égarements du cœur et de l'esprit* (1736–8) he produces his most satisfactory narrative. The young hero, Meilcour, gradually acquires experience in love, fluctuating between an experienced woman and a young girl. He is advised by the confident, successful 'petit-maître', Versac, and learns that one must separate affairs of the head and heart to avoid painful and untidy relationships. The first-person narrative is,

C 5480   F

however, often clumsy, as Meilcour is looking back on his youth and interpreting events at the moment when he describes them. Also, since the characters are little more than representatives of various attitudes and feelings, the total structure is rather loose and episodic.

Though Crébillon and Laclos describe similar patterns of social behaviour, their attitudes to the underlying problems are markedly different, and indeed Crébillon writes as if no problem exists. Whilst his diffuse observations suggest a superficial acceptance and enjoyment of libertine affairs, *Les Liaisons dangereuses* reflects its author's awareness of the social situation of woman and presents three main characters totally involved in a conflict which leads to their destruction. Laclos also wrote three short essays on the education of women in which his evaluation of the differences between their natural, primitive state and their contemporary social situation clearly reflected Rousseau's ideas. Of particular interest to the reader of the novel is the unfinished 'Discours', written in 1783, a year after the publication of *Les Liaisons dangereuses*, in which Laclos asserts that there can be no improvements in the education of women as long as social manners and the law reinforce their subordinate position. Addressing his female reader directly, he says that she has chosen humiliation and degradation rather than the 'vertus plus pénibles d'un être libre et respectable'. But if she now accepts the challenge, ashamed of her losses and misfortune, she must take the initiative against man. As the champion of female emancipation he calls on woman to act: '... si vous brûlez du noble désir de ressaisir vos avantages, de rentrer dans la plénitude de votre être, ne vous laissez pas abuser par de trompeuses promesses, ... apprenez qu'on ne sort de l'esclavage que par une grande révolution.'

That spirit of revolution is upheld for most of the novel by the Marquise de Merteuil who, considering herself intellectually superior to men, refuses to be dominated. And although her struggle with Valmont is central to the action, *Les Liaisons dangereuses* is as much a study of the contrasting attitudes and behaviour of its female characters. Valmont, Danceny, and even Prévan are important, but the reader's, and perhaps Laclos's, sympathy is directed more towards the women. The Marquise and the Présidente de Tourvel are opposites, the former a brilliant intellectual schemer, the latter a woman motivated by deep and sincere feelings, and between them there is the naïve Cécile, her mother who fails fully to understand what is happening, and Valmont's aged aunt, Mme Rosemonde, who has retired from society and can only give sympathy and advice to the victims of its battles.

The Marquise is a revolutionary figure in that she chose, from an early age, to control her language, actions, and gestures quite deliberately in an attempt to defeat man at his own game. In her famous letter 81 in the novel she describes in detail how, with considerable energy and dedication, she achieved the complete self-control which deceives everyone. Before her feelings were aroused, this intellectual discipline had given her considerable powers of insight, so that when she married she already combined a writer's mind with the talent of an actor. Her desire always to preserve the initiative made her task more difficult than the male's, since she wanted to choose when to submit, whilst allowing the man to believe in his conquest. She could easily assert her authority and control over an inexperienced lover, combining the lucidity of the male with the physical submission of the female, but her decision to destroy the experienced 'libertin' Prévan presented a challenge which, if mishandled, threatened utterly to destroy her in the eyes of society. However, it is above all with Valmont, the only man she had really desired, that she reveals her supreme skill. As equals they confide in each other and she also promises herself to him as the reward for his conquest and rejection of the Présidente, thus valuing herself more highly. But when Valmont claims his prize, the Marquise refuses to be taken for granted and demands that he win her. In her refusal to renounce Danceny in his favour she provokes the battle which leads to their destruction, and proves, on one level, that as intellectual equals neither can fully dominate the other. To this extent the Marquise explodes the game by refusing the accepted role of the female.

Throughout the novel, the Marquise and Valmont ruthlessly use their power against the other characters. The Marquise inspires many of the crimes, but Valmont is the agent of both the Présidente's and Cécile's downfall. From the beginning he is determined to conquer and then reject his special victim, the virtuous Présidente, and looks forward to a long, slow struggle in which she will yield gradually and suffer agonies of conflicting remorse and passion. For Valmont it is to be the perfect libertine kill, and he confidently expects her to fall in love with him and finally give herself quite willingly. With his carefully stylized letters, obedience to her wishes, and show of false charity and piety, he plays on her feelings and makes her responsible for his future happiness. And yet Valmont is not a completely cold, calculating villain, for, though he will not admit it to the Marquise, he loves the Présidente and is angry when he realizes just how dependent he is on her. And it is perhaps because the Marquise both injures his pride and hints at the truth in her mocking condemnation of his softness and subservience, that Valmont deals so cruelly with the Présidente. In his desperate attempt to dispel any idea of emotional dependence on her, he merely displays his subservience to the Marquise's whims and is himself another kind of victim. Valmont has neither the intellectual control of the Marquise nor the sincerity and devotion of the Présidente. Having all the social advantages of the male, he stakes everything on regaining the Marquise, and loses; but the fact that he can finally bring about her downfall is, to a large extent, an illustration of the social inequality of the sexes when the chips are down.

In their naïvety and ignorance the other characters are frequently the victims of Valmont's and the Marquise's schemes. Présidente de Tourvel is a sincere, generous character who, whatever Valmont may think, cedes essentially to love. He simply smoothes her path and calms her fears as her passion grows. Her situation, all the more intense and terrible because she commits herself to Valmont's happiness in spite of her remorse, is described with sympathy and sensitivity by Laclos. Tragically, her positive qualities of love and trust are opposed and debased by the destructive forces of the libertine society. Danceny and Cécile are simply clay in the hands of others. Both are candid, ingenuous, and impulsive in their love, easily tormented by doubt and suspicion in their complete dependence on each other. Whilst Cécile both feels guilt and is strangely attracted to Valmont, Danceny is as easily captivated by the Marquise and restored to Cécile again, and together they demonstrate the vulnerability of their naïve sensibility.

Les Liaisons dangereuses, the most profound study of libertinism in the eighteenth century, is a highly controlled and ordered novel. In the skilful juxtaposition of letters, Laclos allows his characters to describe their feelings and reactions so that the reader alone is fully aware of their misunderstandings and appreciates the ironic effect. Equally important, however, is the way in which Valmont and the Marquise, through their advice and influence, motivate the action, and their intellectual perception creates within the action of the novel itself a psychological perspective which is normally established by a narrator or the novelist. Laclos conveys a sense of time and reality by selecting the salient features of a situation and describing them, often with a keen wit. Also, by allowing the action to develop between letters, he preserves an urgency and movement in the narrative.

In the final upheaval and destruction of *Les Liaisons dangereuses* there is something of a male victory, and the revolutionary fire of letter 81 is dampened, for, in spite of Valmont's downfall, his deathbed pact with Danceny is the final act of male complicity. The gallant atmosphere which surrounds their duel contrasts markedly with the wretched, delirious torment of the Présidente's death scenes. Entrusted with the Marquise's letters, Danceny sees it as his social duty to expose her and, with no word of condemnation for Valmont, blames her for the corruption of Cécile. As a result of the ensuing scandal she is jeered at by the same group which welcomes the social return of Prévan. As the one rival whom Valmont admired and feared, it is ironical that he should be reinstated, presumably to continue his former activities and almost as a replacement for Valmont, and that the Marquise should be so completely ostracized, a tragic victim in her financial ruin and disfigurement. The final crushing irony is contained in the last letter, in which Mme de Volanges blindly trusts Mme Rosemonde's advice, ignorant of the real reasons for Cécile's departure to the convent, and comments with stunned horror at the events which have taken place. The position of woman is starkly revealed and, although *Les Liaisons dangereuses* is not a *roman à thèse*, its ending implies that a revolution in the attitude of men is essential for the emancipation of women.

Amongst other eighteenth-century novelists, Restif de la Bretonne is often considered a libertine writer, but his curious preoccupation with sexual prowess, which ranges from humorous boasting to the perverted fantasy of *L'Anti-Justine* (1798), is rarely described in terms of the social game and is of much greater significance as a feature of his autobiographical work.

A shrewd commentator on the eighteenth century, Duclos was also a novelist of some merit, and despite its artistic defects *Les Confessions du Comte de * * * * (1741) suggests interesting possibilities for breaking the libertine impasse. Largely composed of a loose sequence of adventures illustrating different kinds of behaviour, it explores in some detail the problems of establishing and maintaining a settled relationship. It is through generosity and selflessness that Mme de Selve draws the Comte away from short-lived affairs to a state of calm friendship. One problem which is clearly raised, but which Duclos fails to take up, is the significance of time in the Count's different relationships. In their initial desire to preserve their undying love, he and Mme de Selve fail to account for the inevitability of change in time, and it only imposes itself on them through the Count's return to a series of restless liaisons. Their final renunciation of the world and total contentment with each other's company is, one feels, an imposed, idealistic solution which projects into the future a frozen state of new-found harmony. Thus Duclos, in keeping with other writers of the century, conceives relationships only in terms of limited, constantly changing desires, or of undying, unceasing love. Seemingly there is no possibility of a lasting relationship which grows and develops in time, and pleasures are, therefore, presented as either fixed or fickle.

If Duclos seeks to re-establish a way of life based on anti-libertine values, Sade is the most articulate defender of crime and systematic destruction. Several of his novels describe the ultimate libertine relationship in which a woman is cruelly used and tortured by men who only seek the greatest pleasure for themselves in this infliction of pain. Sade's preoccupation with negative forces may in part be explained by his long imprisonment. Though he admits to libertine tendencies in his letters, and will not renounce his ideas, he strongly denies committing any crimes. Trapped and physically frustrated, it is as a philosopher that he defends his mental freedom and describes the way in which confinement has forced him to seek an outlet for his feelings through his imagination. And it is the strange fruits of this imagination which he orders and describes, at times almost dispassionately, in a considerable body of writing, of which at least half is unobtainable: '... vous avez échauffé ma tête, vous m'avez fait former des fantômes qu'il faudra que je réalise... Monsieur le 6,[1] au milieu d'un sérail serait devenu *l'ami des femmes*; il aurait reconnu et *senti* que rien n'est plus beau, plus *grand* que le sexe et qu'hors le sexe il n'est point de salut' (*L'Aigle, Mademoiselle*).

Sade's ideas, based on the motive force of egoism and the destructive impulses of the individual, are essentially antisocial, denying both Christian values and the subservience of the individual's interests to the common good. Since man is self-sufficient on earth and controls his own destiny, there is no place for God and religion, and Sade vigorously denounces Christianity on the grounds that it operates both as a tyrannical restraint and as a self-defensive system for the victim figure. Together with charity and generosity, its lessons of humility are rejected by the philosopher in favour of more positive physical pleasures. For Sade, charity satisfies only those who practise it and humiliates the recipient, and virtue generally involves too much renunciation. The most egoistical creature is Sade's male character who, corrupt in a corrupt century, believes that nature has made him superior to woman and demands that she devote herself to satisfying him; since their pleasure would be shared— and his own pleasure thereby diminished—if he were prepared to make sacrifices, he demands complete subservience to his desires. He renounces love, because it would make him dependent on woman, and also suspects the sincerity of expressions of love and pleasure. The sophisticated delights of a libertine affair are thus rejected in favour of more positive reactions which he provokes in woman, an object in his hands. Through the infliction of pain—which prompts a reaction more intense and more obvious than that produced by love—the male enjoys his superiority and establishes a gulf between himself and his victim.

[1] Sade referred to himself as 'Monsieur le 6' as he occupied cell number 6 in the prison of Vincennes.

Sade's total disregard for the value of the individual stems from his view of nature as the amoral, impersonal force which shapes the world. A man's life is simply a minute part of a much larger cycle which depends on destruction for the creation of more life. Thus, murder is not an offence against nature since it coincides with her reorganization of matter. Nature would not give us impulses harmful to herself. Similarly, because man is conditioned by his environment, his actions are beyond his control and perversions are, therefore, no more punishable than physical deformities. With this view of man as an impersonal cipher, Sade demands that he accept a necessary balance of good and evil in the world, and defends both rich and strong who preserve their superiority, and the criminal who strives to redress his personal disadvantages. The more he develops his ideas on impersonal, destructive forces, the more he devalues the meaning of human life embodied in the individual and yet, paradoxically, the individual always remains the agent of these negative forces.

In his *Idée sur les romans* Sade says that the human heart is nature's most curious work and, with nature herself, 'toujours sublime, toujours majestueuse', represents the true subject of fiction. As a thinker Sade was certainly engrossed by the complexity of both nature and the human heart, but the artistic embodiment of his ideas is far from satisfactory. Though he is often defended as an essentially anti-literary writer, one cannot overlook the fact that he mainly chose the novel as his medium of expression. The frequent repetition of ideas, the disjointed nature of his episodic narrative, and the crudely simple presentation of characters do much to weaken the impact of his work. Of the available longer novels, *Justine* (1791), the story of a virtuous girl who is the victim of a succession of evil people, does, however, suggest a gradation of crime and achieves some intensity in the statuesque descriptions of the perverted orgies in the monastery. But as with Crébillon it is in several of the short and very amusing *Historiettes, contes et fabliaux* (which reflect the influence of Boccaccio) that he reveals a certain control and deftness.

The scenes of torture and extreme sexual perversion in Sade's novels complete the circle which began with the elegant yet patently cruel encounters of Crébillon's characters. From the beginning, libertinism contained the seeds of this total breakdown and negation of positive social values. It is man's capacity for violence and domination, which man rarely admits even to himself, that Sade brings to the level of consciousness and language, revealing the destructive, libertine urges which are latent in us all.

NOTE

CLAUDE PROSPER JOLYOT DE CRÉBILLON, 1707–77, usually known as Crébillon *fils*, was the son of the dramatist of the same name. He wrote tales and dialogues reflecting the vices of high society and was dramatic censor for a period. A witty conversationalist, he founded a dining society in 1752.

CHARLES PINOT DUCLOS, 1704–72, mixed with writers, 'philosophes', actors and 'libertins'. He succeeded Voltaire as national historiographer and was elected to the Academy in 1755.

PIERRE CHODERLOS DE LACLOS, 1741–1803, had a military education and made his career as an artillery officer. In 1788 he served the Duc d'Orléans and in 1790 joined the Jacobin Club.

DONATIEN-ALPHONSE-FRANÇOIS DE SADE, 1740–1814, was sentenced to death in 1772 and, after escaping, was rearrested in 1777, and imprisoned first in Vincennes and then in the Bastille. In 1789 he was transferred to the lunatic asylum of Charenton.

Modern editions. The last complete edition of Crébillon's works was published in the collection 'Le Livre du divan' (1929–30). *Les Égarements du cœur et de l'esprit* is, however, available in a 'Bibliothèque de Cluny' edition and in a Pléiade collection, *Romanciers du XVIIIᵉ siècle* (1965). Duclos's *Considérations sur les mœurs* was published by the Cambridge University Press (1946), and *Les Confessions du Comte de* * * * is available in the above-mentioned Pléiade collection. Laclos's complete works are published in a single Pléiade volume, and *Les Liaisons dangereuses* is also available in a Garnier edition. Pauvert have published Sade's complete works, but several novels are unobtainable. *Historiettes, contes et fabliaux* is also obtainable with *Les Infortunes de la vertu* in a 'Monde en 10/18' paperback edition.

Criticism. C. Cherpack, *An Essay on Crébillon fils* (1962), is an excellent introduction to Crébillon. D. Thelander, *Laclos and the Epistolary Novel* (1963), and J.-L. Seylaz, *Les Liaisons dangereuses* (1958), are detailed studies of Laclos's novel, whilst M. Turnell, *The Novel in France* (1962), also contains an interesting essay on the same author. More particularly, the 'mechanisms' of libertinism receive very intelligent analysis in R. Vailland's *Laclos par lui-même* (1959). In *Lautréamont et Sade* (1963), M. Blanchot gives a short, lucid account of Sade's ideas. An essay on Sade in G. Bataille, *La Littérature et le mal* (1957), and P. Klossowski, *Sade mon prochain* (1947), are also useful studies.

Of particular interest in connection with the background of libertinism and the novel are the Goncourts' book, *La Femme au XVIIIᵉ siècle* (1862), G. May, *Le Dilemme du roman au XVIIIᵉ siècle* (1963), and V. Mylne, *The Eighteenth Century French Novel* (1965).

11. Epigram and Salon Literature

FOR the eighteenth-century man of letters, the salon tended to be a suspect institution. Initially the artist's suspicion was based upon social issues, and in literature the emergence of an increasingly articulate middle-class voice, conscious of its potential and impatient with past restrictions, meant that the salons had to adapt themselves radically in order to meet the insistent demand for recognized status from men of high talent in the face of men of high birth. It was some time before the artist could finally destroy the image which traditional salon philosophy had of him as 'un simple amuseur', a court jester, as Voltaire was to find out in the course of his painful dealings with the Chevalier de Rohan. The salons did adapt, however, to the nascent changes in the balance of class structure, and re-established themselves as flourishing arenas of discussion, congenial to the writer and seminal to the development of the period's literature. As a formative influence on style and aesthetic practice, the salons were to remain in the forefront of literary life in France until the outbreak of the Revolution.

Out of what was said in the salon developed what was written: epigrammatic literature in both verse and prose, the scientific *politesse* of Fontenelle, the aggressive-amusing mental challenge of the Voltairean *conte*, the dilettantism of the *Encyclopédie* itself, all palpably reflect the stamp of salon conditioning and stimulation. It was to salon audiences that the drama of political opposition, social protest, and general intellectual dissent was first played out, since the salons were able to furnish the artist with one of the few effective outlets for the free expression of ideas, and to frustrate to some extent an otherwise formidable censorship machinery. The salon in effect provided the artist with an accessible audience and a flattering mirror. However, the social emancipation of the artist in the eight-eenth-century salon did not, as the testimony of Rivarol's portraits indicates, always serve the long-term interests of literature itself. Excess of attention would focus upon the person of the artist, upon his performance as a salon personality, rather than upon the intrinsic merits of his art. Whilst in one way this was to add a fruitful dimension to the literary criticism of the period, it did entail a distortion of literary values resulting in the creation of a number of extravagant reputations which posterity has been unable to endorse. There was ample opportunity for plausible mediocrity to flourish. Nevertheless, the 'république des lettres' acquired a new social dignity as the artist found his niche in the salon, acting as public conscience and purveyor of progress and enlightenment. The function of the man of letters, so Malesherbes proclaimed to the Academy in 1775, was that of the 'orateurs de Rome et d'Athènes au milieu du public assemblé'.

Yet it was against this background of increasing social flexibility in the salon, allowing the artist to perform freely in an atmosphere of intellectual brilliance, that dissenting voices were to be heard. The frivolity and intrigue still integral to salon life were to produce a reaction amongst certain perceptive moralists who experienced their effects at first hand. As the Revolution approached, awareness of the debilitating influence of the salon on moral values, on art, on society itself, became sharper. Ironically, this growth of apprehensive hostility to salon culture was to find a most effective expression in literary genres nurtured within the salon itself: the epigram, the maxim, the aphorism, and the portrait—the 'written conversation' of the salon. It was here, in a literature indigenous to the salon environment, that a reflection of salon influence and, at the same time, a judgement upon that influence, emerged with pungent clarity.

One of the earliest, but neglected, warnings to be sounded against salon activities and values came from Vauvenargues, a writer who, for a variety of reasons—military commitments, ill-health, and a natural reserve—remained very much on the fringe of Parisian salon circles. Apart from Voltaire and Marmontel, his friends were few and his society contacts negligible. Moreover, his premature death prevented the completion of much of his work. Nevertheless, his *Introduction à la connaissance de l'esprit humain* (1746), published together with the *Réflexions sur divers sujets*, the *Paradoxes mêlées de réflexions et de maximes*, and a number of *Caractères*, provides an unpretentious, but penetrating, commentary upon the withering effects of salon rationality and brilliance upon the individual's sensibility. With his appeal for a return to the emotional truths and natural values of the heart in a society preoccupied with the exaltation of reason as a guide to progress, Vauvenargues foreshadows attitudes to be taken up and extended by Jean-Jacques Rousseau and the proponents of 'sensibilité' in the second half of the century. His maxims lack the surgical precision of La Rochefoucauld's tone and avoid the starkness of the Pascalian aphorism, but with epigrammatic qualities of sharp wit and uncontrived elegance they reflect instead a freshness and spontaneity sometimes absent in the carefully worked products of more celebrated predecessors. The tone of his work is exploratory; he is able to distil, with a total unconcern for external effect, the essence of a problem whilst avoiding dogmatic solutions and pontifical attitudes. Pursuing his search for a basis to moral action, Vauvenargues investigated 'le cœur' as the true source of moral beauty and virtuous conduct, and the focal point of his thought is indicated by two of his capital maxims: 'Les grandes pensées viennent du cœur' and 'Connaître par sentiment est donc le plus haut degré de connaissance'. The subordination of reason to sentiment, of reflection to natural impulse, is fundamental to his whole philosophy, and marks an important early manifestation of the change of emphasis from rationalism to the intuitive values of 'sensibilité' which was to gather momentum in the decades after Vauvenargues's death. 'On doit se consoler de n'avoir pas les grands talents, comme on se console de n'avoir pas les grandes places; on peut être au-dessus de l'un et de l'autre par le cœur.' Vauvenargues was concerned to resist the rationalist preoccupations of his time, which for him were threatening to replace natural emotions with the brittle artifice of a salon culture in which even poetry was subject to the rules of 'géométrie'. Without the spontaneous guidance of 'les sentiments du cœur', reason alone was an insufficient guarantee of virtue:

L'esprit est l'œil de l'âme, non sa force. Sa force est dans le cœur, c'est-à-dire dans les passions. La raison la plus éclairée ne donne pas d'agir et de vouloir. Suffit-il d'avoir la vue bonne pour marcher? Ne faut-il pas encore avoir des pieds, et la volonté avec la puissance de les remuer?

Dans l'enfance de tous les peuples, comme dans celle des particuliers, le sentiment a toujours précédé la réflexion, et en a été le premier maître.

The emphasis on the efficacity of 'sentiment' related in Vauvenargues's thought to a parallel emphasis on the role of nature as a guide to virtuous action. If not an absolutely sure basis for morality, nature was at least a more dependable source of moral enlightenment than reason: 'La raison nous trompe plus souvent que la nature.' 'L'esprit ne fait pas connaître la vertu.' The sterility of eighteenth-century salon society weighed heavily upon Vauvenargues's mind, but his philosophy was not one of resignation to the situation. Here he consciously parted company with the 'pessimistes', and in particular with La Rochefoucauld and Pascal, against whom he directed many of his maxims and epigrams. His solution lay in the rehabilitation of human nature, and especially of the passions, which had not yet emerged from the Pascalian shadows. 'Le mépris de notre nature est une erreur de notre raison.' Rousseau's later glorification of the virtues of nature finds a striking precedent in Vauvenargues's thought. He was able to forecast the coming changes in attitude towards man's stature as a moral being: 'L'homme est maintenant en disgrâce chez tous ceux qui pensent, et c'est à qui le chargera de plus de vices; mais peut-être est-il sur le point de se relever et de se faire restituer toutes ses vertus, car la philosophie a ses modes...' The passions, previously regarded as the source of man's downfall, were now reconstituted as potential sources of noble action. 'Amour-propre' itself was reinstated: 'Est-il contre la raison ou la justice de s'aimer soi-même? Nous sommes susceptibles d'amitié, de justice, d'humanité, de compassion et de raison. O mes amis! qu'est-ce donc la vertu?' Vauvenargues was opposing a world view, prevalent in French moralist traditions of the seventeenth century, of fragile man pursuing a tragic destiny at the mercy of a hostile environment and a vulnerable human nature. 'La pensée de la mort nous trompe parce qu'elle nous fait oublier de vivre.' Death, the proof of man's physical limitations, is a reality, even a necessity—'la plus amère de nos afflictions'—with which man has to come to terms, yet it should not be allowed to dominate the individual's will to action: 'Pour exécuter de grandes choses, il faut vivre comme si on ne devait jamais mourir.' For Vauvenargues, man should be the victim neither of his passions nor of his environment.

His glorification of action in the exercise of the passions suggests almost a Stendhalian cult of energy. Certainly, with Vauvenargues, man was a being born for action and the pursuit of 'gloire', and in action, based upon the promptings of the heart and the guidance of reason through 'sentiment', lay the possibility of progress, of triumph over limitations, and of the achievement of a true state of virtue: 'La plus fausse de toutes les philosophies est celle qui, sous prétexte d'affranchir les hommes des embarras des passions, leur conseille l'oisiveté, l'abandon et l'oubli d'eux-mêmes.' The inactivity and negativity of the frivolous social world, with its emphasis on passive discussion rather than application of ideas, horrified Vauvenargues: 'Les conversations du monde rendent l'esprit paresseux, pesant et l'endorment en quelque sorte dans l'oisiveté.' Society, reason, religious dogma, empty moral codes, all were rejected by Vauvenargues as barriers to free action. Morality was no longer a question of the repression of the passions, or of rationalizing them out of existence, but of canalizing them along positive and socially useful lines. The action which results from this reorientation was not futile 'divertissement', but the key to fulfilment: 'Laissez croire à ceux qui le veulent croire, que l'on est misérable dans les embarras des grands desseins. C'est dans l'oisiveté et la petitesse que la vertu souffre, lorsqu'une prudence timide l'empêche de prendre l'essor, et la fait ramper dans ses liens.'

If Vauvenargues stood apart from society and salon life, the 'disease of the age', Chamfort's work is rooted in a direct experience of the literary and philosophic salons of the latter half of the century. Chamfort was active as a dramatist, poet, and literary critic, as well as being one of the most incisive of the salon moralists. Whereas Vauvenargues's work is the product of detached reflection away from the debilitating influence of an 'inactive' society, Chamfort's work as a moralist and social commentator reflects a carefully observed experience of the salon scene. He did not set out to speculate upon a vast metaphysical canvas, but confined himself to the study of man in a specific social context. Unlike the polished perfection of the maxims of La Rochefoucauld, with whom he is most often compared, Chamfort's work survives largely in note form, and consists of day-to-day jottings on events as they occurred. Despite the casualness of approach and the occasional banality, his *Maximes et pensées* and *Caractères et anecdotes*, published after his death under the title *Produits de la civilisation perfectionnée* (1795), provide a fresh and authentic insight into French society right up to the eve of the Revolution. His epigrams and portraits, animated with the skilled use of dialogue, recapture vividly the banter and conversation of the salons, recreating in close focus the personalities of the salon scene. In the *Caractères et anecdotes* Chamfort provides a sensitive reproduction of the idiosyncrasies of salon culture, in which the critical element is present, but not obvious. Some of the apparently inconsequential conversation pieces take on the sting-in-tail qualities of the epigram, and aim to reflect the brittle wit of the anti-religious barbs thrown by the salon *philosophes*: 'A propos des choses de ce bas monde, qui vont de mal en pis, M. * * * disait "J'ai lu quelque part qu'en politique il n'y avait rien de si malheureux pour les peuples que les règnes trop longs. J'entends dire que Dieu est éternel; tout est dit."' Occasionally Chamfort moves away from the immediate social background to sound an explicit moral note. On these occasions he dispenses with the recorded dialogue technique, and addresses the reader directly: 'La nature, en nous accablant de tant de misère et en nous donnant un attachement invincible pour la vie, semble en avoir agi avec l'homme pour un incendiaire qui mettrait le feu à notre maison après avoir posé des sentinelles à notre porte. Il faut que le danger soit bien grand pour nous obliger à sauter par la fenêtre.' These moments of abstract speculation are rare in the *Caractères et anecdotes*, however, and the work is more interesting for the social and historical insight that it provides into the period.

In the *Maximes et pensées* the closeness to events and personalities is still perceptible, but the author's own viewpoint clarifies. He no longer conceals himself behind a neutralizing shield of dialogue and, as a result, his observations become tinged with an element of involvement and moral reaction. The mere reportage of eighteenth-century drawing-room conversation and incidents now gives way to the wider perspective of 'la France, pays où il est souvent utile de montrer ses vices, et toujours dangereux de montrer ses vertus'. An astringency of tone, together with an attitude of deep pessimism, barely detectable in the *Caractères et anecdotes*, now predominates: 'L'homme vit souvent avec lui-même et il a besoin de vertu; il vit avec les autres, et il a besoin d'honneur.' 'L'espérance n'est qu'un charlatan qui nous trompe sans cesse, et pour moi, le bonheur n'a commencé que lorsque je l'ai eu perdue.' The hope and optimism contained in Vauvenargues's pursuit of virtue through action had no attraction for Chamfort: 'Les hommes sont si pervers que le seul espoir et même le seul désir de les corriger, de les voir raisonnables et honnêtes est une absurdité, une idée romanesque qui ne se pardonne qu'à la simplicité de la première jeunesse.' The growth of a profound disillusionment with the artifice and futility of salon life, whose traits he represented with deceptive tolerance and amusement in the *Caractères et anecdotes*, emerges as one of the most salient features of the *Maximes et pensées*.

The contrast with Vauvenargues is sharp; Vauvenargues had seen a way of escape from society's corruptive influence in the cultivation of sentiment and the voice of the heart. Chamfort affirmed the other point of view: 'Le premier des dons de la nature est cette force de raison qui vous élève au-dessus de vos propres passions et de vos talents et de vos vertus.' The promptings of the heart can lead only to the false security of illusions: 'Le plaisir peut s'appuyer sur l'illusion, mais le bonheur repose sur la vérité.' The consolation which truth provides becomes for Chamfort one of the few constant and dependable factors in life: 'La pensée console de tout et remédie à tout. Si quelquefois elle vous fait du mal, demandez-lui le remède de ce mal, et elle vous le donnera.' In the salons Chamfort had observed a 'public... absurde, atroce et plat', and to some extent the relevance of his outlook remains linked to this milieu. Essentially his maxims and epigrams belong to the salon, and represent a specific reaction to it, but this localized framework does not frustrate entirely the emergence of wider implications concerning the predicament of man in the face of modern conditions. The sardonic pessimism of certain of his maxims recalls the abyss with which Pascal had confronted readers of an earlier salon age: 'Vivre est une maladie dont le sommeil nous soulage toutes les 16 heures. C'est un palliatif. La mort est le remède.' At its best, his work impresses with its immediacy and penetration. The sombre colours in which his vision of man, and of man's future in society, was painted, stood out dramatically in an age which had placed its faith in confident doctrines of progress and rational optimism.

Rivarol was a moralist whose work also crystallized out of a close involvement with the social scene prior to the Revolution. He started from a position of relative detachment as a pungent but undistinguished observer of the social scene, and ended as a morally and politically engaged writer embroiled in the thick of revolutionary tumult. Despite the increasing political commitment of his writings, Rivarol never abandoned his acute sense of artistry; throughout his career he remained a highly skilled and controlled stylist. His reputation as an exponent of language and style, established with the publication of his *Discours sur l'universalité de la langue française* (1784), tends, in fact, to overshadow his stature as a thinker and moralist. It was not until the appearance of a later work, the *Petit Almanach de nos grands hommes* (1788), that an indication of his talent as a delicate exponent of the arts of portrait and prose epigram can be seen. As with other moralists of the period, the stultifying effects of salon society during the last decades of the *ancien régime* provide the bedrock material for his observations. The *Petit Almanach* embodies Rivarol's judgement upon numerous minor literary figures of the salon scene. He sets about their destruction with a detailed, and at times cruelly incisive, survey of literary pretentiousness in the salon, in which he also includes savage attacks on the less trivial reputations of Delille and Beaumarchais. His technique is that of the epigram: the intermingling of personal banter with a scathing attack upon the artist's work. His effects were achieved through a combination of laconic exaggeration, damagingly excessive eulogy, and pointed understatement, all couched in a framework of coldly controlled irony. His entry against the name of Gillet is typical: 'Ses Couplets de Jean à Jeanne sont un monument de l'Almanach des Grâces. Il faut avoir un talent bien particulier pour éviter avec tant de précaution la poésie, l'esprit et l'harmonie et faire pourtant des couplets si aimables. C'est que M. Gillet a saisi le genre.'

The aggressive techniques of the *Petit Almanach* were perfected within a political context in the portraits and epigrams contained in a work published two years later in 1790: the *Petit Dictionnaire des grands hommes de la Révolution*. As a vehicle for the expression of Rivarol's disenchantment with the Revolution, the portrait here becomes a political weapon of considerable refinement. One of the principal targets is Mirabeau:

Ce grand homme a senti de bonne heure que la moindre vertu pouvait l'arrêter sur le chemin de la gloire, et jusqu'à ce jour, il ne s'en est permis aucune .. Il n'a regardé l'honneur et la probité que comme deux tyrans qui pouvaient mettre un frein à son génie, et il s'est rendu sourd à leur voix; il a renoncé à toute espèce de courage, pour ne pas rendre sa destinée trop incertaine; enfin il a profité de son manque d'âme pour se faire des principes à l'épreuve des remords .. [il] n'en passe pas moins pour un des meilleurs ouvriers de la révolution, et il ne s'est pas commis un grand crime dont il ne se soit avisé le premier.

Rivarol's moral and philosophical ideas are to be found in the *Prospectus d'un nouveau dictionnaire* (1797) and its accompanying essay *De l'homme intellectuel, ou discours préliminaire du nouveau dictionnaire de la langue française*, the *Lettres à M. Necker* (1788), the *Journal politique national* (1789–90), and the notebooks, from which were published the *Pensées inédites*. All were composed during a period of social breakdown and civil violence, and reflect both disillusionment with the society and culture of a moribund *ancien régime*, and dismay at the political and social consequences of the death of that regime. His pessimism tends at times to be even more radical than that of Chamfort: 'Les hommes se lassent d'aimer, ils se lassent même de se battre, et ne se lassent pas de se haïr. C'est que l'amour et la guerre ont des causes; la haine a ses raisons; c'est que si l'amour et la guerre ont leurs fureurs, ils ont aussi leurs périodes; la haine a sa patience.' Even in times of apparent progress and enlightenment, the darkness of latent human wickedness was never far away. The values of civilization needed protection from the base, immoral forces lurking within each individual, and constantly menacing human happiness. Neither the narcissistic society of the salons nor the revolutionary State of Mirabeau could provide this protection. Rivarol was therefore suspicious of the doctrines of liberty and equality under the cover of which disorder and social collapse had set in. Good and evil, in the individual and in the State, had degenerated into relative concepts founded on expediency: 'En législation, comme en morale, le bien est toujours le mieux.'

Unlike Joubert, Rivarol did not have recourse to a reassertion of Christianity as a remedy for the disintegrating effect of events. He rejected theological doctrine as such, but nevertheless his thought marks a further stage in the movement away from eighteenth-century rationalist doctrines. The pattern of events during the excesses of political revolution had, for Rivarol, their source in the intellectual revolution of the salon *philosophes*, whose influence he condemned 'pour avoir ignoré le poison des germes qu'ils semaient'. The enthronement of the Goddess of Reason was for him too closely involved with the persecutions and bloodshed of the Terror. Enlightenment and the war against 'l'infâme' had emerged as a destructive and negative movement with its own brand of fanaticism. The result, as Rivarol experienced it, had been the creation of conditions favourable to the unleashing of vicious forces normally held in check in times of social stability. As a realist and a rationalist, therefore, Rivarol reappraised the sources of social stability. Whilst not retracting his opposition to the mystical aspects of Church doctrine, he perceived in the institution of the Church an indispensable instrument for the reconstruction of moral values, and the re-creation of a stable political situation. Religion, whatever its other disadvantages, had at least demonstrated its worth as a bastion against the destructive forces of human nature: 'La philosophie divise les hommes par les opinions; la religion les unit dans les mêmes dogmes et la politique dans les mêmes principes; il y a donc un contrat éternel entre la politique et la religion. Tout état, j'ose le dire, est un vaisseau mystérieux qui a ses ancres dans le ciel.' For the moralists of the Revolution, enlightenment had proved to be an impasse; reason had broken faith with its promise of the better life. Worship of the Supreme Being merely imposed a question mark over the eighteenth-century achievement: 'le genre humain a-t-il souffert de toutes les guerres de religion autant que de ce premier essai du fanatisme philosophique?' With Rivarol, the implications of this question were to be answered in a political defence of an otherwise discredited institution, but from now on moralist thought, as the nineteenth century approached, was to concern itself increasingly with a return to traditional sources of authority, not merely on a politically expedient level, but on a wider moral and more spiritually committed basis.

Joubert was one of the last eighteenth-century moralists. With his *Pensées* (posth. publ. 1838), the wheel of reaction against eighteenth-century attitudes turns full circle. The early maxims reflect the influence of the 'salons philosophiques', under whose wing he spent the initial stages of his career in Paris, and express the fashionable anti-religious and anti-monarchical attitudes of the period. On the eve of the Revolution Joubert was a man convinced of the rightness of revolt, an adherent of Rousseau's views on the immorality of property and the evil caused by the uneven distribution of wealth. Even at the height of his association with the last great names of eighteenth-century enlightenment, however, he retained an independence of mind and an objectivity in which indications of his later hostility to philosophic rationalism can be detected.

In addition to his apprenticeship with the *philosophes*, Joubert also came under pre-Romantic influence with its emphasis on 'sensibilité' and exoticism—developments which had formed part of Rousseau's legacy and found expression with writers such as Bernardin de Saint-Pierre. Much of Joubert's reaction as a moralist focused upon the age of Enlightenment during its closing 'sentimental' phase. He drew attention to the unfortunate effects resulting, in his view, from the desperately contrived attempts on the part of the rationalists to find consolation and escape from their own aridity in the cultivation of 'sensibilité'. In the *Pensées* he referred disparagingly to 'la vie sans actions, toute en affections et en pensées demi-sensuelles... inutile et paresseuse activité, qui engraisse l'âme sans la rendre meilleure'. The cult of the 'âme sensible' was denounced particularly for its encouragement of an illusory sense of virtue. For Joubert, the key to virtue did not lie in the intellectualized exploitation of sentiment: 'Il faut tenir ses sentiments près de son cœur.

Lorsqu'on accoutume son cœur à aimer les espèces qui n'existent que pour l'esprit, on n'a plus d'attache qu'aux abstractions, et on leur sacrifie aisément les réalités... Ces affections philosophiques qu'on ne ressent point sans effort, ruinent et dessèchent notre capacité d'aimer.'

Joubert's role as a follower of the *philosophes* was a temporary one to be played out until the disillusioning processes of the Revolution had gathered momentum. The events of the last decade of the eighteenth century forced him to reconsider his position, and it was during this period of reassessment that his stature as a Christian moralist began to grow. Unlike certain of his contemporaries who were following the same path, he did not summarily dismiss the rationalist achievement, but his priorities were clearly defined: 'Il n'y a de beau que Dieu, et après Dieu, ce qu'il y a de plus beau c'est l'âme, et après l'âme, la pensée.' His thought now became God-centred, and his moral attitudes formed accordingly:

> Sans le monde religieux, le monde sensible offre une énigme désolante.
> La religion est la poésie du cœur... elle nous donne le bonheur et la vertu.
> La piété est au cœur ce que la poésie est à l'imagination, ce qu'une belle métaphysique est à l'esprit: elle exerce toute l'étendue de notre sensibilité.

The former associate of Diderot and d'Alembert now became the ally of Chateaubriand in his affirmation of specifically Christian guides to conduct. Only religion could guarantee virtue and happiness; outside religion 'la morale n'est que maximes et que sentences; avec le dogme elle est précepte, obligation, nécessité'.

As a moralist, Joubert's approach differed from that of his contemporaries and predecessors. His *Pensées* reflected neither the cruel trenchancy of the laconic Rivarol, nor the caustic pessimism of Chamfort. To the oblique and often wordy portrait, he preferred the penetrating 'saillies de philosophie', formulated, in the tradition of the epigram, with a view to easy retention. He lacked the aggression of the seventeenth-century moralists. He made no Pascalian attempts to horrify or depress. Confronted with extremist doctrines and social and political outrage, he displayed neither the cold anger of La Rochefoucauld nor the disenchantment of La Bruyère. The distinctive tone of his criticism is one of compassion; his philosophy exalts the virtues of moderation and control: 'un peu de tout, rien à souhait: grand moyen d'être modéré, d'être sage, d'être content.' Happiness and serenity involved a balance of extremes: 'Ayez soin qu'il manque toujours dans votre maison quelque chose dont la privation ne vous soit pas trop pénible, et dont le désir vous soit agréable. Il faut se maintenir en tel état qu'on ne puisse être jamais ni rassasié ni insatiable.' In the political sphere, liberty without the balance of order was 'un tyran gouverné par ses caprices'. Only in the discipline and order provided by Christianity could the balance be restored: 'La justice vient de l'ordre, et l'ordre vient de Dieu lui-même.' In opposition to the moral and political anarchy of revolution—'des temps où le pauvre n'est pas sûr de sa probité, le riche de sa fortune, et l'innocent de sa vie'—Joubert pointed to the strength and authority of orthodox Christianity. In his *Pensées* two central purposes to man's existence had been defined: the achievement and preservation of his own virtue, and concern for the happiness of others. On a note of gentle optimism Joubert was, in effect, reposing the question of man's responsibility before his own destiny, a question which had been voiced throughout the eighteenth century. Opposing radically the solutions which had emerged from the age of Enlightenment, Joubert's key to the problem of the achievement of stability and justice in society, and virtue and happiness in the individual, lay in a return to the spiritual resources of faith, and in the rediscovery, after a long absence, of God.

NOTE

LUC DE CLAPIERS, MARQUIS DE VAUVENARGUES, 1715–46, friend of Voltaire, led a retiring life in Paris after a military career which shattered his health and his dreams of glory. His *Introduction à la connaissance de l'esprit humain* was published in 1746, followed by a collection of maxims and reflections.

SÉBASTIEN-ROCH-NICOLAS CHAMFORT, 1740–94, first achieved fame as a dramatist with *La Jeune Indienne* (1764). A profound pessimist, his collection of maxims was published posthumously as the *Produits de la civilisation perfectionnée* (1795). Suspect during the Revolution, he died soon after a suicide attempt.

ANTOINE, COMTE DE RIVAROL, 1753–1801, published two collections of literary and political portraits: the *Petit Almanach de nos grands hommes* (1788) and the *Petit Dictionnaire des grands hommes de la Révolution* (1790). He is remembered also for his essay, *De l'homme intellectuel et moral* (1797), and his *Pensées*, edited from notebooks by his brother (1836).

JOSEPH JOUBERT, 1754–1824, did not enter the Paris scene until 1778. His literary activities span the collapse of the *ancien régime* and the early decades of the nineteenth century. A Christian moralist and well-known literary critic, he published little during his lifetime. The *Pensées* appeared in 1838 under the auspices of Chateaubriand.

Modern editions. D. L. Gilbert's edition of Vauvenargues's works (1857) is still satisfactory. H. Gaillard de Champris's *Œuvres choisies* (Aubier, 1942) is useful and scholarly. Chamfort's maxims have appeared in several modern editions, one of the best being that of P. Grosclaude (Collection nationale des classiques français, 1953). The *Maximes et pensées* and *Caractères et anecdotes* are published together, with introduction and notes by C. Roy, in a 'Monde en 10/18' paperback edition. A compact edition of Rivarol's maxims has been produced by V.-H. Debidour (Grasset, 1956). The standard nineteenth-century edition of Joubert's *Pensées*, edited by P. Raynal (9th edn., 1895) is still dependable, although the *Pensées et lettres*, edited by R. Dumay and M. Andrieux (Grasset, 1954) is more convenient.

Criticism. An informative full-length study of Vauvenargues is that of F. Vial, *Une Philosophie et une morale de sentiment: Luc de Clapiers, Marquis de Vauvenargues* (1938). Chamfort's life and work have been covered by J. Teppe, *Chamfort, sa vie, son œuvre, sa pensée* (1950). A. Le Breton's *Rivarol, sa vie, ses idées, son talent* (1895), remains an authoritative introduction to Rivarol. A short but adequate biography of Joubert is available, J. Evans, *The Unselfish Egoist* (1947), and useful chapters on Joubert's work are contained in vol. ii of A. Monglond's *Le Pré-Romantisme français* (1930: reprinted 1966) and in V. Giraud's *Moralistes français* (1923).

12. The Problem of Evil

'WIT without wisdom'; 'a heartless frivolity alternating with a sentimentality as heartless'—in one form or another, in anger or in irony, these judgements of the Enlightenment by Carlyle and Coleridge have been echoed again and again by critics and historians. Shallow, naïve optimism; buoyant confidence in its own possession of absolute knowledge; presumptuous faith in its capacity to refashion the conditions of life; blind inability to appreciate those areas of experience and explanation (religious, aesthetic, and historical) which lie outside a narrowly philosophic vision; all the political follies of the literary imagination and all the literary inadequacies of the politically motivated—such are the ineradicable features of Enlightenment thought, if the commonly accepted picture is accurate. These are the traits from which stemmed both the sparse literature and the political tragedy of eighteenth-century France. The same temper that produced a didactic art bred ideologues whose passion for the reign of virtue was matched only by an astonishing confidence that it could be inaugurated in an effort of the human will. The Revolution was both the culmination of these habits of thought and, in its sinister linking of boundless moral ambition with physical terror, a conclusive proof of the ethical flaws and social menace hidden within the rationalist optimism of the age.

Of course, no interpretation with so long a vogue can be completely without foundation. It gains substance from the notion of progress dominant by the last quarter of the century. In its usual form, this notion spread the faith that men could reshape the world and themselves, that they could so mould the pattern of their existence by the use of reason as to remove those impediments to perfection in this world which were long regarded as endemic in the human condition. In a more radical form, favoured by Condorcet, it predicted an inevitable advance of mind and morals as a result either of a foreordained historical flow or of the necessarily cumulative benefits of scientific investigation.

Yet faith in progress was by no means universal. It was not posed in an articulate and assertive form until, late in the century, Turgot and Condorcet gave it shape and force. Indeed, a strong strain of pessimism runs through the thought of many *philosophes*, and some of the central figures of the age—Montesquieu, Voltaire, and Diderot—expressed vigorous reservations about the constructive capacity of reason, and considerable scepticism about the practicality of even those ideals they shared with others. Nevertheless, although there was more variety in historical philosophies than is often appreciated, the idea of progress was no eccentric sport but was closely related to deep-rooted aspirations and beliefs. As their best-known and most typical venture—the *Encyclopédie*—shows, the *philosophes* were votaries of knowledge and reason, passionate, if inconstant, believers that men now had the techniques by which to see reality as it really is. In their most hopeful moments they believed that this new clarity of vision could provide practical insights and show fresh routes to that highest of values, happiness. For the prudent exploitation of knowledge, of the natural world as a whole but more particularly of man as a creature in nature, could transform the conditions of life and in consequence human nature itself. With the evolution of scientific modes of thought, men had the intellectual tools to remodel the world; if there were doubts, they were whether those with the capacity would have the opportunity, or those with the opportunity would have the will, to reform. It was this weaker faith in the possibility, rather than the certainty, of progress that emerged most typically from the rationalist credo.

Even this qualified and subdued optimism was not achieved without struggle. The *philosophes* did not bask in a comfortable and assured scepticism. Of course, in pressing the claims of individual reason, they challenged old authorities, beliefs, and hierarchies. But, even where the conflict was bitterest, in the assault upon Christianity, they had to fight on the enemy's ground and attack attitudes and concerns defined by the Christian tradition. All had a Christian upbringing; many were originally destined for the priesthood; none was free of tensions between present doubts and past certainties. The damage that intellectual uncertainty inflicted on their emotional balance can clearly be seen in the lives of Rousseau, Diderot, and even Voltaire, so often taken as the paradigm of the urbane, unruffled, and self-confident critic. The genuine anguish that so frequently rocked their intellectual composure rose from a haunting sense of responsibility, a feeling that they must reconstruct a moral and social order which they realized their own critique was—properly—undermining. This practical end, it was felt, required them to face and answer all those problems on which theological explanations had so long been weighed. Thus the Christian tradition largely determined those themes to which the age constantly returned—free will, happiness, mind and body, luxury. Nowhere is this more apparent than in the persistent and ardent debate over the theodicy question.[1] To Voltaire, it was a central and unfortunately unavoidable problem: 'Voici une question des plus difficiles et des plus importantes. Il s'agit de toute la vie humaine' (*Dictionnaire philosophique*). The depth of his concern was not unusual. Nor is it surprising, for the mysticism and quietism of the Christian explanation offended fundamentally the Enlightenment's faith in science and its hopes for reform.

The dilemma was by no means new; as Hume pointed out, it was at least as old as Epicurus. How could the existence of evil be reconciled with the existence of God? How could the only too apparent physical and moral ills besetting mankind be explained in a God-ordained universe? If happiness was a good in itself, as who could doubt it was, how could the author of so much misery possibly be vindicated? The Christian reply, characterized before the Enlightenment by Pascal's tragic vision, placed the guilt on man himself, on this dualistic creature who, given free will as a necessary condition of moral action, had wilfully chosen his fall and wilfully refused the gift of God's grace. The stigma of original sin was the direct cause of all the misery arising from man's inhumanity to man

---

[1] i.e. the problem of the relationship between a just God and a world in which evil and suffering exist (from Gk. *theos*, a god, and *dikē*, justice).

and, in requiring punishment and retribution, the indirect cause of physical scourges. Two examples, from Bayle and Hume, are sufficient to illustrate a general resentment and rejection of this dogma. As in so many cases, Bayle set the terms of the eighteenth-century argument. Typically, in the *Réponse aux questions d'un provincial* (1704–6), the innocence of his conclusion barely hides the bitterness of his real assault. He demonstrates his respectable enough thesis, that reason is unable to resolve the problem of evil, by pointing to the absurdity of previous Christian answers. In particular, he rejects the claim that God had to allow the possibility of bad choices if he was to concede man a status as a moral being. Hume posed the dilemma at its sharpest in his *Dialogues concerning Natural Religion* (publ. 1779). Given the perpetual and undiminishing anguish of all existence, how could human attributes such as benevolence or mercy be ascribed to God? 'Is he willing to prevent evil but not able? then is he impotent. Is he able, but not willing? then is he malevolent. Is he both able and willing? whence then is evil?'

The object of both Bayle's and Hume's attack was not so much the traditional Christian doctrine as the fashionable theory of optimism formulated by King and Leibniz, taken up by many Christian apologists and given its most influential form by Pope. Despite its title, the theory offered few blessings and little hope. Its purpose was not to cure or diminish evil but to explain it or, in the crudest formulation, to deny its existence. In their main lines, the ideas of King and Leibniz coincide. Of all metaphysically possible worlds, this is the one which reaches nearest to perfection. The greatest good on a universal scale can only be achieved within an economy which allows evil in its particular parts; all creation is linked and all in it is necessary to all else. God is not the author of evil, for evil is simply a negative, a limitation or deficiency of perfection. He has created a universe of limited or deficient beings because, given the propriety of creation itself, a perfect universe must enclose a complete spectrum. It must give form to all that can exist without contradiction, and explore all the infinite permutations of deficiency. In the *Essay on Man* (1773–4), Pope enlarged on both these themes— the cosmic utilitarianism which saw all partial evil as contributing to a general good, as well as the principle of plenitude which offered the dubious consolation of a universe logically, and even aesthetically, perfect in its harmony and comprehensiveness. So strongly does he call these bland hosannas that he condemns suffering humanity for voicing its unreasonable complaints, for failing to appreciate the universal order to which its torments necessarily contribute. There was little solace in this comfortable theory and certainly there were few hopes of improvement. The conservative, quietist moral it drew was the virtue of submission to a scheme of things whose very existence was sufficient reason for praise. When it came under fire in the mid-century, it was precisely its practical consequences— its easy denial of men's burdens and its comfortable call to acceptance—that seemed to merit the deepest scorn.

Curiously, the general temper of Christian optimism was reflected in materialist thinking. In denying the reality of the problem of evil, materialists also stressed the necessity of things as they are. For deists such as Voltaire (and Newton himself), the Newtonian 'discovery of fixed and constant laws in physical nature demonstrated a rational *telos* in the universe. But for materialists like La Mettrie, Diderot, and d'Holbach, no such divinely ordained purpose was implied or revealed by scientific advance. They saw in the natural world a perpetual state of flux whose dynamics was determined by chance, the random conjunction of unconnected elements or circumstances, or by the powers of living creatures to adapt to new environments. Given that men had now the means to move towards an understanding of the mechanics of events in nature, they could deflate all the mystic and mythical pretensions with which the past had surrounded forces it could neither comprehend nor control. Earthquake, flood, famine, tempest—all such phenomena could now be stripped of their metaphysical, theological, and moral trappings and be seen in the stark light of material causes rather than the obscurity of final purposes. If the order of nature was no proof of divine intent, there was equally no acceptable evidence of divine violations of the laws of nature, those miracles which the ignorant solicited in prayer and the learned quoted as demonstrations of the beneficent intervention of Providence. For the materialist, the terms of the argument—evil, retribution, sin, punishment—had simply no application to a universe void of moral meaning. All was necessary and had to be accepted, not because this was the best of all possible worlds but because it was the only possible world.

But of course the ripples spread wider than this. For the evils that original sin and optimism purported to explain were moral as well as physical; greed, lust, cruelty, pride—as much as natural disasters—needed a consoling gloss. Here again, although certainly with less confidence and consistency, the materialists argued the irrelevance of the traditional controversy. Once again this brought them paradoxically close to Christian positions. Man, too, was part of nature and was moved by natural necessities and determined forces. An empirical examination of human behaviour showed that traditional doctrine was right in asserting a natural disposition towards what was commonly called evil. Hobbes had opened the case, but La Mettrie put the argument at its baldest and most radical. Self-interest and self-love, cruelty and indifference to others, the attainment of his own goals at the expense of his fellow men, these are basic elements in man's nature. Here La Mettrie was doing no more than extend the psychological commonplaces of the age, for the assumption that the pursuit of happiness was the foundation of all motivational drives went virtually unchallenged. Where he diverged was in dissolving the significance of all moral discourse by this argument. If men were as they were and could be no other, if the instincts and passions that moved them were as fixed and unalterable as the paths of the stars, then what part had praise or blame, approval or disapproval, in our reaction to them? Why should moral judgements intrude on what was solely a psychological, even a physiological matter? Of course few thinkers were willing to follow through this train of argument to its ultimate moral nihilism. La Mettrie himself tried to fit this hedonism within a framework of utilitarian ethics. Diderot, emotionally torn by the intellectual force of the materialist argument, continually fell back upon conscience and feeling as the source of a moral instinct. Indeed, unless Sade is taken to be a serious representative of Enlightenment thought, the *philosophes*—even those most attracted by materialism—continued to treat moral evil as an evil and to seek explanations, if not cures, for man's inhumanity. The general effect of their doctrine was not

to encourage the denial of all values but, like Christian and
deistic optimism, to nurture the passive acceptance of the fact of
evil.

The unholy alliance was apparent at the time. In his *Poème sur le
désastre de Lisbonne* (1756) Voltaire coupled, perhaps unconsciously,
these unlikely partners, linking in common abuse 'tout est bien' and
'ces immuables lois de la nécessité'. Voltaire illustrates well the unhappy, tormented concern with the theodicy problem, and the growing
disillusionment with the optimist solution. A facile assurance that
bears little relation to the sombre Leibnizian doctrine emerges from
his earlier writings. Evil exists in the world but, in the balance, there
is a preponderance of good over evil or, what was to him the same
thing, pleasure over pain; this was his first easy answer. By the time
he wrote *Zadig*, he was engaged more directly with the problem. He
had read and admired Pope's *Essay on Man*, and his tale of destiny
reflects, albeit crudely, Pope's optimism. He does not recklessly
abandon his early faith in a favourable balance sheet. The bluntly
stated moral of the tale is the final victory of patience, common
sense, loyalty, and courage over all adversities of fortune and all the
prejudice and irrational hostility of men. But some doubts cloud the
pleasant prospect. In the parable of the angel Jesrad, Voltaire both
states and mildly questions the theory of optimism. Just when
Zadig is beginning to rebel against his misfortune and murmur
against Providence, he meets the angel disguised as a hermit. The
hermit's wicked and inexplicable acts, his return of theft, arson, and
murder for generosity, are fully explained only when he reveals his
true identity. Each separate act of apparently gratuitous evil is
shown to have prevented an even greater evil: 'Mais quoi! dit
Zadig, il est donc nécessaire qu'il y ait des crimes et des malheurs?'
Yes, for every evil gives rise to a good and the existence of a tainted
world is necessary to the variety of God's creation. Zadig's final 'but',
before the angel disappears, leaves some uncertainty; yet in the end
Zadig, all murmurs against Providence dispelled, falls on his knees
worshipping in true submissiveness. Despite the 'but', this is an
optimism beyond the optimists, calculating not just an over-all
balance of good but a direct return of good on each individual
investment of evil. The doubts were to triumph, however. In his

appalled reaction to the Lisbon earthquake,[1] Voltaire rejects optimism with all the vigour of a recent apostate. Yet, beneath the
violence and sincerity of his passion, there is confusion:

> Tout est bien, dites-vous, et tout est nécessaire.
> Quoi! l'univers entier, sans ce gouffre infernal,
> Sans engloutir Lisbonne, eût-il été plus mal?

He repudiates the comforting theory, but remains with the dilemma
that prompted the theory. Only the inhuman could deny the justice
of the complaints of the maimed and dying. Only the blind could
deny the power of God:

> Il est libre, il est juste, il n'est point implacable.
> Pourquoi donc souffrons-nous sous un maître équitable?

He is back full circle with 'Epicurus's old questions', having rejected the optimists' denial of the reality of evil and the materialists'
denial of the reality of God. Another age, another man might have
urged defiance of a malign Providence. Voltaire counsels merely
that we should accept the mystery as insoluble: 'le livre du sort se
ferme à notre vue.' And, whilst patiently acknowledging the radical
imperfection of our present lot, we must maintain faith in the
future: 'Un jour tout sera bien.' This call was to have revolutionary
implications for other thinkers with a sharper view of the cause of
human misery. Voltaire offers no more than the hope, without any
reasonable grounds for holding to it. His practical advice was to
accept and to submit:

> Humble dans mes soupirs, soumis dans ma souffrance,
> Je ne m'élève point contre la Providence.

All the fury, all the passionate disavowal of optimist explanations,
end only in an exhausted echo of optimist conclusions. The same
root uncertainty invades the most brilliant of his attacks upon
optimism, *Candide* (1759). Unlike Zadig, Candide reaches no final
happiness after his trials. Nothing satisfies, even the achievement of
his most cherished and persistent aims, for which all the pleasures

---

[1] The earthquake of 1755 prompted Voltaire's *Poème sur le désastre de Lisbonne*
(1756).

of Eldorado had been sacrificed. He marries Cunégonde, but only
when both beauty and desire have melted. The final wisdom offered
to us is a stunted creature. Let us win some peace by limiting our
hopes and stifling our questions. We cannot avoid pain but we can
curtail it by exercising grand ambitions and restless doubts. Submission is advised less patiently, but Voltaire can advise little else.

However typical Voltaire's obsessive concern with the problem of
evil, a more impatient and active temper dominated Enlightenment
thought by the mid-century. So long as the problem was set in
a theological context, men were caught in the dilemma of the
justice of their ills or the injustice of God. But the context changed,
and increasingly social causes were found for the moral flaws which
had been seen as endemic disorders of the soul. Theology gave way
to a social psychology which, no matter how tangled and primitive,
sparked expectations previously deadened by the conviction that
vice and cruelty sprang from imperfections no human agency could
remove. Stated crudely, the change is startling and revolutionary.
What had been imputed to radical defects in each individual soul
was now ascribed to removable defects in society; what had been
thought the awful effects of God's judgement now became the less
profoundly menacing effects of man's misjudgement; what had
been a permanent shadow on existence, lightened only by prayer
and prostration, became a mist which could be dispelled by the
full light of reason. This new conviction that we must look to society,
not to God or the soul, for the source of human misery, forced
a massive reassessment of the role of politics in human life. The
Christian tradition did not speak of this with any clear voice. The
Pauline dualism of flesh and spirit, as interpreted by Augustine,
relegated social institutions, and particularly the state, to a watch-
dog role. Social institutions could cage the rapacious demands of
man's instinctive drives, curbing what was degraded, but they could
not, any more than the instincts themselves, aid the fulfilment of
man's highest aspirations to God. The virtues of renunciation were
challenged in Thomist thought. Government, the family, property
—all the institutions that regulated yet conceded the claims of
instinctive life—were not simply negative restraints on human

bestiality but positive means towards moral progress. Although this more humane Aristotelianism gave a moral role to the state unknown to the Augustinian tradition, it was still far from the position of the later Enlightenment. For now the state and political action were not just routes by which to turn to good instincts that are potentially evil, but means by which to alter instinctive life itself. On to society was thrust a new moral responsibility for the pains men suffer and the vices they carry in them. Government became more than an arbiter in the peripheral conflicts of self-interested men, more even than a translator of God's law into civil law. With the full powers given by newly acquired knowledge, it emerged as the master of human nature itself, a new creator which could take the feeble, divided creature of Christian theology and make of him a wholly virtuous man. This persistently moral urge to reform most distinctively marks the social thinking of the *philosophes*, and this is owed to the theological origins of its ambitions. The belief of the *philosophes* in the possibility of reform, their belief that men had now the tools to refashion society, derived from the pervasive faith in scientific method; but their immense expectations of reform drew life from the conviction that for the first time men had an answer to the problem of evil which allowed them not merely to explain the world but to change it.

The breach with the Christian answer was at its widest in the thinker who most vigorously declared his attachment to the old faith and most violently denounced the scepticism of his fellow philosophers. In his *Confessions* (written 1764–70), Rousseau reveals both his break with the past and the strength of the new moral ambition:

J'avais vu que tout tenait radicalement à la politique, et que, de quelque façon qu'on s'y prît, aucun peuple ne serait jamais que ce que la nature de son gouvernement le ferait être; ainsi cette grande question du meilleur gouvernement possible me paraissait se réduire à celle-ci: Quelle est la nature du gouvernement propre à former le peuple le plus vertueux, le plus éclairé, le plus sage, le meilleur enfin, à prendre ce mot dans son plus grand sens.

In this indirect response to the theodicy problem, he made a much more substantial, radical, and influential statement than when he

addressed it directly. In the *Lettre sur la Providence* (1756), he answered
what he saw as Voltaire's complaint against God by reiterating the
optimist commonplaces. Pain is not predominant, and the divine
economist limits evil though he cannot logically exclude it. It is
imperfect man, not an impotent or unjust God, who is guilty of
the flaws in creation. Yet even here a novel note is struck, for it is
man in general, rather than men as individuals, who stands accused.
Corrupted men are as innocent as God himself, for the blame lies
on the corrupting agent, society. It was not Voltaire's rebellion that
was the root offence; it was his lack of hope. And the hope Rousseau
offered was that what man had done he could undo; deliverance
would come not through God's grace but through man's endeavours.

The simple attribution of evil to social causes in itself settled
little, for it left unanswered the prior question of how the social
distortion that brought about moral deformity had occurred. But it
did determine the character of the answer. If men were not corrup-
ters of society but corrupted by it, if it was social institutions that
prevented the full realization of the potentialities of man in the
abstract, man in nature, an explanation of his decline had to be
sought in history rather than in metaphysics or theology. What, in
the course of social development, had obstructed moral progress and
given birth to those vices so alien to mankind's true nature? One
crude, stark, and (if its persistence is any guide) attractive answer
came from the theory of conspiracy. The mass of men are deluded
and vicious because it has been in the interests of other men so to
debase them. D'Holbach, whose thought seemed 'so grey, so chim-
erical, so deathlike' to Goethe, and who was yet so passionate a
rationalist, links his atheism to his social radicalism by this theory.
To maintain their power and position, kings and clerics have
created and perpetuated the ignorance on which moral corruption
feeds: 'L'homme fut une pure machine entre les mains de ses
tyrans et ses prêtres, qui seuls eurent le droit de régler ses mouve-
mens: conduit toujours en esclave, il en eut presqu'en tout temps et
en tous lieux les vices et le caractère. Voilà les véritables sources de
la corruption des mœurs' (*Le bon sens*, 1772). The corrupting few
and the corrupted many, the innocent multitude threatened or sub-
verted by conspiratorial machinations—this simple theme, effective

perhaps because of its simplicity, has been a political clarion-call from Robespierre and Barruel to Stalin and McCarthy.

However, the Enlightenment had other and more subtle answers to the paradox of moral man in immoral society. These did not rely on the destructive effects of class conflict and exploitation to explain social degeneracy. They pointed, as the causes of moral discord, to divisions and tensions within the individual psyche brought about by a clash between instinctive (or 'natural') energies and the pressure of social conformity. A disharmony of social arrangements, requiring men's suppression of their most deeply felt urges and the frustration of their highest aspirations, was reflected in individual alienation, in an inner schism that estranged men from their social environment and left them feeble in their purposes and uncertain of their true identity. Two writers above all explored this novel conception of the origins of evil: Diderot and Rousseau.

In the *Supplément au Voyage de Bougainville* (written 1772), Diderot takes the image of the innocent, uncorrupted Tahitian and uses it to decipher the ills of civilized man. The confused, divided, and tortured Western man (represented inevitably in the chaplain), whose moral promptings constantly war with the demands of his instincts, is contrasted with the emotionally balanced and morally stable primitive, whose happy social state asks of him no actions that run counter to his passions. This ideal society, whose moral code reflects and satisfies actual human needs, fosters the virtues of love, sympathy, and kindness. Civilized society, opposing duty to natural impulse, breeds men driven by the opposite but complementary vices of pride and false shame.

By escaping the easy inversion of nature and culture, primitive and civilized, Rousseau extends and deepens this argument. In the *Discours sur l'inégalité* (1754), he rejects the use of natural, pre-social man as a stick with which to beat civilization. He attacks the notion implicit in previous social contract theories that men were conscious creators of society and could conceive outside it the sort of purposes which can be pursued within it. Man becomes a moral being only by living in a community. It is only within a situation of stable relationships that settled claims and duties can grow, and only there that men can begin to recognize themselves as moral persons, recipients of rights and owners of obligations. Society is not an artificial construct made by far-sighted men of nature, nor are moral codes merely rules of prudence designed to reach more efficiently constant and persistent ends. For the emergence of men as social creatures involved another resurrection, the death of natural, amoral man with no conception of good or aspiration towards it and the birth of moral man who feels the need not only to satisfy his desires but to lead a worthwhile life, and who is self-critical because he is self-conscious. Thus the development of society presents men with opportunities and capacities previously closed to them. At the same time, the societies that have historically arisen, though they have given men a conception of good, have not inclined them towards it. Largely because of the inequality on which they are based, they have been corrupting influences, nurturing vanity and aggressiveness and so creating desires which deprive their members partially of their ability to act well; but only partially, for there remains within men (and this is the sense in which they are 'naturally' good) a desire for love, benevolence, and justice in their relations with others. This desire, this conscience as Rousseau calls it, is not extinguished by a perverted society. It is not strong enough to prevent the hegemony of avarice and ambition, but it is never so weak that vice can enjoy ease. From the opposing promptings of conscience and social *mores* arises the disquiet of men who feel that they are acting traitor to their own best selves and who are haunted by the sense that they do what they would not and do not what they would. From this inner conflict springs that feeling of self-betrayal, that divorce between the individual and his human environment, which Hegel and Marx were to call alienation. Yet it was precisely from this dissatisfaction that Rousseau could draw hope, for the existence of this tension suggested that, no matter how urgently driven by social pressures, men always retained an impulse to virtue which could be used both to discover and to create a new moral and social order.

Despite his notorious paradoxes and ambiguity, Rousseau was the most articulate and sensitive exponent of the view that social dislocation was the root of moral evil. This diagnosis, common by the mid-century although usually less subtly argued, dictated a cure more thorough and complete than Christian repentance. Previously, the disease had been relieved by the palliative of divine grace; now it could be eradicated by swift political surgery. At this point the consensus broke down, for, whilst most *philosophes* agreed that social reorganization would bring incalculable moral benefits, they could not agree on how society should be reconstructed or even on what the criteria for reconstruction should be. What was the good society, and how could it be discerned? These were questions that prompted a variety of answers.

The obvious frame of reference was the traditional theory of natural law, and it was in the French and American declarations of rights that this theory gained its most obvious practical victories. Yet no concept was more confused in eighteenth-century thought than 'nature', and no criterion less capable of providing a coherent or agreed social blueprint. In its older Christian formulation, natural law was the order God had ordained for the universe. That part of the divine order relating to man differed from the laws governing the brute or inanimate creation, in that it did not determine behaviour but simply suggested proper action. Unlike animals, men possessed the divine gift of free will, but they were not left floundering in uncharted seas. By the use of the other divine gift of reason they could discover how they ought to live in order to fulfil God's purposes. Already in the seventeenth century this scheme had been modified. In the first place, it had narrowed down to a theory of natural rights. The Thomist tradition had seen natural law as laying down duties and obligations. By the use of inborn reason, *lumen naturale*, men could appreciate the ends of terrestrial life and in consequence their responsibilities to others. In the thought of Locke, for example, reason taught them rather what claims they could make against others. It was largely in this form that the Enlightenment inherited the theory, and it was used in the main to erect a protective dyke between the individual and government. Seventeenth-century thinkers as different as Hobbes and Grotius also divorced natural law from the will of God. By arguing that it had an inherent validity and a self-evident rationality which made it convincing even without divine instruction, they enabled the theory to survive even when its old theological basis was questioned. It was this concession that persuaded philosophic deists and atheists to cling to a theory in many ways alien to their most cherished ideas. For the belief in the rational discovery of *a priori* truths ran directly counter to the Enlightenment's much vaunted commitment to the methods of empirical inquiry and to the sensationalist epistemology which was thought to be both the basis and a consequence of these methods. No truths seemed so unequivocal as those announced by Bacon, Newton, and Locke—that we can know with certainty only what experience or experiment teach us and that our ideas are all either impressions of the external world received through our senses, or deductions we make from those impressions. The tension is apparent in Locke who, despite his attack on innate ideas, retains natural law as a central theme in his social theory. In France, it shows in the reluctance of Voltaire, perhaps the most ardent apostle of British empiricism, to discard the comforting ethical stability provided by natural law. Although he accepted that there are no moral ideas instinct within men, throughout his life he insisted that a universal morality, perceptible and valid at all times and in all places, arises from common human reactions to a common human condition. The similarity of our experience gives birth to commonly held ethical norms by which we can judge both ourselves and our society.

In this way, Voltaire tried to maintain a natural (in the sense of universally valid) morality, together with a sensationalist theory of knowledge. In doing so he moved towards a criterion for social reconstruction that was to prove more generally acceptable than natural law. Closely associated with sensationalism was a hedonist psychological theory: just as men derived their ideas from the senses, so they were moved to action by their desire to maximize pleasurable, and to minimize painful, sensations. 'The pursuit of happiness' was sufficiently ambiguous a description of human motivation to stimulate a complex and confused debate, but behind the controversy lay a few root assumptions. All experience teaches us that attraction to pleasure and aversion to pain determine the courses men pursue. It is also in this pursuit that they form moral feelings. When they come into contact with other men, they are forced to recognize the claims that others have upon them, either because they can sympathetically substitute themselves for others and share their pains or because they realize the achievement of their own happiness requires a prudential regard for the interests of others. So hedonism provided an account of men's motives and of the origins of moral feelings. Still more was demanded of it, for it became the basis of a prescrip-tive moral theory. It offered, in utilitarian philosophy, a clue not only to the reasons men act as they do and how they come to make moral judgements, but to the proper basis for those judgements. Helvétius's disciple, Bentham, puts the dual role of the pleasure-pain principle succinctly: 'Nature has placed mankind under the governance of two sovereign masters, *pain* and *pleasure*. It is for them alone to point out what we ought to do, as well as to determine what we shall do' (*Introduction to the Principles of Morals and Legislation*, 1789). Here, plainly, psychological description is translated into moral prescription. And, given a much narrower definition of pleasure than the moral philosophers would have allowed, it justifies the credo of Rameau's nephew, of Valmont, and of other libertine heroes. The philosophers did not intend to sanctify all felt desires, for they had a much wider point of reference than the individual when they talked of pleasure or happiness. As a moral theory, utilitarianism took all the effects of an action into account when reckoning its moral worth, not just the effects upon the actor him-self. Virtue is not that which adds to my happiness but that which benefits all mankind, and the interest to be protected by moral codes is not self-interest but the general interest: 'Ce n'est pas l'intérêt personnel et passager d'un individu, d'un prince, d'une nation qui doit être la mesure des jugements que nous portons sur la conduite des hommes, c'est l'intérêt permanent de l'homme; c'est l'utilité constante de la Société, de l'espèce humaine, qui doivent fixer nos idées' (d'Holbach, *Système social*, 1773). So moral anarchy was avoided, but a yawning gap was left between description and prescription, between the 'is' and the 'ought'. Why should men, constitutionally absorbed in the pursuit of their own happiness, follow 'l'utilité constante de la Société'?

The gap was bridged in different ways. Some refused to recognize its existence, claiming that, in the pursuit of their own happiness, men automatically further the general good. Mandeville's dictum, 'private vices, public benefits', found its most influential advocates in Adam Smith and the Physiocrats and its most lasting monument in the new science of political economy. Others argued with Rousseau that, as our desires are essentially social and sympathetic, our true or our fullest happiness can be attained only along the path of virtue. Virtue, because it is lovable, is useful or conducive to happiness. However, the dominant argument, particularly amongst the Encyclopedists, was that virtue, because it is useful, is lovable. If we understood our interest aright, we would see the indissoluble connection between our happiness and the interest of all. To maximize our own welfare, we must take the well-being of others into account. If we follow our enlightened self-interest in this way, the old tensions between duty and desire, instinct and obligation, will disappear.

This moral theory was critical as well as explanatory. It sought to give a standard for assessing different moral codes and, in a corrupt society, for reconstructing them. By the same token, it provided a measure by which to judge government and legislation, whose ends were identical with those of morality: 'Unir l'intérêt au devoir, voilà le grand art de la morale et de la législation' (*Système social*). The greatest happiness was the proper objective of the legislator; and, because he could now know the real springs of action, he could ensure the reconciliation of duty and interest, pushing people here, restraining them there, by the judicious use of reward and punishment.

If the standard was clear, the implications were not. There was little agreement on what laws or institutions would create the general happiness, despite the continual assertion by different writers that their recommendations, and only their recommendations, were immediately obvious to universal reason. Some wished to restrict the scope of politics, others to extend it; some wanted to divide power, others to consolidate it; some saw salvation in an enlightened monarch, others in the advent of democracy. Yet behind the confusion there can be heard a common theme. Man's quest for happiness defines what the ideal community should be and indicates how it can be attained.

This confidence reached its height in the writings of d'Holbach and Helvétius. They have attracted, and perhaps deserved, much of the criticism levelled against Enlightenment thought. If the charges of shallow optimism and meanness of vision can be made at all, they should be directed against these extreme utilitarians. Nevertheless, even when faced with their broad and unmitigated hopes, it would be wrong to characterize the Enlightenment's expectations as the fruit of insensitive blindness to moral dilemmas which have racked other ages. The very intensity and scope of the philosophers' dreams stemmed from their belief that they had successfully confronted the problem of evil. Their ideas can only be understood against the background of this obsessive moral concern. They were revolutionary because they predicted that a final solution was at best inevitable and at worst possible. But these hopes of a total transformation were not born of a simple and sunny disregard for moral complexity and the difficulties of social change. Indeed, they relied on dissatisfaction and a sense of moral inadequacy as the motive force of change. They rested on the fundamental conviction that we can fruitfully exploit, rather than passively accept, the doubts, ambiguities, perplexities, self-blame, and bewilderment that beset us when we examine our involved moral experience.

NOTE

Some primary sources. Bayle, *Dictionnaire historique et critique* (1697, revised 1702), especially the articles on 'Manichéens' and 'Pauliciens', *Réponse aux questions d'un provincial* (1704–6); Pope, *Essay on Man* (1733–4); Hume, *Dialogues concerning Natural Religion* (1779); Voltaire, *Zadig* (1747), *Poème sur le désastre de Lisbonne* (1756), *Candide* (1759), *Dictionnaire philosophique* (1764), especially articles 'Bien, souverain bien', 'Bien, du bien et du mal, physique et moral', and 'Bien, tout est bien'; La Mettrie, *L'Homme machine* (1748); Diderot, *Le Neveu de Rameau* (written 1762), *Supplément au Voyage de Bougainville* (1796, written 1772); d'Holbach, *Système social* (1773); Rousseau, *Discours sur l'inégalité parmi les hommes* (1754), *Lettre sur la Providence* (to Voltaire, 8 August 1756), *Du contrat social* (1762).

Secondary sources. T. Besterman, 'Voltaire et le désastre de Lisbonne: ou, la mort de l'optimisme' in Besterman, ed., *Studies on Voltaire and the Eighteenth Century*, vol. ii (1956); P. Hazard, 'Le problème du mal', *Romanic Review*, vol. xxxii (1941); J. Hick, *Evil and the God of Love* (1966); A. O. Lovejoy, *The Great Chain of Being* (1936), Chapter VII, 'The Principle of Plenitude and Eighteenth Century Optimism'; A. D. Sertillanges, *Le Problème du mal* (1948–51: 2 vols.);

R. A. Tsanoff, *The Nature of Evil* (1931); C. Werner, *Le Problème du mal dans la pensée humaine* (1946).

General studies on the Enlightenment. C. Becker, *The Heavenly City of the Eighteenth Century Philosophers* (1959); E. Cassirer, *The Philosophy of the Enlightenment* (1951); A. Cobban, *In Search of Humanity* (1960); L. G. Crocker, *The Age of Crisis* (1959), *Nature and Culture* (1963); P. Gay, *The Party of Humanity* (1964); P. Hazard, *La Pensée européenne au XVIIIe siècle* (1946).

CHRONOLOGY

History	French literature	English and German literature
	Fénelon, *Télémaque* (1699)	
		Dryden died, 1700
		Congreve, *The Way of the World* (1700)
War of the Spanish Succession, 1701–13		
Camisard rebellion in Cévennes, 1702–5		
French defeat at Blenheim, 1704		
French defeat at Ramillies, 1706		Farquhar, *The Recruiting Officer* (1706)
	Lesage, *Le Diable boiteux* (1707; rev. edn. 1726)	Farquhar, *The Beaux' Stratagem* (1707)
	Regnard, *Le Légataire universel* (1708)	
French defeat at Malplaquet, 1709	Lesage, *Turcaret* (1709)	
		Steele and Addison, *The Spectator* (1711–12)
		Pope, *The Rape of the Lock* (1712)
Bull Unigenitus, 1713		Addison, *Cato* (1713)
Peace of Utrecht, 1713–15		
Louis XIV died, 1715 (reigned, 1643–1715)	Lesage, *Gil Blas* (1715–35)	Pope's translation of *Iliad* (1715–20)
Accession of Louis XV, 1715		
Regency of duc d'Orléans, 1715–23		

Painting and music	Criticism and aesthetic theory	Ideas and philosophy
		Newton, *Philosophiae Naturalis Principia Mathematica* (1687)
Corelli, 1653–1713 (*Concerti grossi, c.* 1713)		Locke, *Essay concerning Human Understanding* (1690)
Largillière, 1656–1746		Locke, *Treatises of Government* (1690)
A. Scarlatti, 1660–1725		Bayle, *Dictionnaire historique et critique* (1697)
Couperin, 1668–1733 (4 *Livres de clavecin*: 1713–30)	Boileau, *Lettres à Perrault* (1700)	
Vivaldi, *c.* 1676–1741		
Piazzetta, 1682–1754		
Rameau, 1683–1764 (*Les Indes galantes*, 1735; *Castor et Pollux*, 1737; *Dardanus*, 1739)		
Watteau, 1684–1721	Swift, *The Battle of the Books* (1704)	Newton, *Optics* (1704)
		Berkeley, *Essay towards a new Theory of Vision* (1709)
	Boileau, *Trois nouvelles réflexions sur Longin* (1710)	Berkeley, *The Principles of Human Knowledge* (1710)
		Leibniz, *Theodicy: Essays on the Goodness of God, the Freedom of Man and the Origin of Evil* (1710)
	Pope, *An Essay on Criticism* (1711)	
	Addison, *The Spectator* (1711–14)	Berkeley, *Three Dialogues between Hylas and Philonus* (1713)
J. S. Bach, 1685–1750 (*Brandenburg Concertos*, 1721; *St. Matthew Passion*, 1729; *Mass in B minor*, 1733?–8)		Abbé de Saint-Pierre, *Projet de paix perpétuelle* (1713–17)
D. Scarlatti, 1685–1757		Leibniz, *Monadology* (1714)

History	French literature	English and German literature
Law's Bank and East India Company, 1716		
	Marivaux, *L'Iliade travestie* (1717) and *Le Télémaque travesti* (written 1717)	
		Defoe, *Robinson Crusoe* (1719)
	Marivaux, *Annibal* (1720) Montesquieu, *Lettres persanes* (1721)	
	Marivaux, *La (Première) Surprise de l'amour* (1722)	Defoe, *Moll Flanders* (1722)
Reign of Louis XV, 1723–74		
	Marivaux, *L'Île des esclaves* (1725)	Pope's translation of *Odyssey* (1725–6)
Cardinal Fleury chief minister, 1726–43		Swift, *Gulliver's Travels* (1726)
	Prévost, *Mémoires et aventures d'un homme de qualité* (1728–31)	Gay, *The Beggar's Opera* (1728) Pope, *Dunciad* (1728)
	Marivaux, *Le Jeu de l'amour et du hasard* (1730)	Thomson, *The Seasons* (1730)
Treaty of Vienna, 1731	Marivaux, *La Vie de Marianne* (1731–41)	
	Prévost, *Manon Lescaut* (1731)	
	Prévost, *Le Philosophe anglais ou l'histoire de M. Cleveland* (1732–9)	
Outbreak of War of the Polish Succession, 1733		
	Marivaux, *Le Paysan parvenu* (1734–5)	Pope, *Essay on Man* (1734)
	Saint-Simon, *Mémoires* (1734–53)	

Painting and music	Criticism and aesthetic theory	Ideas and philosophy
Handel, 1685–1759 (*Water Music*, 1717; *Messiah*, 1741; *Music for Royal Fireworks*, 1749)		
Nattier, 1685–1766		Keill, *Introductio ad veram*
Geminiani, 1687–1762		*astronomiam* (1718)
Lancret, 1690–1743	Du Bos, *Réflexions critiques sur la poésie et la peinture* (1719)	
Daquin, 1694–1772		's Gravesande, *Physices Elementa* (1720–1)
Tiepolo, 1696–1769	Marivaux, *Le Spectateur français* (1722)	
Hogarth, 1697–1764		
		Vico, *La scienza nuova* (1725–30)
		Fontenelle, *Éloge de Newton* (1727)
		Pemberton, *A View of Sir Isaac Newton's Philosophy* (1728)
	Gottsched, *Versuch einer critischen Dichtkunst vor die Deutschen* (1730)	
Canaletto, 1697–1768		Maupertuis, *Discours sur les différentes figures des astres* (1732)
	Voltaire, *Le Temple du goût* (1733)	Pope, *Essay on Man* (1733–4)
		Voltaire, *Lettres philosophiques* (1734)
		Montesquieu, *Considérations sur les causes de la grandeur des Romains et de leur décadence* (1734)

History	French literature	English and German literature
	Prévost, *Le Doyen de Killerine* (1735–40)	
	Marivaux, *Le Legs* (1736)	
	Crébillon *fils*, *Les Égarements du cœur et de l'esprit* (1736–8)	
Fall of Chauvelin, 1737	Marivaux, *Les fausses confidences* (1737)	
Treaty of Vienna, 1738		
Death of Emperor Charles VI, 1740	Marivaux, *L'Épreuve* (1740)	Richardson, *Pamela* (1740)
Frederick II becomes King of Prussia, 1740 (reigned 1740–86)		
Franco-Prussian Alliance (1741)	Duclos, *Les Confessions du Comte de **** (1741)	
War of the Austrian Succession, 1741–8	La Chaussée, *Mélanide* (1741)	
	Prévost, *Histoire d'une Grecque moderne* (1741)	
	Voltaire, *Mahomet* (1742) Crébillon *fils*, *Le Sopha* (1742)	Young, *Night Thoughts* (1742)
France declares war on England, 1744		
Victory of Maréchal de Saxe at battle of Fontenoy, 1745		
French conquer Madras, 1746	Vauvenargues, *Œuvres* (1746)	
	Voltaire, *Zadig* (1747)	
Treaty of Aix-la-Chapelle ends War of the Austrian Succession, 1748	Diderot, *Les Bijoux indiscrets* (1748)	Klopstock, *Der Messias* (1748–73)
		Smollett, *Roderick Random* (1748)

Painting and music	Criticism and aesthetic theory	Ideas and philosophy
Chardin, 1699–1779	Desfontaines, *Observations sur les écrits modernes* (1735–43)	Linnaeus, *Systema Naturae* (1735)
		Deslandes, *Recueil de différents traités de physique* (1736)
Longhi, 1702–85		
		Hume, *A Treatise of Human Nature* (1739–40)
	Fontenelle, *Réflexions sur la poétique* (1742)	
Boucher, 1703–70		
		La Mettrie, *Histoire naturelle de l'âme* (1745)
	Batteux, *Les Beaux-Arts réduits à un seul principe* (1746)	Diderot, *Pensées philosophiques* (1746)
		Condillac, *Essai sur l'origine des connaissances humaines* (1746)
		Diderot, *Promenade du sceptique* (written 1747, publ. 1830)
		Montesquieu, *De l'esprit des lois* (1748)

History	French literature	English and German literature
		Richardson, *Clarissa Harlowe* (1749)
		Fielding, *Tom Jones* (1749)
	Marivaux, *La Colonie* (1750)	
		Smollett, *Peregrine Pickle* (1751)
		Gray, *Elegy Written in a Country Churchyard* (1751)
	Voltaire, *Micromégas* (1752)	
	Crébillon *fils, Les heureux orphelins* (1754)	
Lisbon earthquake, 1755 (30,000 killed)	Crébillon *fils, La Nuit et le moment* (1755)	
Seven Years War, 1756–63	Voltaire, *Poème sur le désastre de Lisbonne* (1756)	

Painting and music	Criticism and aesthetic theory	Ideas and philosophy
La Tour, 1704–88		La Mettrie, *L'Homme machine* (1748)
Pergolesi, 1710–36 (*Stabat Mater*, 1736)		Buffon, *Histoire naturelle* (1749–88)
Boyce, 1710–79		Diderot, *Lettre sur les aveugles* (1749)
Guardi, 1712–93		Condillac, *Traité des systèmes* (1749)
	Johnson, *The Rambler* (1750–2)	Duclos, *Considérations sur les mœurs* (1750)
		Turgot, *Discours en Sorbonne* (1750)
		Rousseau, *Discours sur les sciences et les arts* (1750)
Ramsay, 1713–84	Fontenelle, *Traité sur la poésie en général* (1751)	Voltaire, *Le Siècle de Louis XIV* (1751)
		Publication of *Encyclopédie* (1751–72)
		Hume, *An Enquiry concerning the Principles of Morals* (1751)
Rousseau, *Le Devin du village* (1752)		
	Buffon, *Discours sur le style* (1753)	
	Grimm, *Correspondance littéraire* (1754–73)	Diderot, *Pensées sur l'interprétation de la nature* (1754)
		Rousseau, *Discours sur l'inégalité parmi les hommes* (1754)
		Condillac, *Traité des sensations* (1754)
Wilson, 1714–82		Morelly, *Code de la nature* (1755)
	Warton, *Essay on the Genius and Writings of Pope* (1756 and 1782)	Burke, *A Philosophical Inquiry into the Origin of our Ideas of the Sublime and Beautiful* (1756)
Gluck, 1714–87 (*Orfeo*, 1762)		Voltaire, *Essai sur les mœurs* (1756)

History	French literature	English and German literature
	Diderot, *Le Fils naturel* (1757)	
Choiseul Foreign Secretary and effective First Minister, 1758–70	Diderot, *Le Père de famille* (1758)	
French defeat at battle of Minden and loss of Quebec, Guadeloupe, Martinique, etc., 1759	Voltaire, *Candide* (1759)	Johnson, *Rasselas* (1759)
French naval defeats at Lagos and Quiberon Bay, 1759		
	Diderot, *La Religieuse* (written 1760, publ. 1796)	Sterne, *Tristram Shandy* (1760–7)
		Macpherson, *Fragments of Ancient Poetry translated from the Gaelic (Ossian)* (1760)
	Marmontel, *Contes moraux* (1761)	
	Rousseau, *Julie, ou la Nouvelle Héloïse* (1761)	
Calas executed, 1762	Diderot, *Le Neveu de Rameau* (1762)	Macpherson, *Fingal* (1762)
Catherine II of Russia reigned, 1762–96		
Peace of Paris, 1763		*Temora* (1763)
Dissolution of Jesuits in France, 1764	Rousseau, *Confessions* (written 1764–70, publ. 1782 and 1789)	Walpole, *The Castle of Otranto* (1764)

Painting and music	Criticism and aesthetic theory	Ideas and philosophy
	Marmontel: article 'Critique' in the *Encyclopédie* (1757)	
C. P. E. Bach, 1714–88	Montesquieu: article 'Goût' in the *Encyclopédie* (1757)	
	Diderot, *Entretiens sur le Fils naturel* (1757)	
Reynolds, 1723–92	Rousseau, *Lettre à d'Alembert sur les spectacles* (1758)	Helvétius, *De l'esprit* (1758)
	Diderot, *Discours sur la poésie dramatique* (1758)	
		Diderot, *Lettre sur les sourds et muets* (1759)
Greuze, 1725–1805		
Gainsborough, 1727–88		
Fragonard, 1732–1806		
Haydn, 1732–1809 (*Military* and *Clock Symphonies*, 1794; *Creation*, 1798)	Diderot, *Éloge de Richardson* (1761)	
		Rousseau, *Du Contrat social* (1762)
		Rousseau, *Émile* (1762)
J. C. F. Bach, 1732–95		
		Voltaire, *Traité sur la tolérance* (1763)
	Wincklemann, *Geschichte der Kunst des Alterthums* (1764)	Voltaire, *Dictionnaire philosophique* (1764)
		Reid, *Inquiry into the Human Mind* (1764)

History	French literature	English and German literature
	Sedaine, *Le Philosophe sans le savoir* (1765)	Percy, *Reliques* (1765)
Lorraine becomes part of France, 1766		Goldsmith, *The Vicar of Wakefield* (1766)
		Wieland, *Geschichte des Agathon* (1766–7)
Bougainville circum-navigates world, 1767–9	Beaumarchais, *Eugénie* (1767)	
		Sterne, *A Sentimental Journey* (1768)
Maupeou reform of Parlement, 1770	Beaumarchais, *Les deux amis* (1770)	Goldsmith, *The Deserted Village* (1770)
	Crébillon *fils, Lettres athéniennes* (1771)	Smollett, *Humphry Clinker* (1771)
		Klopstock, *Oden* (1771)
	Diderot, *Jacques le fataliste* (written 1773, publ. 1796)	Bürger, *Leonore* (1773)
		Goldsmith, *She Stoops to Conquer* (1773)
		Goethe, *Götz von Berlichingen* (1773)
Accession of Louis XVI, 1774 (executed 1793)		Goethe, *Die Leiden des jungen Werthers* (1774)
Ministries of Turgot (1774–6) and Necker (1776–81)		

Painting and music	Criticism and aesthetic theory	Ideas and philosophy
	Diderot, *Essais sur la peinture* (written 1765, posth. publ. 1795)	
	Diderot, *Salon de 1765*	
Zoffany, 1733–1810	Lessing, *Laokoon* (1766)	
	Beaumarchais, *Essai sur le genre dramatique sérieux* (1767)	
Romney, 1734–1802	Lessing, *Die Hamburgische Dramaturgie* (1767–8)	
		Diderot, *Le Rêve de d'Alembert* (written 1769, publ. 1830)
J. C. Bach, 1735–82		D'Holbach, *Système de la nature* (1770)
		First edition of *Encyclopaedia Britannica* (1771)
		Helvétius, *De l'homme* (posth. publ. 1772)
		Diderot, *Supplément au Voyage de Bougainville* (written 1772, publ. 1796)
Grétry, 1741–1813	Diderot, *Paradoxe sur le comédien* (written 1773–8, publ. 1830)	D'Holbach, *Système social* (1773)
Goya, 1746–1828		
		Diderot, *Éléments de physiologie* (1774–80)

History	French literature	English and German literature
American War of Independence (1775–83) (Declaration of Independence, 1776; France enters war, 1778)	Restif de la Bretonne, *Le Paysan perverti* (1775) Beaumarchais, *Le Barbier de Séville* (1775) Rousseau, *Rêveries du promeneur solitaire* (written 1776–8)	Sheridan, *The Rivals* (1775)
		Sheridan, *The School for Scandal* (1777)
	Restif de la Bretonne, *La Vie de mon père* (1779)	Lessing, *Nathan der Weise* (1779)
		Wieland, *Oberon* (1780)
	Diderot, *Est-il bon? Est-il méchant?* (1781)	Schiller, *Die Räuber* (1781)
	Rousseau, *Dialogues* (1782)	
	Laclos, *Les Liaisons dangereuses* (1782)	
Peace of Versailles, 1783		Schiller, *Fiesko* (1783)
	Beaumarchais, *Le Mariage de Figaro* (1784)	Schiller, *Kabale und Liebe* (1784)
	Restif de la Bretonne, *La Paysanne pervertie* (1784)	
Death of Frederick the Great, 1786		Burns, *Poems* (1786)
	Bernardin de Saint-Pierre, *Paul et Virginie* (1787)	
	Rivarol, *Petit Almanach de nos grands hommes* (1788)	
Fall of Bastille, 1789 *Déclaration des droits de l'homme*, 1789		Blake, *Songs of Innocence* (1789)
	Rivarol, *Petit Dictionnaire des grands hommes de la Révolution* (1790)	

Painting and music	Criticism and aesthetic theory	Ideas and philosophy
David, 1748–1825		
		Gibbon, *Decline and Fall of the Roman Empire* (1776)
		Adam Smith, *The Wealth of Nations* (1776)
Clementi, 1752–1832		
	Johnson, *The Lives of the Poets* (1779–81)	Hume, *Dialogues concerning Natural Religion* (1779)
		Diderot, *Essai sur Sénèque* (1779)
Mozart, 1756–91 (*Don Giovanni*, 1787; *Jupiter Symphony*, 1788; *Magic Flute*, 1791; *Requiem*, 1791)		Kant, *Kritik der reinen Vernunft* (1781)
Raeburn, 1756–1823		
	Rivarol, *Discours de l'universalité de la langue française* (1784)	Herder, *Ideen zur Philosophie der Geschichte der Menschheit* (1784–91)
Blake, 1757–1827		Reid, *Essay on the Intellectual Powers of Man* (1785)
Crome, 1768–1821	Alfieri, *Del principe e delle lettere* (1788)	Kant, *Kritik der praktischen Vernunft* (1788)
Laurence, 1769–1830		Bentham, *Introduction to the Principles of Morals and Legislation* (1789)
		Burke, *Reflections on the French Revolution* (1790)

History	French literature	English and German literature
Death of Mirabeau, 1791 Flight to Varennes, 1791	Sade, *Justine, ou les malheurs de la vertu* (1791)	Boswell, *The Life of Samuel Johnson* (1791)
September Massacres, 1792 French victory at Jemappes, 1792	Beaumarchais, *La Mère coupable* (1792)	
Vendée revolt, 1793		
Assassination of Marat, 1793		
Fall of Robespierre, 1794	Chénier, *Iambes* (1794)	Mrs. Radcliffe, *The Mysteries of Udolpho* (1794)
Rule of Directoire begins, 1795	Chamfort, *Les Produits de la civilisation perfectionnée* (posth. publ. 1795)	Goethe, *Wilhelm Meister* (1795–6)
	Sade, *Aline et Valcour* (1795)	
	Sade, *Le Philosophe dans le boudoir* (1795)	
French victory at Lodi, 1796	Restif de la Bretonne, *Monsieur Nicolas* (1796–7)	
French victory at Rivoli, 1797	Sade, *La nouvelle Justine* (1797)	Hölderlin, *Hyperion* (1797–9)
French expedition to Egypt, 1798	Restif de la Bretonne, *L'Anti-Justine* (1798)	Wordsworth, *Lyrical Ballads* (1798)
French victory at the Battle of the Pyramids, 1798		Austen, *Northanger Abbey*, 1798
French naval defeat at Aboukir Bay, 1798		Schiller, *Wallenstein* (1798–9)
Bonaparte's *coup d'état* (18th brumaire, 1799)		
		Schiller, *Maria Stuart* (1800)

Painting and music	Criticism and aesthetic theory	Ideas and Philosophy
		Paine, *The Rights of Man* (1791–2)
Beethoven, 1770–1827 (*Symphony No. 1*, 1799)		
		Paley, *Evidences of Christianity* (1794)
		Condorcet, *Esquisse d'un tableau historique des progrès de l'esprit humain* (1794)
Girtin, 1775–1802	Mme de Staël, *Essai sur les fictions* (1795)	
	Schiller, *Über naive und sentimentalische Dichtung* (1795)	
		Malthus, *An Essay on the Principle of Population* (1798)
		Schleiermacher, *Reden über die Religion* (1799)
	Sade, *Idée sur les romans* (1800)	
	Mme de Staël, *De la littérature* (1800)	
	Wordsworth: preface to the second edition of *Lyrical Ballads* (1800)	

Index

Académie des Sciences, Fontenelle and, 20; Beaumarchais and, 127.

Agricultural Revolution, 17.

Alembert, Jean le Rond d' (1717–83), viii, 100; and the Enlightenment, 16; on Newton, 22; on Newton and Locke, 24; and Diderot, 77; on Descartes, 87; co-editor of *Encyclopédie*, 102.

    Works: *Discours préliminaire* (to *Encyclopédie* 1751), 21, 24, 98, 102; *Traité de dynamique*, 64.

Amélie (mistress of Beaumarchais), 129.

Arland, Marcel, and Marivaux, 118, 121–2.

Augier, Guillaume Victor Émile (1820–89), adopts Diderot's ideas for the stage, 113.

Bacon, Francis, Baron Verulam of Verulam, Viscount St. Albans (1561–1626), 103; respected in eighteenth-century France, 85; and the Enlightenment, 86; and sensationalism, 191.

Barber, E. G., on the bourgeoisie, 94.

Bastide, Maurice, critic of Marivaux, 121, 132.

Bayle, Pierre (1647–1706), agrees with Locke, 24; and the Enlightenment, 86; and religion, 87.

    Works: *Dictionnaire historique et critique*, 98, 194; *Réponse aux questions d'un provincial*, 180, 194.

Beaumarchais, Marie-Louise, and the Clavijo affair, 127.

Beaumarchais, Pierre Augustin Caron de (1732–99), vii; and the contemporary theatre, 73; on morality and the theatre, 76; his background, 81; and Marivaux, 126, 131; his history, 127–9; failure of his *drames*, 130; at his best, 130–1; a 'professional Beaumarchais', 131–2; notes on, 132–3; Rivarol attacks, 170.

    Works: *Eugénie*, 126, 130, 131; *La Mère coupable*, 79, 126, 131; *Le Barbier de Séville*, 64, 74, 129, 130, 131, 133; *Le Mariage de Figaro*, 128, 129, 130, 131, 133; *Les deux amis*, 79, 126, 130, 131; *Mémoires*, 127, 129; *Tarare*, 130.

Benozzi, Zanetta Rosa (Silvia), in Marivaux's comedies, 121.

Bentham, Jeremy (1748–1832), and heritage of the Enlightenment, 28; on role of pain and pleasure, 192; *Introduction to the Principles of Morals and Legislation*, 192.

Bernard, J. F., *Réflexions morales, satiriques et comiques*, 31.

Bernard, Jean-Jacques, and Marivaux, 126.

Bernoulli, Jean (1667–1748), opposed to Newtonianism, 20.

Blache, Comte de la, 127.

Boccaccio, Giovanni (1313–75), and the *conte*, 13; influences Sade, 160.

Boileau-Despréaux, Nicolas (1636–1711), and utility in literature, 62.

Bonnet, Charles (1720–93), 105.

Bordeu, Théophile de, 105.

Bossuet, Jacques-Bénigne (1627–1704), Voltaire and, 10, 13; his sermons, 64; *Discours sur l'histoire universelle*, 75.

Boucher, François (1703–70), Diderot and, 113.

Boulainvilliers, Henri, Comte de (1658–1722), supports Locke, 24.

Bourgeoisie, eighteenth-century French, and the Enlightenment, 17; defined, 93–4; and the intelligentsia, 94, 95; ambitions of, 94.

Bretonne, Restif de la, vii; *L'Anti-Justine*, 158.

Buffier, Claude (1661–1737), *Traité des premières vérités*, 24.

Buffon, Georges Louis Leclerc, Comte de

subject-matter for *Clavigo*, 127; on d'Holbach, 187.

Goëzmann, Counsellor, 127, 129, 130.

Goëzmann, Madame, 127, 129.

Goncourt, Edmond de (1822–96) and Jules de (1830–70), on 'l'amour et la volupté' in eighteenth century, 149; on seduction, 150; *La Femme au XVIIIᵉ siècle*, 149, 162.

Government, Voltaire's view of, 9; Montesquieu's ideas on, 39–41; Diderot and, 115; Rousseau's suspicions of, 137; the general interest the criterion for, 193.

Gravesande, Willem Jakob Storm van 's, accepts Newtonianism, 20; Voltaire and, 21; his *Physices Elementa*, 20.

Greuze, Jean Baptiste (1725–1805), Diderot and, 113.

Grimm, Friedrich Melchior, Baron (1723–1807), on salutary effect of the *drame*, 74.

Grotius, Hugo (Huig van Groot, 1583–1645), 38; and moral law, 36; and Natural Law and laws, 38; natural law and theology, 190.

Haller, Albrecht von (1708–77), 105.

Hazard, P., on the *philosophes* and Nature, 90.

Hegel, Georg Wilhelm Friedrich (1770–1831), the *philosophes* precursors of, 88; and 'alienation', 189.

Helvétius, Claude Adrien (1715–71), viii, 8, 91, 193; and the Enlightenment, 16; his theory of human psychology, 25–6; d'Holbach and, 27; and the future, 27; influences Bentham, 28; notes on, 29; Diderot and, 105, 111.

Works: *De l'esprit*, 8, 25, 98; *De l'homme*, 25, 26.

Hobbes, Thomas (1588–1679), 37; human nature and the tendency towards evil, 182; and natural law, 190.

Holbach, Paul Heinrich Dietrich, Baron d' (1723–89), viii, 16, 100, 193; and Helvetian thesis, 26–7; and the future, 27; notes on, 29; and Voltaire, 71; rejects idea of divine control, 181; and theory of conspiracy, 187; on determination of ideas for the general interest, 192.

Works: *Le bon sens*, 187; *Le Christianisme dévoilé*, 98; *Politique naturelle*, 27; *Système de la nature*, 27; *Système social*, 27, 192, 193, 194.

Horace, Quintus Horatius Flaccus (65–8 B.C.), on poetry, 62.

Hôtel Colbert, Mme Lambert's salon at, 119.

Humanism, and traditional culture, 85; Diderot and, 115.

Hume, David (1711–76), Rousseau and, 147; and the question of theodicy, 179; *Dialogues concerning Natural Religion*, 180, 194.

Industrial Revolution, the, 17.

Intellectuals, eighteenth-century French, an occupational group, 80; social status and economic independence of, 81; causes of prestige of, 81–3; concerned to change the world, 83; and society, 83–4, 91–2; a modernizing élite, 92–3.

Intelligentsia, eighteenth-century French intellectuals prototype of, 83–4; universal background to, 84; eighteenth-century French intelligentsia, 86; and the bourgeoisie, 94, 95; and socialism, 94–5; concern with the individual, 96.

Jansenists, hostile to Locke's ideas, 24.

Jesuits, friendly to Locke's ideas, 24.

Joubert, Joseph (1754–1824), and Christianity, 172; and Revolution, 173; denounces cult of 'l'âme sensible'; 173–4; a Christian moralist, 174; compared with contemporaries, 174–5; assessed, 175; note on, 176; *Pensées*, 173, 174, 175.

Kant, Immanuel (1724–1804), the *philosophes* precursors of, 88.

Keill, John, Maupertuis and, 21; *Introductio ad veram astronomiam*, 20.

King, Revd. William, and theory of optimism, 180.

La Barre, J. F. Lefebvre de, Voltaire and, 1, 8.

La Bruyère, Jean de (1645–96), 31; and utility in literature, 62; Montesquieu and, 70, 71; Joubert and, 175.

Laclos, Pierre Ambroise François Choderlos de (1741–1803), and woman's emancipation, 154, 157; notes on, 161; *Les Liaisons dangereuses*, 56, 154–7; 161.

La Fayette, Marie-Madeleine Pioche de Lavergne, Comtesse de (1634–93), *La Princesse de Clèves*, 47, 149.